T0330185

DEALING IN UNCERTAINTY

Insurance in the Age of Finance

Arjen van der Heide

BRISTOL
UNIVERSITY
PRESS

First published in Great Britain in 2023 by

Bristol University Press
University of Bristol
1–9 Old Park Hill
Bristol
BS2 8BB
UK
t: +44 (0)117 374 6645
e: bup-info@bristol.ac.uk

Details of international sales and distribution partners are available at bristoluniversitypress.co.uk

© Bristol University Press 2023

British Library Cataloguing in Publication Data
A catalogue record for this book is available from the British Library

ISBN 978-1-5292-2135-0 hardcover
ISBN 978-1-5292-2136-7 ePub
ISBN 978-1-5292-2137-4 ePdf

Cover design: Qube Design
Front cover image: Shutterstock/Vlad_Chorniy
Bristol University Press uses environmentally responsible print partners.
Printed and bound in Great Britain by CPI Group (UK) Ltd

FSC
www.fsc.org
MIX
Paper | Supporting
responsible forestry
FSC® C013604

Contents

List of Figures

Acknowledgements

The journey from which this book emerged began in my time as a master's student in the Cultures of Arts, Science and Technology programme at Maastricht University. As part of this programme, I spent one semester on a research internship at the University of Edinburgh, where I had the luxury of pursuing my own research interests. Like many others, I was drawn to the social studies of finance by the formative experience of the global financial crisis. Looking for a good topic to study, I became aware that the European Union had just passed a directive for insurance companies that in style and substance pretty much resembled the banking regulations that had become discredited after the global financial crisis. Once I sunk my teeth into this, I could not let it go and started on a long journey exploring a topic I had never imagined I would become so interested in, discovering along the way the joy of unearthing obscure stories and details about a world that most who were not part of had any clue about, including myself.

I didn't make this journey alone, of course, nor indeed could I have done so. First and foremost, I owe a great debt of gratitude to Donald MacKenzie, who is not only a great mentor but also an exemplary scholar. In a status-based profession, it's rare to find such scholars who manage to pair academic brilliance with modesty and kindness. Thanks are due also to Nathan Coombs, Iain Hardie, Julius Kob, Liz McFall, Charlotte Rommerskirchen, Matthias Thiemann, Leon Wansleben and Natascha van der Zwan, who at various stages of this project have provided me with feedback, were a source of intellectual inspiration and encouragement, and/or enabled me to continue working on the project even after having completed my PhD. There are many more former colleagues at the University of Edinburgh and the Max Planck Institute for the Study of Societies whose names I could mention, but … well, you know who you are! At Bristol University Press, there is Paul Stevens, who has been extremely encouraging and a pleasure to work with, as were his colleagues Emma Cook and Georgina Bolwell. I also owe a debt of gratitude to the anonymous reviewers, who have kindly given their time to review previous drafts of the book – their work shall remain anonymous but not unacknowledged. Of course, writing this book also wouldn't have been possible without the generosity of my interviewees, many of whom took out extended periods of time from their busy work schedules to speak to me about all things insurance in cafés, restaurants, office buildings or even their homes. Special thanks are due to John Hibbert, Sandy Sharp, Craig Turnbull and David Wilkie, who helped me get to grips with the complex and sometimes rather abstract seeming world of insurance and actuarial science. Finally, the knowledge and expertise of the Institute and Faculty of Actuaries' librarians David Hood and David Raymont proved invaluable. They have helped me retrieve archival sources, get hold of my interviewees and generally find the data I needed. I thank them dearly for that.

1

Life Insurance in the Age of Finance

How societies organize uncertainty is often seen as one of their defining features. Contemporary capitalist societies, for instance, are held together by extensive welfare arrangements that define, measure and redistribute the costs and risks associated with (un-)employment, illness and death. While most scholarly attention tends to be devoted to public insurance arrangements of this kind, private insurance is an almost equally pervasive phenomenon that is present in many spheres of social life, even if just in the background. Apart from the various state-organized social insurance arrangements, including disability, accident, old age and unemployment insurance, private insurers provide protection against a large variety of risks, including liability, flood, cyber, trade and credit risk.

The societal importance of insurance is also reflected by the economic weight of the insurance industry. In the UK, for instance, annual insurance premiums amounted to nearly 12 per cent of GDP in 2019. Insurers, moreover, are sizable investors, owning a large stake in both domestic and foreign economies (in 2017, British insurers had nearly £2 trillion assets under management).[1] And to the extent that the economic risks associated with climate change, pandemics and cyber threats are unlikely to subside any time soon, private insurance will continue to play an important role in organizing uncertainty in contemporary capitalist societies going into the future. Insurance is also a moral technology that exudes the liberal virtues of individual responsibility and entrepreneurial risk taking. By allowing individuals to pool resources to gain compensation in the case of some pre-specified adverse event, it provides a mechanism through which individuals may gain economic independence and enables entrepreneurs or large businesses to take risks they might otherwise not take (Knights and Vurdubakis, 1993; O'Malley, 2000; Baker and Simon, 2002). It is therefore not too much of an exaggeration to say that we live in an insurance society.

Despite the centrality of insurance in contemporary capitalist societies, few scholars have investigated how the institution of private insurance fared in the age of financial capitalism. Social science scholarship on insurance either focuses on the historical antecedents of contemporary insurance arrangements – showing, for instance, how deeply ingrained the insurance technology is with the history of capitalism (Levy, 2012; Kingston, 2014; Bouk, 2015; Horan, 2021) – or on the more recent introduction of new technologies such as genetic testing, big data analytics and behavioural pricing in the 21st century (Van Hoyweghen, 2007; Meyers and Van Hoyweghen, 2018; McFall, 2019; Cevolini and Esposito, 2020). Among the most salient developments in contemporary history, however, is the onset of neoliberalism in the 1970s and the rise of finance as a dominant sphere in society more generally. A by now vast literature on the rampant processes of neoliberalization and financialization has documented, for instance, how the increased prevalence of financial actors, logics and motives has altered the fabric of contemporary capitalist societies, with a lasting structural impact on the nature of welfare states, the way that corporates are governed and the way that housing is organized (see Mader et al, 2021). Studies of how the insurance sector has evolved in this period, however, are few and far between (for notable exceptions, see Jarzabkowski et al, 2015; François, 2021).

This book takes up the task of investigating how private insurance has fared in the age of finance. It does so through a detailed empirical study of how evaluation practices in British life insurance have changed since the 1960s and '70s. The book focuses exclusively on life insurance because business practice in life insurance tends to be different from non-life insurers. Life insurers typically offer long-term contracts triggered by an event that will happen with certainty: the death of an individual (or the end of the contract, if it comes earlier). Because insurers invest the premiums they receive in financial assets, investment is thus typically an important aspect of any life insurance arrangement. Life insurers therefore also manage much more money than non-life insurers typically do, making the issue of financial risk especially pertinent in the context of life insurance. All this also means that the question of financial risk plays out quite differently in life insurance compared to non-life insurance.

Life insurance, as Ericson and Doyle (2004) put it, has 'evolved into an institution for the prolongation of prosperous lives and the management of civilized death' (p 22). In its 'modern' form – that is, with long-term contractual arrangements and actuarial risk-based pricing – life insurance developed in the UK from the late 18th century onwards in conjunction with statistical theory, which radically transformed life insurance as an institution (Porter, 1986; Daston, 1988; Hacking, 1990; Alborn, 2009). While statistical theory enabled the development of a theoretically informed technology of risk that facilitated differentiated insurance pricing according to age, life insurance in turn provided an important use case for early statistical theory. As Daston (1988, chapter 3) argues, the transition towards statistically informed governance of the life insurance business, which was accompanied by the rise of the actuarial profession, was by no means entirely smooth and required prior beliefs and values about uncertainty and risk to be turned on their heads.

The events described in this book tell the story of another more recent episode of cultural change in the British life insurance industry and how insurers deploy the technology of risk and uncertainty, one whereby the traditional actuarial methods, techniques and norms to deal with uncertainty have been displaced by or supplemented with the technical repertoire of modern finance theory. Scholars have documented how the rise of modern finance theory has contributed to the transformation of financial markets (MacKenzie, 2006; Wigan, 2009; Brine and Poovey, 2017). Less well known, however, is that modern finance theory also had a significant impact on insurance, with subtle but important implications for what private insurance is and does going into the future. To get a sense of the scope of the changes I have in mind, it is useful to look at two snapshots of the life insurance business, first in the 1970s, and then as it is now.

Life insurance, then and now

At the beginning of the 1970s, life insurers earned most of their £1bn annual premium income from individual business, either in the form of whole-of-life (providing life cover for the entire lifespan), term assurance (providing life cover for a limited period), endowment assurance (paying a benefit upon death or at a pre-specified date, for instance at the date of retirement) or annuity business (providing an income until death in exchange for a lump sum payment up front). These policies were typically sold to middle-class policyholders for a variety of purposes, for instance to cover burial expenses, to repay any outstanding debts upon death, the loss of household income due to the policyholder's death or – in the case of annuities and endowment assurance – to supplement retirement income (Bennet et al, 1984). A second mainstay of 20th-century insurance was industrial life insurance, a type of insurance that revolved around agents collecting premiums from working- and lower middle-class customers typically in industrial areas (hence the name) to cover funeral expenses. Industrial insurance emerged in the late 19th century and became hugely successful in the early decades of the 20th century (McFall, 2009). Although at the start of the 1970s, industrial insurance was already in retreat, it still made up a quarter of the industry's premium income. The final category was pension business, which formed nearly a third of the industry's premium income. Some of the pension business was directly sold to individual policyholders in the form of personal pensions, but most of it was sold to occupational pension funds, who bought insurance either to cover for the mortality risk embedded in pension contracts, or to take over all of their risk (Bennet et al, 1984). Although personal and group pensions already formed a substantial share of insurers' premium income, most of their premium income derived from more traditional forms of ordinary and industrial insurance.

Most insurers were so-called 'with-profits' insurers, selling a combination of non-profit and with-profit contracts. In a non-profit insurance arrangement, both premiums and benefits are determined up front. In a with-profits arrangement, however, policyholder benefits depend on a bonus system, allowing policyholders to participate in the profits of a firm. Insurers promised with-profits policyholders payment of a guaranteed 'sum assured' that was typically below what was promised to non-profit policyholders but would be supplemented by periodical 'reversionary' bonuses and a 'final' or 'terminal' bonus at the end of the contract. In exchange for the added uncertainty, with-profits policyholders could expect to receive on average more than what was promised to an equivalent non-profit policyholder. With-profits policyholders, in other words, were a kind of hybrid between standard non-profit policyholders and shareholders, whose capital could be used as a buffer for unforeseen financial adversity.

The traditional character of the life insurance market was not just reflected in the types of policies that were sold, but also in the organization of the life industry itself. For example, the actuary – a central figure in the Hollywood noir *Double Indemnity*, who, equipped with statistical knowledge, sees what is really going on behind the world of appearances, intrigue and shady romance – still takes up a prominent position in British life insurance. The structure of insurance business was such that actuarial expertise was required not just to calculate individual policyholders' mortality risk but also to make key decisions about the level of prudence needed to keep life insurers financially sound or about how insurers' financial surpluses should be distributed across policyholders and (if an office was proprietary rather than mutualized) shareholders. The importance of actuarial expertise for the insurance business was reflected in the organizational structure of most life offices. By law, for instance, companies were required to have an appointed actuary whom regulators held responsible for ensuring that policyholder interests were protected (Daykin, 1999). Actuaries, moreover, often occupied senior positions within the insurance business. In the 1970s, some even argued that '[i]n a large well-run life assurance office the Appointed Actuary will normally be the chief executive and will have served for many years in less senior positions' (Thornton, 1979, pp 27–8). Anecdotal evidence suggests that actuaries tended to take up positions throughout the entire organization, ranging from board-level positions to heads of marketing and IT (O'Brien et al, 2015).

Figure 1.1: Total new premiums written per business segment, 1999–2019

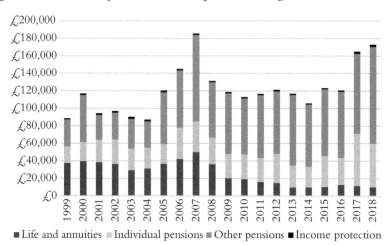

Source: Association of British Insurers

Looking at the life insurance industry today, the picture changes drastically. Although the industry as a whole grew significantly, to an annual premium income of around £147bn in 2016 (amounting to more than 5 per cent of GDP, a significant increase compared to the 0.7 per cent of GDP in 1970), industrial life insurance completely disappeared (Carter and Falush, 2009; Association of British Insurers, 2018). Retirement income business is now by far the most important source of insurers' premium income, amounting to more than 90 per cent of total new business written today (see Figure 1.1). With-profits insurance arrangements, moreover, have been displaced by unit-linked arrangements that tie policyholder benefits directly to the financial market performance of underlying investment funds. Rather than participate in the firm, unit-linked policyholders participate in financial markets.

Growth in the industry as whole was also accompanied by the emergence of a few large insurance groups, such as AVIVA and Legal & General, who figure as weighty investors in today's capital markets. Notable, too, is the pension 'de-risking' industry, in which often newly established insurers like the former Goldman Sachs subsidiary Rothesay Life and the Pension Insurance Corporation take over the risks of defined benefit pension schemes, often in mind-bogglingly large transactions. In June 2019, for instance, Rolls Royce passed on pension obligations to 33,000 (former) employees to Legal & General in a £4.6bn transaction (Ralph and Pfeifer, 2019). The emphasis in the insurance industry has thus shifted from traditional insurance contracts to retirement income provisioning and asset management, a development that was epitomized in 2017 by the long-established insurer Standard Life's decision to sell off its insurance business to the Phoenix Group – an entity that hoovers up legacy insurance and pension schemes – and merge with Aberdeen Asset Management (Ralph, 2018). Rather than dealing *with* financial uncertainty through organized solidarity, in other words, British life insurers have become increasingly focused on dealing *in uncertainty*, seeking profitable investment opportunities while leaving the burden of financial uncertainty at the level of individual policyholders. Although they might still provide protection against the economic risks of early death or long lives, the level of protection depends directly on investment performance.

This shift in emphasis was accompanied by organizational changes. While the traditional policies dominant in the 1970s organized financial uncertainty through the practices of prudence and profit participation, today financial uncertainty is dealt with at the level of individual policyholders and through risk-based capital reserving. The function of the Appointed Actuary has disappeared, and although actuaries are still a key professional group within the insurance business, there tend to be fewer of them in high-level positions such as executive boards (O'Brien et al, 2015). As a whole, the actuarial profession grew. While in 1984, for instance, the Faculty of Actuaries and the Institute of Actuaries combined counted around 3,000 fellows among their members, this figure had increased to over 10,000 from 2010 onwards (see Figure 1.2). This growth, however, was due mostly to actuaries increasingly

Figure 1.2: Membership of the British actuarial profession

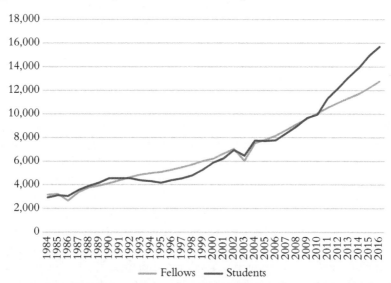

Note: The figures represent combined membership of the Institute and Faculty of Actuaries, which merged in 2010. Not included in the figures are types of memberships other than fellows or students, such as honorary fellows and associates.

Source: Institute and Faculty of Actuaries, courtesy of David Raymont

finding employment outside the traditional jobs at life insurance and pension schemes. While in 1994, 82 per cent of actuarial fellows were still employed in the fields of life insurance and pensions, by 2009 this figure had dropped to 62 per cent and by 2016 to 52 per cent. A corollary of this trend has been the rise of the consulting actuary. While in 1984 only 350 actuaries were employed as consultants, by 1994 there were 1,150. In 2016, 4,234 actuaries were employed as consultants, providing advice primarily to life insurance companies and pension trustees not only on traditional valuation issues but also increasingly on things like enterprise risk management.[2] Although many within the actuarial profession experienced the final decades of the 20th century as a period in which traditional forms of actuarial expertise were under threat, not least by the ascendancy of modern financial economics, the actuarial profession expanded significantly as actuaries increasingly became employed in 'wider fields'.

Actuaries had to revise their career expectations too. This is perhaps best illustrated by one of my interviewees' reflections on her career:

> 'The idea of the old-fashioned actuary as maybe overly prudent and a bit plodding and stuff, you can't do that [any more]. ... we've had to change a bit our expectations of what our careers were going to be like. When I started I thought ... I was gonna build up, do my exams, become a scheme actuary, and then be a scheme actuary to bigger schemes maybe. And that was going to be me. But, you know, that rug got pulled from under me.' (Perrella interview)

With an increasingly large proportion of actuaries working outside traditional actuarial forms of employment, the need to acquire expertise outside traditional forms of actuarial knowledge grew too. Indeed, actuarial expertise changed substantially, most significantly with the incorporation of models and techniques from modern finance theory. In the early 1980s, the renowned actuary Frank Redington observed that '[t]he actuary of 1945 was closer in spirit to the William Morgan of 1800 than to the actuary of today' (Redington, 1981, p 361), pointing at a trend that would continue until today. Rather than managing insurance business, most actuaries are now quantitative experts with expertise in financial economics who play a key role in the modelling of economic value and risk required by the newly established European regulatory framework of Solvency II. In other words, with the introduction of modern finance theory in the life insurance business, the epistemic authority of the actuary was replaced by the epistemic authority of the market.

What to make of these snapshots? In this book, I want to suggest that the changes occurring in the 50-odd years that separate them amount to a remaking of the 'value model' (Christophers, 2015) of private life insurance and a shift in the boundary between finance and insurance – a shift whereby insurers have become increasingly subdued to the epistemic authority of financial markets and whereby the differences in the identities of investment companies and insurers have started to fade (Preda, 2009). The dominant evaluation culture has shifted from the traditional actuarial practices of prudence and profit participation to a culture of exactitude in financial quantification and financial risk management. Insurance, in other words, has been subjected to financialization, whereby the traditional actuarial logics and motives have been displaced by financialized ones (see further François, 2021; Fytros, 2021; Van der Heide, 2022). This development has been accompanied by shifting relations of control over insurance capital too, from a model centred on the actuarial profession to a model dominated by shareholder interests.

The financialization of the insurance sector has been especially visible in life insurance, which is the book's main focus. This is because life insurance contracts typically tend to be long term, with premiums and benefits defined at the start of the contract. Throughout a contract's lifespan, life insurers collect premiums, which they then invest in capital markets to generate sufficient income to pay policyholders and – in the case of a stock company – shareholders as and when payments are due. To ensure they can live up to their financial commitments, life insurers may adopt a range of different strategies, ranging from prudently calculating the premiums needed to meet obligations to making policyholder benefits dependent on the performance of underlying investments. By looking at the strategies life insurers use to deal with uncertainty, we can understand in what sense life insurers have become financialized: the strategies life insurers use today are more closely aligned than 30 years ago with the preferences of shareholders and those policyholders that buy life insurance as an investment product. The shift in evaluation practices thus concerns not just a change in organizational culture but also involves a shift in the organization of capital and risk and its distribution across the different stakeholders in the insurance business.

Financialization in the making

Much has been written about the term 'financialization', and most agree that at the very minimum the term denotes 'how an increasingly autonomous realm of global finance has altered the underlying logics of the industrial economy and the inner workings of democratic society' (Van der Zwan, 2014, pp 99–100). Defined as such, financialization may encompass a variety of interrelated processes that gained hold with the increased liberalization of financial markets from the 1970s onwards. It is, in other words, a variegated phenomenon encompassing the rise of an international financial system and its complex interactions with the various institutions of contemporary capitalist societies, such as welfare states, occupational pensions and corporate governance (Mader et al, 2021), which also pushes individual households increasingly to 'embrace' the risk of capital markets (Baker and Simon, 2002; Martin, 2002). This book examines how this process unfolds outside the centres of financial modernity, in what many consider the periphery of the financial sector.

Life insurance, as noted earlier, hasn't been immune to the rise of financial capitalism. Indeed, changes in the organizational practice of life insurance may perhaps be interpreted as a rational response to the changing nature of the broader political economy since the 1970s. Since then, the world has seen unprecedented financial market volatility, which has manifested itself in the amplification of the 'financial cycle' (Drehmann et al, 2012), violent exchange rate fluctuations (Strange, 1997) and the proliferation of financial crises (Kindleberger, 2015). This volatility famously led Susan Strange (1997) to describe the global financial system as a 'casino', the erratic nature of which posed significant political and economic challenges to policymakers around the globe. For the diverse actors in financial markets, financial market volatility posed both challenges and opportunities. For insurers, things were no different. Making money from uncertainty in the age of finance, however, required a reorientation of insurers' business models away from traditional forms of insurance built in varying degrees of mutuality and towards a rationalized form generating reliable revenue streams for shareholders.

Yet, this story is somewhat simplistic and the reasoning circular. Indeed, an important difficulty in dealing with terms like financialization is that 'they stand simultaneously as subject and object of analysis – something to be explained and a way of making sense out of what is going on around us' (Martin, 2002, p 8). The financialization of contemporary capitalism provides the context in which changes in the insurance industry take place. It is, however, also a development that begs for an explanation. How is it that finance seems to have such an outsized influence on the core institutions of capitalist societies? And how does the rise of an international financial sector reshape the logic of economic security? What are the pathways, in other words, through which finance exercises influence over economy and society alike? To address questions like these, I propose examining 'financialization in the making'. Focusing on the British life insurance sector, I investigate how actors in the insurance industry responded to changes in the broader political economy; how, in other words, the rise of finance and the institutionalization of modern finance theory created new opportunities and challenges for insurers and insurance practitioners alike.

To address the how and why of financialization in UK life insurance, I conceive of financialization as a social process that can be studied with sociological tools. Central to my endeavour is a focus on evaluation practices – how insurers evaluate 'economic value' and 'risk' – and how these practices have changed over time. By focusing on evaluation practices, I follow a strand of scholarship that has come to understand financialization as the diffusion of quantification conventions (Chiapello, 2015; Chiapello and Walter, 2016) in areas of financial market practices such as accounting (Chiapello, 2016; Baud and Chiapello, 2017), risk management (Coombs and Van der Heide, 2020) and credit rating (Carruthers, 2015; Besedovsky, 2018). The institutionalization of calculation conventions rooted in modern finance theory, I suggest, has reshaped life insurers' value model and the social relations underpinning the financial risks of retirement and death (Christophers, 2015). It has created a direct link between financial risk (in its mathematical form) and the value of an insurance contract, folding calculated financial risk into the insurance commodity.

More on this will be said in the following section. For now, it suffices to say that evaluation practices provide a useful focal point for any analysis that seeks to uncover changes in the governance of the life insurance industry itself. In broadly following this approach, this book examines how and why the evaluation culture in insurance came to revolve around the financial evaluation practices mostly associated hitherto with modern finance theory and the derivatives departments of investment banks.

The argument

The main argument of the book, simply put, is that insurers' appropriation of financialized evaluation practices to quantify and manage financial risk consolidated a broader set of developments that redefined the boundaries between finance and insurance. While finance and insurance were often regarded as separate spheres of economic activity – each with distinct structures of governance, characteristic business models, distinctive bodies of expertise and indeed largely unconnected bodies of experts – the boundaries between the two fields gradually became more porous from the 1970s onwards as actors, capital and ideas increasingly traversed the boundaries between them. The increased permeability also involved the migration of modern finance theory into the domain of life insurance, where its core models have been appropriated, adapted and institutionalized primarily – though not exclusively – through regulatory reform. The institutionalization of modern finance theory in the life insurance sector in turn congealed the porous boundaries between finance and insurance, facilitating the flow of actors and capital between the two fields. While the value model of insurance – earning premiums in exchange for the transfer of risk – has seeped into the world of finance (Christophers, 2015), the value model of insurance itself has been remade.

Permeability between the two domains, I suggest, was not simply the result of financiers colonizing insurance. A key factor driving the financialization of insurance was the competitive pressure among a well-established group of incumbent insurers and a group of smaller challenger firms, often though not always backed by banks and investment funds, that first introduced unit-linked insurance. As noted earlier, unit-linked insurance arrangements tied policyholder benefits directly to the market value of underlying units of investment. The savings and investment component of life insurance had always been one of its main attractions, especially in the UK (Alborn, 2009; Lehtonen and Liukko, 2010), and in times of booming stock markets, unit-linked insurance seemed to offer superior investment capabilities compared to more conventional life insurance arrangements because it eliminated actuarial discretion. In response to the rise of unit-linked insurers, the traditional insurers changed the way they managed their with-profits schemes to look more like unit-linked insurance. Unit-linked insurers, in contrast, only partially lived up to their promise to eliminate actuarial discretion. With actuarial discretion reduced and with increased post-Bretton Woods financial market volatility, the hybrid insurance arrangements of the 1970s and '80s increasingly got into trouble by the end of the century, epitomized by the collapse of the Equitable Life Assurance Society.[3] Equitable's downfall raised questions about the adequacy of actuarial expertise in the management of financial risk.

Although many agreed that life insurers needed new techniques to measure and manage financial risk in the wake of 'Equitable', the crisis in the life insurance industry does not by itself explain why modern finance theory became such a potent force in reshaping the life insurance field. Several proximate causes made the embrace of modern finance theory possible and even likely. The first has to do with changes in the structure of the actuarial profession and actuarial employment. Historically, actuaries were employed in the fields of life insurance and pensions, and they were often affiliated with one specific company or one specific pension scheme. In the 20th century, however, actuaries have increasingly become employed as consultants, often advising multiple schemes and companies at once; *and* also venturing outside the traditional domains of actuarial work into finance. Moreover, towards the end of the century, a gulf of mergers, acquisitions and demutualizations enveloped the insurance industry, which put the question of economic value front and centre of actuarial work. As a result of these developments, a new generation of younger actuaries emerged who in one way or another had become familiar with modern finance theory. These actuaries perceived the appropriation of modern finance theory as essential for the survival of the actuarial profession and the maintenance of its jurisdictional claims within the life insurance business.

Second, the expansion of a British regulatory state created new opportunities for proponents of modern finance theory to make the case for market-consistent valuation. A crucial factor, for instance, was the integration of insurance and banking supervision within the single supervisory agent the Financial Services Authority towards the end of the 20th century. While the previous regulatory structure was dominated by actuaries, who were socialized in a system of governance revolving around the principle of 'freedom with publicity', the new regulatory organization was increasingly dominated by regulators who had earned their stripes in banking supervision. For them, the models of modern finance theory promised to provide a more transparent and objective knowledge base for the governance of insurance, which allowed them to take some of the epistemic authority away from the actuarial profession. Actuarial proponents of modern finance theory, in turn, found new allies in the newly established regulatory body to push epistemic practice in the direction of modern finance theory, which functioned as a 'hinge' strategy between the groups.

A third proximate cause can be traced to the increased exposure of the British insurance industry to international developments in insurance regulation and accounting standardization. On the one hand, there was the context of European market integration. In the early 2000s, the European Commission joined forces with the newly emerging large European insurance groups that were eager to enhance cross-border access to foreign insurance markets. When it became clear that a harmonized regulatory regime for insurance would be established on a risk-based and market-consistent framework, British insurance regulators had an incentive to front-run European developments by implementing a similar regime when the domestic insurance sector was in crisis. On the other hand, by the late 1990s international accounting standard setters had embraced the concept of fair value as the core principle for new accounting standards, and they were also keen on developing a fair value standard for insurance. Regulators and supervisors perceived it as desirable that the domestic regulatory regime would be based on the international accounting framework, therefore embracing the concept of fair value. That the development of a fair value accounting standard for insurance was split off from the accounting standard setter's main project and was only agreed upon in 2017 hardly mattered in this respect – just the promise of fair value accounting for insurance contracts strengthened the arguments of proponents of modern finance theory.

Combined, the increased employment of actuaries outside life insurance, the integration of insurance and banking supervision, and the promise of a fair value accounting standard for insurance all made it more likely that modern finance theory would have an impact on the governance of risk in the life insurance sector. And the crisis in British life insurance in the late 1990s and early 2000s formed a window of opportunity for proponents of modern finance theory to reform the governance system.

The appropriation and institutionalization of modern finance theory through regulatory reform was itself not without consequences. I will highlight two of these consequences here. First, with the introduction of new quantitative practices, life insurance governance now revolved around the dictum of financial risk management. This shift was characterized by the rise of financial risk management functions and chief risk officers, and an increased emphasis on the quantification and active management of not only financial risk but also of other forms of non-diversifiable risk. Since the early 2000s, for instance, various attempts have been made to launch instruments that allow insurers to trade 'longevity risk', which, in contrast to mortality risk, does not measure the diversifiable uncertainty around the death of individual policyholders, but measures the non-diversifiable process whereby long-term longevity trends (improvements in life expectancy, for example) diverge from current expectations. Although insurers' increased use of active risk management tools such as derivatives may contribute to increased financial stability under some circumstances, it may also increase the systemic complexity of financial markets more generally and foster speculative behaviour among the more adventurous insurance companies. Overall, these attempts point to the increased privileging of capital considerations and shareholder interests in insurance decision making.

A second and related point is that the institutionalization of modern finance theory in the insurance industry has impacted how the pensions of many (retired) British workers are secured. Most notably, the 'economic' view of insurance liabilities has facilitated the wholesale transfer of defined benefit pension liabilities from legacy occupational pension schemes to insurance firms. The financial economic view of pension liabilities facilitated this transfer because it changed the question of pension valuation from one focused on the funding of pension promises to a question of value and hence allowed pension liabilities to be *priced*. But the structure offered also changed: although there is a great variety of products on offer today, in the absence of mechanisms to carry financial risk at the level of the collective, this risk tends to be located at the level of individual policyholders. Thus, as private life insurers play an increasingly important role in the provisioning of retirement income, individualized forms of retirement saving have become increasingly entrenched. I return to these issues in the conclusion.

Sources

In making these arguments, the book takes the form of a historical narrative that traces the emergence of contemporary life insurance arrangements in the UK to the 1960s and '70s. It is also a sociological narrative, because it seeks to explain how and why insurers' evaluation practices changed the way they did, not as a function of some internal logic, but – loosely following the tradition of the sociology of scientific knowledge (Barnes et al, 1995) – as at root a social process. Methodologically, this means that I adopt a stance of methodological relativism, which is to say that 'the same types of causes would explain, say true and false beliefs' (Bloor, 1991, p 5).

The historical-sociological narrative is based primarily on 44 semi-structured oral history interviews with people involved in the UK's insurance industry, oftentimes directly so, in other cases more indirectly, for example through their involvement in international organizations. These include interviews with company actuaries, regulators and supervisors, consultants and model providers, academic actuaries, actuaries working for investment banks, and people who currently have another position, such as non-executive director or who are currently in retirement. Many of my interviewees have taken up at least two or more of the above positions in their career.

Some of my interviewees have had long careers and were involved in many of the events described in this book. Others were at a relatively early stage in their career. The nature and length of the interviews varied accordingly. In some interviews, I asked my interviewees to walk me through their careers and to describe both routine practice and specific events that they considered pivotal. These interviews tended to take up relatively more time, typically between 1.5 and two hours (the longest being 4.5 hours). In other cases, the interviews were more concise (typically between 45 minutes and 1.5 hours). These interviews tended to serve a direct purpose. Although I still asked interviewees about their individual careers, I steered the interviews more intently towards specific events and asked interviewees about particular routines. Follow-up interviews were used to clarify some of the more technical aspects of evaluation, leading in four cases to a repeat interview. The interviews allowed me to identify key events, to situate them in a historical order and to grasp as adequately as possible the technical nature of the evaluation practices in which my interviewees have been involved.

One of the major pitfalls of oral history interviews is that memory tends to be rather fickle, which raises the issue of the validity and reliability of oral history data (Ritchie, 2003). A particularly important problem is that interviewees' accounts of past events may be self-serving. I used various means to try to ascertain the validity and reliability of interview data. First, most of the interview questions concerned routine practice, memory of which tends to be more reliable than memories about specific events (Thompson, 1988). Second, where I was interested in specific events, I tried to gauge the extent to which interviewees had retold memories about specific events on earlier occasions. Although this is likely to make memories more reliable, it is also likely to decrease their validity, because the purpose of those earlier retellings may have influenced the account in ways that may serve interviewees' self-interest (Thomson, 2010). Third, and most importantly, I tried to corroborate key data points, first with the memories of other interviewees, and secondly with alternative sources including an extensive set of primary and secondary documentary material.

For reasons of availability and reliability, interview coverage is skewed towards events from the late 1990s onwards (Chapters 6, 7, 8 and 9). Earlier chapters are based more heavily on a set of primary documentary material, which has also been used to supplement the interview data where it was available. A crucial set of documents includes articles published in the actuarial journals, the *Journal of the Institute of Actuaries* and the *Transactions of the Faculty of Actuaries*, which merged in 1993 to form the *British Actuarial Journal*. Conveniently, these journals publish transcriptions and summaries of professional debates alongside articles. This allowed me not only to trace the inception of new ideas but also to gauge their reception among peers. Other documents include regulatory communication (including speeches, newsletters, briefings, consultation papers, 'Dear CEO' letters and so on), articles in newspapers, magazines and professional journals, occasional papers, consultancy reports, individual companies' annual reports and yearbooks of the actuarial profession (which include, for example, actuarial exams).

Overview of the book

A story about how insurers' evaluation practices changed over time may be a challenging read for those without prior knowledge of the insurance business. Yet I have sought to make this book accessible, especially to non-experts. This is not an actuarial book, nor a history of actuarial thought (for this, see Turnbull, 2017) but a sociological examination of changes in life insurers' calculative machinery and the implications thereof for the governance of risk and the organization of uncertainty. The book takes the form of a historical narrative, with broadly chronologically structured parts composed of more thematic chapters. One of the book's main objectives is to highlight the social and political nature of seemingly technical issues. I have therefore sought to explain relevant technical notions throughout the book as straightforwardly as I can. The mathematics underlying key concepts are left out.

Apart from the introductory and concluding chapters, the book consists of a theoretical chapter (Chapter 2) and three substantive parts containing an additional seven chapters (Chapter 3–9). In the next chapter, I lay the theoretical foundations for this study, outlining my approach to studying cultural change in the insurance industry. I briefly review the social science literature on financialization and insurance, literature in the social studies of finance, sociological field theory and the sociology of professions. From these various bodies of literature, I outline an integrated perspective that seeks to capture the drawn out and long-winded process of institutional change in the British life insurance sector.

The first part of the book covers the period from the late 1960s until the 1990s. It examines the traditional business model of life insurance and how this business model was challenged by the emergence of newly founded life insurance companies specializing in unit-linked insurance. It also reviews debates within the actuarial profession on the nature of financial risk and the limits of traditional actuarial methods for dealing with financial uncertainty. Chapter 3 explores how the structure of life insurance arrangements started to change in the 1970s, focusing especially on the emergence of newly established life insurers who sought to challenge the dominant position of the long-established incumbents by selling unit-linked insurance. The chapter examines how proponents of unit-linked insurance envisioned a model for life insurance arrangements that would reduce reliance on actuarial discretion and enable life insurance to be seen primarily as an investment product. The chapter concludes by arguing that the competitive challenge from unit-linked insurance led to the emergence of hybrid forms of insurance, combining elements from traditional forms of with-profits insurance and unit-linked insurance, as the dominant mode of insurance provisioning.

In Chapter 4, the book's analytical focus moves to the actuarial field and examines how changes in the structure of life insurance arrangements led actuaries to reconsider the nature of financial uncertainty. The chapter starts by identifying a key moment in debates about financial risk: the presentation by Sydney Benjamin of a new way of modelling the financial risk in unit-linked insurance contracts, using stochastic simulation techniques. While traditional actuarial modelling was mostly 'deterministic', representing the future merely according to point-based estimates, stochastic simulation modelling ascribed a likelihood to different scenarios and thereby allowed actuaries to account for the spread of possible outcomes. After describing Benjamin's novel approach and identifying the sources of its contentiousness, the chapter continues to review the ensuing actuarial debates about whether and how financial uncertainty should be modelled and then places this debate in the broader context of the actuarial field, showing how actuaries struggled not only over financial risk, but also over the question of the appropriate place for mathematics and computing in actuarial thought and practice. The chapter concludes by considering how the introduction of this new mode of modelling financial risk – stochastic modelling – influenced life insurance and actuarial science more broadly.

Chapter 5 builds on the two preceding chapters and examines how many of the questions about financial risk and actuarial discretion continued to surface throughout the 1980s and '90s. The chapter first describes how declining interest rates put pressure on the capital base of insurance firms. One company in particular ended up with serious difficulties: the Equitable Life Assurance Society, a mutual company whose practices exemplified *in extremis* the problems in British life insurance more generally. I suggest in this chapter that the dramatic collapse of Equitable Life in 2000 gave rise to the perception that actuarial expertise had failed to keep up with the realities of financial capitalism. The chapter ends by describing how this crisis of actuarial expertise in turn provided a window of opportunity for proponents of modern finance theory to push for reforms in the calculative machinery of life insurance, drawing on the core models of modern finance theory and the derivatives departments of investment banks. The downfall of Equitable Life, which resulted from the competitive dynamic between incumbent with-profits insurers and the newly established unit-linked insurers, thus prepared the way for life insurers' evaluation machinery to be overhauled more generally.

In the second part of the book, I investigate the subsequent remaking of life insurers' evaluation machinery in the late 1990s and early 2000s, specifically focusing on the appropriation of modern finance theory. Chapter 6 describes how – once it became clear that UK regulators required life insurers to use models from modern finance theory to calculate their balance sheets – insurers sought to adapt these models to the specificities of insurance contracts. First, the chapter examines the specificities of the models of modern finance theory (and the derivatives departments of investment banks) and how they differ from traditional actuarial modelling. The chapter proceeds with an examination of how these models were appropriated in the context of life insurance and reviews the key decisions that were made around the appropriate extension of modern finance theory to the context of insurance. Finally, the chapter asks to what extent we can speak of insurers' appropriation of modern finance theory and the concomitant transition towards market-consistent modelling as a process of cultural change.

Chapter 7 moves to the rise of quantitative approaches to financial risk management in insurance. While the market-consistent valuation models discussed in Chapter 6 seek to estimate the economic value of insurance contracts, given their financial risk, risk models seek to estimate the likelihood that the economic value of insurers' liabilities fall below their assets, which requires the quantification of non-diversifiable risk factors, including risks associated with improvements in life expectancy and financial risks. The chapter examines the rise of financial risk management practices in insurance and scrutinizes the development of models to quantify longevity risk. It also addresses the question of how the rise of risk management affects the power relations between the different actors within the field of life insurance.

In the third part of the book, I examine how the subterranean conflicts and tensions between traditional insurance practice and financial logics remain present in contemporary life insurance. While Chapters 6 and 7 focused on the implementation of market-consistent valuation and risk-based capital regulation in the British insurance industry in the 2000s, Chapter 8 shifts the focus to the complicated relationship between the British insurance sector and Solvency II. The anticipation of Solvency II played an important role in the British decision to move ahead and implement a market-consistent framework in the early 2000s. In subsequent years, British insurers also came to play a lead role in the development of Solvency II, taking key positions in various working groups. Already before Solvency II finally went live in 2016, however, various elements of the framework were criticized for being 'overengineered', first by insurers and later also by supervisors. Pleas for changes to be made to some of the key features of Solvency II subsequently fed into Brexit narratives about 'taking back control'. This chapter ultimately shows how in the EU context, implementation of principles-based regulation caused not a regulatory race to the bottom but a push to fix the meaning of regulatory concepts and rules, which was perceived as a poor fit with the British reliance on market-based finance.

Chapter 9 examines the emergence of the pension de-risking market, which is in many ways exemplary of the changes in the insurance industry more generally. The chapter provides a brief historical overview of what became known as the 'pensions crisis' that led to the closure of many defined benefit pension schemes, leaving the legacy defined benefit pension liabilities to be picked up by insurance companies. The chapter then analyses the structure of this newly invigorated market field before analysing the ties with this field and the adjacent market field of asset management. The chapter concludes by arguing that this development illustrates the changing logics underpinning private pensions: from a relational model based on trust to one that revolves around the financial logic of risk-based capital.

Finally, in Chapter 10, which concludes the book, I return to some of the questions raised in this introductory chapter. I review the key arguments developed in this book, and, in an attempt to understand why modern finance theory has become such a powerful force in reshaping various domains of society, I relate the key arguments of the book to the notion of 'performative power' (Svetlova, 2012). I subsequently address the question of how the institutionalization of modern finance theory may be interpreted as a form of rationalization that, on the one hand, achieves socio-technical closure by making it more difficult to sustain organizational forms of insurance other than large proprietary insurance companies that predominantly sell unit-linked products. I finally raise the question of whether this socio-technical closure should be seen as a desirable development in the context of future needs for economic security.

Financialization, Quantification and Evaluation

The main purpose of this book is to document and explain a process of cultural change in the British life insurance industry away from traditional actuarial practices of prudence and profit participation and towards a system of financialized governance that relies on the explicit quantification of financial risk. This task can be subdivided into three components: (1) a description of how life insurers came to organize uncertainty around the explicit quantification of financial risk; (2) an explanation of why financial risk became incorporated into insurers' evaluation machinery in the way it did; and (3) an examination of the consequences of insurers' changing evaluation machinery. In this chapter, I outline the theoretical approach I follow to study the process of cultural change and the remaking of the boundaries between British life insurance and the financial sector more generally.

The chapter contains three sections. First, I explain what is meant here by financialization, drawing on the work of Eve Chiapello and colleagues, who, in Weberian spirit, link the evolution of capitalism to the tools and instruments employed to render capital visible, deployable and manageable. Second, I review the social science literature on insurance. This section enables us to see how the insurance logic changes with the appropriation and institutionalization of new financial evaluation practices. Third and finally, I outline the theoretical apparatus that underpins the analysis of *how* the boundaries between finance and insurance were remade. I draw on, and integrate, three sociological perspectives: the social studies of finance, field theory and the sociology of professions. Drawing together key lessons from each of these perspectives, I suggest that the institutionalization of new quantification practices and the subsequent evolution of British life insurance occurs at the intersection of the power struggles among insurance companies and the competition between different forms of actuarial and financial professional expertise. Readers not interested in sociological theory per se may wish to skip this final section and proceed directly to the empirical chapters.

Financialization and the three ages of financial quantification

Financialization has been a key term for understanding changes in contemporary capitalism (Van der Zwan, 2014; Mader et al, 2021). In generic terms, financialization refers to the process whereby financial logics, motives and actors have become increasingly prevalent in contemporary capitalist societies. The term encompasses both structural changes in the economy and changes at the level of practice in various spheres of society. Focusing on the structural level, for instance, Krippner (2005) has shown that an increased share of US national income is earned through financial channels. Financialization, in this view, may be seen as a recurring phenomenon that has occurred at various other stages in global history (Arrighi, 1994). Crucially, this structural perspective tends to include insurance among the financial channels through which income is generated, and the expansion of the insurance sector may therefore be interpreted as contributing to the financialization of society.

In this book, however, I follow another approach, focusing on financialization as a phenomenon taking place at the level of practice. As the vast literature on financialization has shown, the rise of finance has been accompanied by the diffusion of financial actors, logics, motives and value models in various spheres of contemporary capitalist societies, ranging from corporate governance (Erturk, 2020) to the art world (Velthuis and Coslor, 2012) and from housing (Aalbers, 2016) to – indeed – finance itself (for example, Besedovsky, 2018; Coombs and Van der Heide, 2020). Arguably among the most prolific studies of financialization in practice have been those documenting the increased power enjoyed by shareholders in the governance of the private sector. Their position has been strengthened by the proliferation of ideological maxims and calculative tools propagating the virtues of shareholder maximization – a development that has also been accompanied by the rise of new functions such as that of the Chief Financial Officer, who has not only increased the importance of financial considerations in corporate decision making but has also served as a mouthpiece of shareholder interests on management boards (Zorn, 2004; Fligstein and Shin, 2007). They are in effect the 'symbols of the corporate focus on "shareholder value"' (Zorn, 2004, p 346). Financialization, in this perspective, is thus primarily an organizational phenomenon affecting corporate behaviour by shaping corporate calculations and embedding these calculations into organizational routines.

This approach is akin to a Weberian take on the history of capitalism that perceives the rise of business accounting and its quantitative techniques as a key factor in the history of capitalism (Carruthers and Espeland, 1991;

Bryer, 2000; Berland and Chiapello, 2009). Accounting makes investment decisions amenable to calculation and contributes to the rationalization of business decision making – not necessarily in the sense that it makes business more efficient but in that it allows actors to justify and account for particular actions with logical reasons, enhancing trust in enterprise. The significance of accounting and the associated quantitative techniques has a technical as well as a rhetorical aspect: it structures processes of calculation *and* gives entrepreneurs a rhetorical tool that allows them to present their business plans as rational to both investors and regulators (Carruthers and Espeland, 1991).

The financial quantification techniques business actors use today have a long history. Observing this history, Chiapello and Walter (2016) distinguish three ages of financial quantification. The first age refers to the rise of financial discounting. Discounting is a technique that puts a value on time. It has been used since at least the late 17th century to establish equivalence between £100 today and £100 in, say, ten years from now. Various approaches to discounting have been used, but the one that has become most widespread is compound-interest discounting, which measures the present value of a future value by discounting exponentially (Deringer, 2017). When discounting exponentially, the present value of a distant future value may quickly become rather small. For example, assuming an annual discount rate of 10 per cent, in other words, means that the present value of £100 in one year from now is equal to

$$£100 \star \frac{1}{1.1} \approx 90.90 \, ,$$

while the present value of the same £100 in ten years from now is equal to

$$£100 \star \frac{1}{(1.1^{10})} \approx 38.55 \, .$$

This decline in value the further out an investment is in the future is typically justified by two arguments. First, investments have opportunity costs, and discount rates are a way to take those opportunity costs into account. By investing in a ten-year project, say, an investor chooses not to invest in something else or to earn an interest by depositing the funds at a bank. The discount rate should thus reflect the interest that could have been earned through alternative investment opportunities. Second, a promise to receive £100 in the future is uncertain. In those ten years, many things can happen that may prevent the actual payment from being made, including debtor bankruptcy, for example. Compound interest discounting provides a means to take this uncertainty into consideration.

Despite the shroud of objectivity, discounting is a subjective and somewhat arbitrary affair. Picking a particular discount rate requires some sort of judgement, whether implicitly or explicitly, about an investment's opportunity costs and the degree of uncertainty with which the promise of payment will materialize. This is no easy task. In what Chiapello and Walter (2016) refer to as the second age of financial quantification, which they situate in the 1950s, new concepts and techniques were developed in the context of financial markets investment to estimate the appropriate discount rate for particular investments. With the rise of modern portfolio theory in the 1950s, the investment problem was increasingly presented as a trade-off between the expected returns of the investment and risk that could be optimized by diversifying away idiosyncratic risks. Risk acquired a more precise meaning, finding expression as the volatility of the instrument's price. The riskier the investment, the higher the returns investors would expect and the higher the discount rate should be. The discount rate should thus consist of the investment's opportunity costs – which could be measured simply by picking a reference asset – and a 'risk premium', which is the part of an investment's expected returns that serves as compensation for risk and is proportionate to the asset's volatility.

In the third age of financial quantification, which goes to the heart of the cultural changes described in this book, the subjectivity implied by discounting was further reduced. This age is strongly associated with the rise of options pricing theory from the 1970s onwards and the idea that the market value of instruments represents their true value. Options had been notoriously difficult to value. In 1973, however, the economists Fischer Black, Myron Scholes and Robert Merton came up with a model for pricing European call options that would become paradigmatic in the field of modern finance theory (more on this in Chapter 6). The Black–Scholes–Merton model became an exemplary problem solution on the back of which a wide variety of models were developed for valuing claims that were contingent on some underlying random process (such as derivatives). What Chiapello and Walter (2016) refer to as the market-consistent convention follows from this model and assumes that markets are frictionless, complete and free from arbitrage opportunities. Within these markets, the value of an instrument can be inferred from the market prices of instruments that can be used to 'hedge' against or insulate future price movements of the instrument. The modeller, in other words, may derive a stochastic discount factor, which in contrast to deterministic discounting takes account of the changing value of a contingent or derivative claim depending on the price movements of the underlying asset. To the uninitiated, this might easily seem like impenetrable language, and it is, at this stage, not necessary to fully understand what's going on here (Chapter 6 contains a more detailed explanation for those who are interested in this). What should be clear, however, is that the mean variance and market-consistent conventions turn discounting into a seemingly 'objective' problem – objective in the sense that within the model world of option pricing theory – the market-consistent world – a unique value (and the appropriate discount factor) can be found for any financial instrument traded therein. Market-consistent valuation, in other words, takes away some of the modeller's discretion in judgements about the opportunity costs and risks of an investment, and this exactitude enables the measurement, carving and trading of financial risk.

The diffusion of financial quantification techniques helps make things amenable to investment and links an increasingly broad range of things into financial circuits. Chiapello (2015) therefore suggests that the financialization of capitalism should be understood by studying the progressive diffusion of the three quantification conventions associated with the three ages of financial quantification. This is where the concept of financialization meets the related concepts of economization (Çalışkan and Callon, 2009, 2010) and assetization (Birch and Muniesa, 2020), which have led scholars to investigate how economic objects and assets are created, and how the asset form has become prevalent in contemporary capitalism. The asset form involves control over a particular thing (a piece of machinery, a brand or even a customer relation) and entails the promise of future revenue. In this light, financialization refers to those cases where things are turned into *financial* assets – that is, tradable securities that are bought, sold and held primarily for the purpose of benefitting from capital gains (price appreciation), dividends and interest payments. Financial quantification conventions then help turn things into financial assets by establishing and formalizing actors' expectations about the risk and rewards of purchasing specific financial securities, allowing for rationalized decision making, engendering trust in the asset form itself, and enhancing the security's tradability.

Studying financialization in action, that is, investigating the diffusion of financial evaluation practices that help spread the financial asset form, especially those that belong to the second and third age of financial quantification, also enables us to see how finance itself has become financialized. This seemingly oxymoronic phrase contains the claim made by various scholars that the creation of the international financial system – the system that crashed so violently in 2007–9 and has since struggled to maintain itself – was accompanied by the rapid proliferation in various domains of financial practice of financial evaluation practices rooted in modern finance theory (Lengwiler, 2016; Besedovsky, 2018; Coombs and Van der Heide, 2020). The exactitude of modern financial quantifications – whether financial actors believe them to be true or not – has enabled financial actors and their supervisors to act as if uncertainty can be accurately quantified into risk and as if this risk can be managed rationally (MacKenzie, 2011). The result is well known: a massive proliferation of the financial asset form and the creation of a highly unstable financial system that has not managed without the continued support of governments and central banks ever since. Even if the American insurer AIG played a crucial role in enabling the emergence of a fragile international financial system, few have studied processes of financialization in the context of insurance (for some exceptions, see Jarzabkowski et al, 2015; François, 2021; Fytros, 2021). This is what the book seeks to achieve: to describe and explain how the governance of the British life insurance sector has been transformed via the appropriation of financial evaluation practices.

Viewing financialization as a diffusion of financial actors and motives enables an understanding of how the value model of British life insurers has changed since the 1970s. The traditional premium-based value model of insurance closely corresponds to what Christophers (2015) identifies as one of four ideal-typical 'value models' in financial services: fees, gains, premiums and spreads. Their main source of income are the premiums they receive in exchange for assuming the financial risk associated with some predefined event – in the case of life insurance: death. Insurers are understood to be able to manage this risk through diversification. By *pooling* resources and grouping together uncertain events, they can reduce the overall uncertainty to a level that is more manageable (Lehtonen and Liukko, 2015).[1] Of course, life insurers also invest collected premiums in financial markets to generate additional income, which is a relevant source of income especially for long-term insurance arrangements such as life insurance. But the financial risk associated with these investments was generally not considered an important part of the insurance commodity: it was seen simply as something to be dealt with through actuarial discretion and prudence. With the introduction of modern finance theory in the life insurance sector to govern financial risk, however, insurers' value model also started to change, increasingly becoming similar to the fee-based model more often seen in the investment management industry.

Insurance and the technology of risk

The preeminent sociologist of insurance François Ewald (1991) famously described modern insurance as a set of institutions that operationalize the 'abstract technology of risk' and thereby enable individuals to pool together resources to face economic uncertainty. As various historians have noted, the rise of this technology was intimately tied to the rise of statistical thinking more generally (Daston, 1988; Hacking, 1990; Porter, 1995). In its modern statistical incarnation, risk is an expression of the likelihood that an individual incurs a loss, for instance due to death. While it is almost impossible to predict the death of a specific individual, it is much easier to predict when a group of individuals will die *on average*. Even if insurers cannot know when a specific individual will die, they can still derive an expectation about the likelihood the same individual will die – their 'risk' – from the mortality statistics of a larger population. The law of large numbers, moreover, postulates that the larger the risk pool, the more likely the risk pool's actual mortality will closely follow the mortality of the population at large. By pooling individuals together, in other words, life insurers manage uncertainty through diversification. At least since the late 18th century, insurers have used this abstract technology of risk to rationalize the governance of insurance arrangements and to commodify or economize uncertainty (Lehtonen and Van Hoyweghen, 2014).

The reality of insurance in practice, however, has been a lot messier than this neat account of the insurance logic suggests. The 'making' of risk, as Van Hoyweghen (2007) calls it, is troubled by a wide range of problems that complicate the calculation and application of risk knowledge. Many of these problems pertain to the potential mismatch between the population from which the risk knowledge is derived and the population of insureds included in a given risk pool (in insurance terminology, this is called 'basis risk'). Mortality statistics, for instance, are by necessity based on populations that are no longer alive. The mortality of populations in a specific region, moreover, may diverge from the overall population in a country (Alborn, 2009; Turnbull, 2017). Even more troublesome is the problem of adverse selection, which denotes the basic idea that the largest risks have the biggest incentive to take out insurance, potentially skewing the propensity to die among an insurer's risk pool in a direction unfavourable for the insurer. When insurers don't have the means to distinguish good from bad risks, the idea goes, the pool will fill itself with bad risks, incentivizing the good risks – who would otherwise end up 'subsidizing' the bad risks – to leave (Baker, 2003). Other forms of uncertainty, unrelated to mortality, further reduce insurers' capacity to price according to risk. Life insurers, for instance, invest policyholders' premiums in capital markets, and they may not know in advance how well their investments will perform. Put simply, even with the technology of risk, life insurance is a highly uncertain business (Ericson and Doyle, 2004).

Insurers may adopt various strategies to deal with the uncertainty of their business. A first set of strategies focuses on the underwriting process and the selection of risks, involving the classification of insurance prospects into appropriate risk categories. Prior to the introduction of life tables, risk selection in life insurance often involved rather crude distinctions and, as Porter remarks about American life insurance, was 'rather like admitting someone to a gentleman's club. The company had to be satisfied that the applicant was honourable and trustworthy' (Porter, 2000, p 228; for Britain, see Clark, 1999). Small mutual insurers and friendly societies similarly rely on community ethics to tackle the problem of adverse selection (Van Leeuwen, 2016). Modern life insurance added to this the technique of risk-based pricing, offering differentiated rates to prospects according to their risk and thereby enlarging the pool of potential entrants to an insurance scheme. Age-based pricing is the most obvious example of this (Bouk, 2015). Another example is the professionalization of medical underwriting and the use of medical knowledge to assess the physical condition of insurance prospects (Jauho, 2015; Porter, 2000). Marketing can also play a role in this, selecting risks by leveraging the power of affect and self-selection (McFall, 2011, 2015). Bringing the abstract technology of risk into practice thus involves a wide variety of practices that aim to stabilize the relation between statistical knowledge of risk and the risk pool itself.

A second strategy deployed in modern life insurance to deal with uncertainty is prudence. The inevitable uncertainty involved in risk calculations has allowed the actuarial profession to maintain jurisdictional claims over pricing and reserving, arguing that the application of risk knowledge to the insurance business required a good measure of judgement and prudence (Alborn, 1994; Porter, 1995). In practice, this often meant that insurance companies tended to charge premiums well in excess of what in hindsight would have been 'actuarially fair', building up large reserves that in the case of mutual insurance companies belonged to no one in particular. To distribute these surpluses across policyholders, and to reduce their pricing, insurers invented bonus systems that allowed them to distribute excess reserves post-hoc (Alborn, 2002a, 2009). Via these bonuses, policyholders could participate in the firm's profits in exchange for reduced certainty about the level of benefits they would receive. These were the basic elements of how traditional 'with-profits' life insurers, emerging from the late 18th century onwards, dealt with uncertainty: prudence in calculation and post-hoc bonus distribution of thusly accumulated surpluses (Chapter 3 deals with this topic in more detail).

Applying the technology of risk in practice is anything but straightforward and involves many forms of uncertainty. For Ewald, this implies a specific role for social scientific and humanities research on insurance. 'Where the elaboration of the abstract technology is the work of the actuary', he argued,

> and the creation of the institution that of the entrepreneur, one might say that the aim of the sociologist, historian or political analyst should be to ascertain why at a given moment insurance institutions take on particular shape rather than another, and utilize the technique of risk in one way rather than in another. (Ewald, 1991, p 198)

This is precisely what this book aims to achieve: to add to the sociology of insurance an understanding of how and why the value model of insurance has changed and how the institutionalization of financial uncertainty in the insurance business has changed, away from traditional actuarial modes of dealing with uncertainty towards the individualization of financial risk and financial risk management as the dominant mode of governance.

A sociological perspective on the financialization of life insurance

My approach to studying the evolution of British life insurance and the diffusion of financial quantification conventions therein draws on three different intellectual traditions. First, drawing on sociological field theory, I conceptualize British life insurance as a set of market fields and actuarial science as an epistemic or 'intellectual field' (Whitley, 1984). Doing so opens up a view of how the competitive forces between incumbents and challengers shape the 'rules of the game'. Second, to capture the competitive dynamics among professional groups within these fields, I draw on the ecological perspective that has been prevalent in the sociology of professions. This perspective makes clear, for instance, that members of a profession may operate in different organizational environments that come with different challenges from the profession's jurisdictional claims and claims to special expertise. A profession's internal struggles in response to external challenges in one particular environment impact the jurisdictional claims of the profession in other environments too. These environments are the epistemic and market fields in which members of a profession work. Third, drawing on science and technology studies, I suggest that the enactments of expertise and the institutionalization of evaluation practices in the market field are tied to their material environment, lending them a degree of durability and enabling and constraining the strategies available to field actors and members of professional groups. Insurers' evaluation practices – the way they model and evaluate the economic value and risks of their business – is where the field struggles and professional expertise comes together.

In what follows, I first review each of the three perspectives, briefly summarize their core features and say a few words about what these perspectives have to offer for my study of the insurance sector and how they help address the how and why questions central to this book: how did the financial evaluation practices that belong to modern finance theory become institutionalized in British life insurance and why was this the case? I conclude this chapter with a few considerations on whether and how these perspectives can be integrated.

The social studies of finance

Although the social studies of finance broadly refers to the application of concepts and methodologies from the broader social sciences to the study of finance (de Goede, 2005a), it is often associated with a set of propositions inspired by the social studies of science and technology (and, in particular, actor-network theory) that draw attention to the 'the physicality, the corporeality, and the technicality of markets' (MacKenzie, 2009, p 8).

Foundational in this field is the work of Michel Callon (1998b, 2007), who has made the case for economic sociology more generally to focus on the question of how economic agency is constructed, constituted or shaped, and the role that devices and material artefacts play in this construction. If we are to have an adequate sociological understanding of the economy, this work suggests, we should appreciate the role of economic knowledge and technology in shaping cognition, making calculation possible and constructing economic agency (Callon, 2007; MacKenzie, 2009).

Central in the social studies of finance is the proposition of the 'performativity' of economics, the notion that practices purporting to describe economic reality play an active role in constituting it (Callon, 1998b, 2007; MacKenzie, 2006; Muniesa, 2014; Boldyrev and Svetlova, 2016). Studying economic performativity is especially pertinent in the case of financial markets, which revolve around the buying and selling of seemingly abstract claims or promises on future 'cash flows'. Simply put, the performativity of economics can be understood as follows: to decide whether one should buy or sell a financial product requires some sort of evaluation of its 'value'; and in the case of an economic transaction, which is what the buying of a financial product is, this evaluation will require some form of economic knowledge and takes place within a material environment that provides the stage for this evaluation, as it were. Economic agency is situated in a material environment and is constituted by knowledge of the economy.

Scholars in the social studies of finance have used this basic insight to investigate the role that economic models play in financial markets. MacKenzie's (2006) seminal study of options pricing theory and the rise of derivatives markets, for instance, examined how the rise of options pricing theory, and in particular the Black–Scholes model for pricing financial options, was used in financial markets and how this usage has not only helped to legitimize financial derivatives but also influenced and shaped the pricing patterns. In this study, MacKenzie finds a particular type of performativity, which he calls 'Barnesian performativity', that consists of a feedback loop that makes real-world price patterns conform to the prices 'predicted' by the model (see also MacKenzie, 2001; MacKenzie and Millo, 2003). Later studies have broadened this agenda, examining the various ways in which actors use a wide variety of models in financial markets for the purposes of organizational control, the making of trading decisions and the identification of trading opportunities (Svetlova, 2018). In a recent study, for instance, Beunza (2019) suggests that when models are used for the purposes of organizational control as a source of authority, they may induce 'model-based moral disengagement', 'opening the bank to unrestrained pursuit of self-interest' (p 13).

In this book, I take this basic insight of the social studies of finance – namely that economic models do things and that what they do depends on how they are deployed and institutionalized in practice – as the starting point for my analysis of the evolution of insurance practice. Sociological and historical scholarship on insurance has all but ignored the material dimension of insurance, examining for instance how insurers 'make risks' (of the diversifiable kind) and how they market them (Van Hoyweghen, 2007; McFall, 2009; Ossandón, 2014; Meyers and Van Hoyweghen, 2018). But few have investigated the role that economic models of insurers' assets and liabilities play in insurance governance more broadly. One of the key contributions of this book, then, is to take the social studies of finance to insurance and to investigate how insurers use economic models to evaluate the risks and value of insurance business and what role these models play in systems of internal and external control. This perspective gives us a basic framework for understanding the object of interest in this study – insurers' evaluation practices – and provides the basis for understanding how and why the power struggles and the competitive dynamics among professional groups in the insurance business shape and are shaped by insurers' evaluation machinery.

Markets as fields

The second intellectual resource on which this book draws is sociological field theory, as developed primarily by Pierre Bourdieu (1997, 2005) and Neil Fligstein (1996, 2001; Fligstein and McAdam, 2012). Field theory provides a meso-level account of how social order emerges and evolves in various domains of social life, including markets (DiMaggio and Powell, 1983; Bourdieu, 1997; Fligstein and McAdam, 2012). It presents a relational view of actors, whose position in a given field defines their interests vis-a-vis other actors - a position that must be actively reproduced - and focuses on the role of state agencies in shaping the institutional arrangements that enable and constrain their behaviour. The central analytical divide is that between 'incumbents' - actors whose interests tend to be reflected in the institutional structure of the field - and 'challengers', who may seek to influence the rules of the game (Bourdieu, 1997; Fligstein, 2001; Fligstein and McAdam, 2012, p 13). The crucial analytical advantage of the notion of fields is its ability to account for the interaction between the institutional structures of a given field and the agency of the actors that populate it. For instance, challengers are not just passive agents that stick to the rules set by incumbents; they may also seize on events external to the field (a technological innovation or a political event, for example) as opportunities for undermining the existing rules of the game. If successful, an alternative social constellation may emerge, which redefines who is on which side of the divide between incumbents and challengers (Fligstein, 1996, 2001; Fligstein and McAdam, 2012).

Field theory provides a powerful set of tools to explain how practices in a given domain evolve as the product of the competitive struggles between actors vying over scarce resources, whatever they may be. This perspective lends itself well to the study of markets, which may be seen as specific types of social arena defined by competition among producers or service providers. It shifts focus from the moment of exchange to the structuring forces that determine the position of actors (Beckert, 2009, p 609) and, in so doing, draws attention to the fact that markets do not exist in isolation but are embedded in a broader social environment that may be conceived of in terms of 'adjacent fields' (Fligstein and McAdam, 2012). Connections to powerful actors in adjacent fields may strengthen the field position of actors in other fields. The state, for instance, may itself be conceived of as a set of strategic action fields that endows those actors who manage to get the state on their side with a powerful resource to strengthen their own position in the market field (Fligstein and McAdam, 2012). Under normal conditions, this relation will typically be based on a congruence of interests between the incumbent groups in state and market fields. In some pivotal moments, however, state actors may perceive it as being in their best interest to link up with the challengers in a market field and help them undermine the existing institutional structures. This may for instance be the case when there are changes internal to the adjacent state fields, such as shifts in the relations between the different actor groups and their positions within the field. Actors' ties to actors in adjacent fields, such as state fields or neighbouring market fields (for example, banking in the case of insurance), thus often play a crucial role in the dynamics of stability and change that shape the evolution of market fields (Fligstein and McAdam, 2012).

The history of insurance is replete with examples where state action has been a decisive factor in stabilizing field relations and in overturning previously stable field settlements. Historians have for instance found that state supervisors have played an important role in the maintenance of insurance cartels in the likes of France, Norway and Sweden by regulating both price and product competition (Hautcoeur, 2004; Larsson and Lönnborg, 2015; Espeli, 2020). While this cartelization allowed incumbent insurers to secure their dominant position in the insurance industry in the face of competition from foreign insurers, Swedish and Norwegian state actors also perceived cartelization as a means of protecting policyholders' entitlements and securing a stable source of investment in the domestic economy (Larsson and Lönnborg, 2015; Espeli, 2020). In the early 1980s, when the economists favouring competition-enhancing policies gained the upper hand within the Norwegian state fields, the insurance supervisor retracted its sanctioning of horizontal price agreements, inaugurating the end of a long-lasting insurance cartel (Espeli, 2020).

State regulation of the British insurance market, however, has traditionally been much more 'light touch' than elsewhere, and many have argued for this reason that the competition among UK insurers has tended to be fiercer, leading to sharper insurance pricing (Finsinger and Pauly, 1986). Others, however, suggest that British insurers have been similarly successful in regulating competition, albeit via other means (Westall, 2006). Incumbent British insurers have relied much more on what Fligstein and McAdam (2012) call 'internal governance units' other than insurance supervisors. Internal governance units are the organizations and actors that ensure compliance with the rules of the game, and, in so doing, help stabilize the 'original settlement' of the field by imposing norms and standards, coordinating the exchange of information between market actors, or representing field actors in policy fields. Even if their existence is often justified by reference to the general interest of the field, incumbents often, though not always, retain a strong degree of control over internal governance units and by extension over the competitive dynamics among field actors. One notable example of such an internal governance unit, for instance, is the Fire Offices Committee, through which incumbents could restrict access to reinsurance facilities and share pricing information. The Fire Offices Committee was set up as early as 1868. 'While never establishing absolute market control', Westall (2006) argues, 'it was an overwhelmingly important price leader across the market for a century' (p 1631). Collusion in the life insurance market never went this far, though there was the Life Offices Association, which imposed limits on commission rates and the timing of the payment of commissions to intermediaries, limiting the capacity of challengers quickly to gain market share (Carter and Falush, 2009, pp 154–5).

In sum, the field-theoretical approach provides a key part of the puzzle for addressing the question of why modern finance theory became institutionalized in the insurance business the way it did. The crucial features of this approach here are, first, the analytical distinction between incumbents and challengers, competition among whom provides the central dynamic through which changes external to the field are filtered; second, an appreciation of actors' ties to adjacent fields as potential power resources; and, third, a focus on the role of internal governance units as part of the fabric of market fields that intermediate the power relations between incumbents and challengers.

Professions and their ecologies

The third intellectual resource this book draws on is the sociology of professions (Macdonald, 1995; Adams, 2015) and especially the framework developed by Andrew Abbott to study professions through the lens of linked ecologies (Abbott, 1988; Abbott, 2005). This framework helps us to capture the social forces that are less easily understood by looking at markets as fields, namely those forces and effects produced by the cross-field alliances among members of professional groups.

Scholars in the sociology of professions have extensively examined the links between professions, their institutional environment, the nature of their work and the methods and techniques used to carry out that work. A central concept in this literature is that of the 'professional project' (Larson, 1977), or the strategies that members of a profession may deploy to strengthen and expand the profession's jurisdictional claims and enhance its status. These strategies may include, for instance, the institutionalization of a formal system of education, licensing and the search for the state's approval to self-organize and -regulate (Macdonald, 1995). In pursuing these strategies, moreover, professions do not just solidify or extend jurisdictional claims but also inadvertently influence the institutional structure of the fields in which they operate. 'Field-level change occurs, largely, in tandem with professionals' efforts to consolidate and advance their own professional projects' (Suddaby and Viale, 2011, p 247; see also DiMaggio and Powell, 1983). Professions, in other words, are among the forces that shape the institutional structure of the fields in which they maintain their jurisdictional claims. Professional expertise mediates the power struggles in a field but cannot be reduced to the field logic.

Processes of 'professionalization' are never entirely complete. Professions must actively maintain their privileged position. They must fend off threats from two main types of competitors: from bureaucratic forms of organization and competing professional groups (Abbott, 1988). These pressures are key to understanding what Larson refers to as 'the dialectics of indetermination and standardization' in the forms of knowledge on which professional groups lay claim (Larson, 1977, p 42) – a dynamic that has been very persistent in the history of the actuarial profession too. In order to legitimize their privileged position in the face of state scrutiny, members of the actuarial profession have veered between claims of scientific and mathematical objectivity and a more subjective form of expertise deriving from practical business experience, which eludes standardization. While emphasizing their mathematical prowess has allowed actuaries to differentiate themselves from other occupational groups such as accountants, their claim of deeply rooted subjective knowledge of the insurance business and mortality statistics facilitated resistance against the intrusion of bureaucracy and the standardization of valuation work (Alborn, 1994; Porter, 1995). In contrast to the accounting profession, the actuarial profession has succeeded relatively well in fending off pressure to standardize and routinize expertise (Porter, 1995).

In Abbott's ecological view of professions, interprofessional competition is the crucial factor for understanding the relation between professions, the work their members do and the knowledge and skills they deploy in so doing (Abbott, 1988). The continuous possibility that a profession may see its jurisdictional claims challenged by neighbouring professional groups means they must engage in sustained efforts to maintain their jurisdictional claims. Drawing on academic knowledge to claim special expertise is one way in which professions may strengthen their jurisdictional claims (Alborn, 1994). Another is through internal governance mechanisms, signalling quality control (Macdonald, 1995). The strength of these claims, however, is not absolute. Whenever doubts arise about the effectiveness of a profession's knowledge base or the reliability of its internal governance mechanisms, rivalling professional groups may effectively challenge the profession's jurisdictional claims and push organizations or policymakers to relinquish its privileged status. Strategies that worked in the past, moreover, may later turn into a liability as the environment changes (Abbott, 1988).

The strategy that professions adopt to fend off challenges to their jurisdictional claims is a product of the internal struggles within the professions in which the variegating work experiences, forms of expertise and positions within professional ecologies shape the preferences of a profession's members (Abbott, 2005; Seabrooke and Tsingou, 2009; Seabrooke, 2014). Professionals located in one ecology may form alliances within or across professional ecologies to make a stronger case for reforming the profession's knowledge base (Abbott, 1995). Especially important here are the 'go-betweens', or those who move across different ecologies, thereby facilitating the establishment of alliances (Seabrooke and Tsingou, 2009). In so doing, they may gain familiarity with different ways of doing things and different kinds of know-how and establish cross-professional networks that facilitate the formation of 'hinges' – or strategies that provide benefits to professionals across multiple ecologies (Abbott, 2005). In the case of the actuarial profession, such rewards may be reflected in the strengthening of the position of members of the profession in their professional ecology.

Professional sociology, in sum, provides a way of understanding how members of a profession may serve as agents of change in the way that work is organized and specific tasks are performed. The need to legitimize jurisdictional claims in ever changing professional ecologies provides an impetus for changing the knowledge base on which the profession stools its claims. Although professions will usually seek to maintain stability even in the face of external changes, some changes are so threatening to a profession's jurisdictional claims that previous settlements may become unsettled. Members of a profession may develop or attach themselves to new professional projects in response, depending on what strategy they think best strengthens their position within given ecologies. These professional reform projects may include the adoption of new internal governance mechanisms, but they may also include reforms of the educational curriculum to include new sources of academic knowledge as part of the profession's knowledge base. The ecological view of professions, in other words, provides a useful way of understanding why particular sources of knowledge and expertise gain legitimacy in performing specific tasks.

An integrated approach

Taken together, these three perspectives offer the conceptual material for the theoretical framework underpinning this book. This framework, as already indicated earlier, conceives of the British life insurance market as a set of interrelated fields that are also tied to the adjacent fields of the state, banking and finance more generally, the epistemic field of actuarial science and, further removed, also modern finance theory. The internal power struggles over the rules of the game within these fields is what drives the dynamics of stability and change. A key force mediating these power struggles is the competition between professional groups, operating across fields. Members of the actuarial profession, for instance, are simultaneously a member of the profession and part of an organization (a life insurance company or an investment bank, for example), and their interests may be in tension with those of other members of the organization. Field dynamics and the dynamic of professional competition may influence each other. The power relations among field actors and the competitive relations among professional groups are both structured by the material (evaluation) practices that enable and constrain actors' strategies.

Scholars have frequently noted the similarity between the field theoretical and ecological approaches, which raises the question of why this distinction between field dynamics and ecology dynamics should be maintained. Both approaches, after all, rely on spatial metaphors, and the location that actors occupy within these spaces is determined by their relations to other actors (Lowrey and Sherrill, 2020). Both approaches, moreover, highlight the importance of isomorphism, noting that the structure of adjacent fields and neighbouring ecologies will likely become more alike over time (Liu and Emirbayer, 2016).

There are, however, also marked differences between the two approaches that justify the adoption of an integrated perspective that accounts for both market fields and professional ecologies. The location of actors in fields is determined primarily by their resources and the unequal relations among actors. The location of actors within professional ecologies, in contrast, is primarily determined by their affiliation with other members of the professional group, the work they do and by the competitive relation to members of other professional groups (Liu and Emirbayer, 2016). While field theory is better equipped to account for the role of power and social structure in determining action, the metaphor of ecologies is well suited for the study of the creative reimagining of a social space in response to disruptions or challenges to prior settlements (Liu and Emirbayer, 2016; Lowrey and Sherrill, 2020). Simply put, while conceiving of social spaces as fields enables the analysis of how actors leverage various resources to jockey for position in the social space, ecological approaches emphasize how the variegated nature of actors' experiences provides the raw input for imagining and reimagining professional identity, which may contribute to processes of institutional change (Suddaby and Viale, 2011).

The social studies of finance, on the other hand, is closely associated with actor-network theory, which has a distinct intellectual tradition that is sometimes thought of as incommensurable with the more conventional (economic) sociological approaches of field theory and professional ecologies. (Indeed, Callon (1998b) articulated his performativity approach in opposition to the 'new economic sociology' of Mark Granovetter; and Neil Fligstein (2001) explicitly says that his theorization of markets as fields was technological determinist.) The issue at stake here is that the different theoretical approaches focus on different units of analysis. While field theory analyses social reality in terms of fields populated by human or organizational actors, actor-network theory instead focuses on socio-material networks – also referred to as assemblages or *agencements* – composed of human and non-human entities that operate as actors or actants.

As some scholars have noted, however, these approaches have much to gain from each other (Gulledge et al, 2015; MacKenzie, 2019). While actor-network theory can benefit from more conventional sociological approaches to conceptualize issues of power and structural advantage, for instance, field theory stands much to gain from the attention paid in actor-network theory to the role of material devices, models and so on in the construction of agency (MacKenzie, 2019). Similarly, the sociology of professions can benefit from actor-network theory by conceptualizing expertise not as something that an individual can possess or not but as something that inheres in the socio-material networks that allow for the performance of expertise (Eyal, 2013). In this book, I follow these lines of thinking and take up Fourcade's (2007) dictum that 'all field struggles are also, always, performativity struggles' (p 1027). The rules of the game, in other words, have no independent existence outside the material machinery that enables actors to conform to or undermine them, and among the rules of the game are the jurisdictional claims of professional groups to perform certain tasks drawing on specific performances of expertise.

3

Shifting Boundaries
between Insurance and Finance

> Why did Hambro Life, Britain's most successful life assurance company, pay £10.4m, or more than four times book value, this week, for Dunbar, a tiny merchant bank whose only claim to fame is that Sean Connery owns 8 per cent of the action and several of sports promoter Mark McCormack's stable are among its client list? It is a question that has been hotly debated over City luncheon tables as analysts try to reconcile the price Hambro Life is paying for an unknown licensed deposit taker with the lowly rating normally accorded to bank shares. (Hall, 1982)

In 1982, this was still a genuine question. Life insurance and banking were distinct markets, each operating with distinct knowledge machineries and distinct systems of supervision. The management of Hambro Life, a relative newcomer to the market, however, thought differently. The company was founded in 1970 by the South African insurance entrepreneur Mark Weinberg, who in 1961 had already successfully set up another company, Abbey Life. Both companies had gained substantial market share by aggressively competing in the market using a large direct sales force. Yet, maintaining such a large sales force – Hambro Life employed over 3,000 sales agents in 1982 – was also expensive. Weinberg therefore envisioned Hambro Life expanding its business operations in a market for financial services at large. 'We feel very strongly that the dividing lines between various financial institutions are going to break down', he was reported saying by a *Financial Times* reporter. 'We are in a strong position to make our life assurance company the hub of an integrated financial services operation on a lower cost basis than either a clearing bank or a building society which have to carry very large high street branch networks' (Hall, 1982).

Regardless of how successful Weinberg's efforts to integrate insurance and banking services were or not, what matters here is that Weinberg perceived life insurance predominantly as a *financial* service. In so doing, Weinberg's ideas about life insurance differed quite substantially from what would have counted as actuarial orthodoxy at the time and the idea that life insurance operated on a different, incommensurable logic relative to finance. Weinberg, who himself had a legal background, perceived life insurance primarily as a savings and investment product, which should require as little interference from actuaries as possible. By tying policyholder benefits directly to the investment performance of underlying funds, unit-linked insurance did just that. The emergence of unit-linked insurance, in other words, entailed not just a competitive struggle between different businesses but also between different conceptions of what life insurance should be and the role of actuarial expertise therein. If anywhere, the story of the changing boundaries between insurance and finance should thus begin with the story of unit-linked insurance and Mark Weinberg's efforts to remake British life insurance.

Upending the market for life insurance

When unit-linked insurance emerged towards the late 1950s and early 1960s, it challenged a traditional model of life insurance that had remained largely unchanged since the mid-1800s. Unit-linked insurers sought to use increased information processing capacities to circumvent the barriers that had traditionally made it more difficult for new firms to enter the life insurance field. In this section, I first examine some of the factors that stabilized competition in the life insurance field before analysing the strategies that unit-linked insurers deployed to challenge the traditional way of doing things.

Fielding modern life insurance

After the tumultuous beginnings of modern life insurance in the Victorian age, competition began to stabilize in the latter half of the 19th century. In the early 19th century, there was still a high degree of specialization among insurers. An important factor in the creation of niches, as indicated by names such as London and Lancashire Life, Manchester Life, and Edinburgh & Glasgow, was geographic location. Another differentiating factor was social class. Some of the older companies like Pelican, Globe, and Royal Exchange, for instance, tended to rely on pre-existing ties to the aristocratic clientele, 'who insured their lives as collateral when their need for credit exceeded what their property was worth' (Alborn, 2009, p 4). In contrast, some of the newly established companies of the mid-19th century, like Prudential, tended to focus on a working-class clientele, to whom it sold 'industrial insurance', mostly to cover for funeral expenses (Alborn, 2009; McFall, 2009). As class structures changed, however, so did the life insurance market.

From the mid-19th century onwards, most insurers competed for the lower middle classes, leading to increased diversification and consolidation, as the fierce competition, especially among London-based firms, drove many companies into bankruptcy.

From the late 19th century onwards, the market stabilized. Though new companies continued to emerge and older companies disappeared, the field of life insurance as a whole remained rather stable. All of the ten largest life offices in operation in 1953 originated from before 1867. Market concentration was modest. In 1913, the ten largest offices conducted only 46.4 per cent of total business, which increased in subsequent decades to 57.8 per cent in 1953. Although the industry as a whole grew substantially – the number of 'ordinary life' policies increased from 2 million in 1900 to more than 9 million in 1953 – the number of companies and the relative distribution of market share remained fairly stable (Johnston and Murphy, 1957). By the late 1800s, in other words, the rules of the game constrained the corrosive pressures of competition while avoiding excessive cartelization. The business of life insurance flourished.

Various mechanisms can be identified that contributed to the relatively stable growth. The imposition of regulatory requirements, for instance, created a barrier to entry. Especially pertinent is the 1870 Life Assurance Companies Act, which required insurers to publish periodical actuarial valuations. Before 1870, 'new life insurance offices frequently promised unrealistically high surpluses, based on overly optimistic projections of future investment yields and low mortality. … [T]he Life Assurance Companies Act almost immediately put a stop to this practice' (Alborn, 2009, p 63). Newcomers had to publish an actuarial valuation once every three years. Incumbents had to publish a similar valuation once every five years. Though the Act did not require any authorization, it did require newcomers to have at least £20,000 starting capital – a requirement that was made more stringent in subsequent decades. In the late 1960s, the Department of Trade asked new entrants to show for at least £100,000 in paid-up capital and, in addition, to provide a business plan alongside evidence that the management was 'fit and proper' (Franklin and Woodhead, 1980).

There were important economic barriers too. First, life insurance is characterized by increasing economies of scale (Hardwick, 1997). The expenses of large offices are relatively small compared to the cost of running a smaller office, for instance, because it is relatively more expensive for smaller companies to sustain a distribution network (Ward, 2002). Second, a key aspect of the economics of life insurance is the phenomenon of 'new business strain'. While the revenue of traditional life insurance materializes over long periods, their costs (for example, commission to sales agents) tend to be concentrated at the start. Writing large volumes of new business can thus be rather costly, putting 'strain' on a company's capital base and dampening companies' growth potential (Franklin and Woodhead, 1980, pp 94–5). Combined, these economic features of modern life insurance put larger offices at a structural advantage, leaving smaller offices to target specific niches.

At least equally important was access to and control over distribution channels. Due to the complex and long-term nature of life insurance products, marketing plays a pivotal role in structuring the field of life insurance. Historically, and with a few exceptions, life insurers did not have an in-house sales force. Rather, they made use of independent sales agents, such as local bank branches or professional groups such as lawyers, who would sell life insurance 'on the side' and only for a limited number of companies (Alborn, 2009). Sales practices, moreover, were regulated by the Associated Scottish Life Offices and the Life Offices Association in England (they later merged into the Association of British Insurers, which still exists today). These organizations served as 'internal governance units' (Fligstein and McAdam, 2012), stabilizing the field by capping sales commissions and constraining the power of sales agents. The sales caps prevented individual offices from aggressively expanding market share by increasing sales commissions (Carter and Falush, 2009, pp 154–5).

Finally, incumbent insurers enjoyed a competitive advantage by virtue of having an 'estate'. Estates were the surplus reserves that belonged to no stakeholder in particular but to the company as a whole. They were accumulated by taking 'tiny slices' of a company's profits and setting them aside. In so doing, incumbent insurers had amassed large reserves. The actuary David Forfar, for instance, suggested that his company's estate comprised around 30 per cent of total assets. Estates were, in a sense, passed on from previous generations of policyholders to the next; the responsible actuary therefore not only had a duty, in law, to the current generation of policyholders but also to future generations. This legal obligation was often accompanied by a strong sense of duty. Forfar, for instance, recalls feeling a sense of "loyalty" to "his predecessors", who he said through "careful husbandry" had "built up the estate" (Forfar interview). Estates gave companies several advantages, including increased flexibility in bonus distribution and the 'smoothing' of policyholder benefits and thus put incumbent insurers at a structural advantage versus challenger firms that did not have the benefit of legacy estates.

Unit-linked insurance and the rise of challenger firms

In the 1950s and '60s, the relative stability of the life insurance field was shaken by the introduction of unit-linked insurance. The number of new entrants in the field of life insurance surged (see Figure 3.1), and some of them attracted large shares of new business. In 1968, for instance, the largest

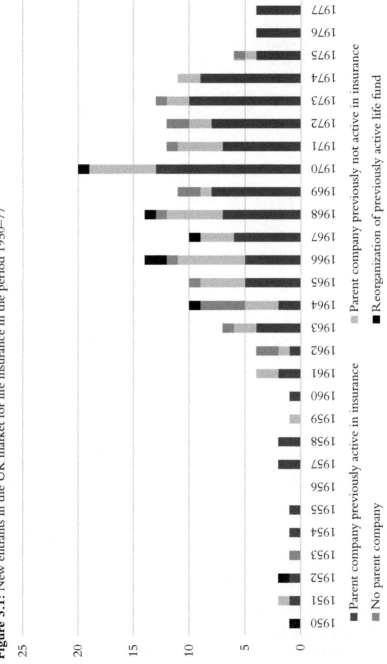

Figure 3.1: New entrants in the UK market for life insurance in the period 1950–77

Source: Franklin and Woodhead (1980, p 97)

share of new business premiums went to Abbey Life, the first of the unit-linked offices founded by Weinberg. Save & Prosper and International Life – two of the other major unit-linked offices – similarly featured among the top ten companies attracting new business (Richards and Colenutt, 1975, p 157). Seven years later, in 1975, the picture had changed even further. The top ten of companies attracting most new business volumes was now spearheaded by Hambro Life, the second of Weinberg's companies. It further included Abbey Life, Hill Samuel and Property Growth – all selling unit-linked insurance (Richards and Colenutt, 1975, p 158).

Weinberg's companies were not the first to sell unit-linked insurance. The first unit-linked contracts were sold by existing insurers who collaborated with unit trust funds. Unit trusts, which are the UK equivalent of American 'mutual funds', were becoming increasingly dominant in the adjacent field of investment management. They first emerged in the 1920s and became increasingly popular after the Great Depression. In contrast to investment trusts, mutual funds and unit trusts were seen as 'transparent' capital pooling mechanisms allowing small-time savers to benefit from capital market investment. To participate, investors could buy 'units' of the investment fund, which moved in price in sync with the underlying investments. While unit trusts were successful in the United States, they remained a relatively fringe phenomenon in the UK well into the late 1950s (Morecroft, 2017, chapter 7). In 1959, total assets under management by UK unit trusts amounted to £100 million, not much of an increase compared to the £84 million 20 years earlier in 1939 (Morecroft, 2017, p 250); in 1960, however, this figure increased to £191 million, and in 1965 increased further to £500 million (Grant and Kingsnorth, 1966, p 17).

Unit-linked insurance emerged as an 'ambiguous innovation' (Funk and Hirschman, 2014) that straddled the divide of investment and insurance. The first unit-linked policies were offered in 1957 by the investment firm Unicorn Trust, which offered 500,000 units of investment (80 per cent of which was invested in 'well-spread ordinary shares'). These units, moreover, were linked to endowment insurance offered by the London and Edinburgh office (Anon, 1957, p 437). In 1958, the life office Northern Assurance started offering insurance contracts based on an in-house unit trust, albeit only to existing customers as a top-up to their existing pension plans (Anon, 1958). Though unit-linked insurance started out as an ambiguous innovation, it was eventually incorporated entirely within the field of life insurance. Insurers enjoyed several competitive advantages relative to unit trusts, which pushed some unit trusts to set up their own life offices (like Save & Prosper and Municipal & General), attracted some existing life offices to the unit-linked market and led to the emergence of new unit-linked insurers (like Abbey Life). Unlike life insurers, for instance, unit trusts were not allowed to market their policies door-to-door (Melville, 1970, p 312). Life insurers, moreover, enjoyed preferential tax treatment through the 'Life Assurance Premium Relief' (Carter and Falush, 2009). As unit-linked insurance grew, the question of whether unit-linked insurance should be treated as investment or insurance gained pertinence. In 1971, the Department of Trade and Industry (the successor of the Board of Trade) therefore commissioned a report by Hilary Scott, a non-executive director of Equity & Law and the Bank of Scotland, who set up a committee to investigate the issue (Scott et al, 1973). Committee members were divided. Although most agreed there was some validity to the proposal to separate the investment and insurance components, doing so was also considered highly impracticable. Even if one member continued to disagree, the commission ultimately settled on treating unit-linked insurance as insurance, a decision that redrew the boundaries of life insurance to include insurers' unit-linked investment funds.

Unit-linked insurance provided challenger firms in the life insurance field with a powerful strategy to challenge the dominant position of incumbent with-profits insurers. Unit-linked insurance enabled challenger firms to circumvent the barriers-to-entry that had contributed to the stability of the life insurance field for so long. For instance, because unit-linked insurance pushes investment risk to policyholders, it is argued to be much less capital intensive relative to with-profits insurance. Weinberg saw this as an important reason why Abbey Life could grow so fast:

> The first unit-linked policy introduced in this country was introduced not for any technical actuarial reason but for a very valid marketing reason, namely that a newly established life office ... recognised that in a savings-orientated market it was difficult for it to compete in the absence of an estate which enabled it to quote competitive with-profits bonuses, and this problem was neatly finessed by linking the policy to units of a Unit Trust. (Weinberg, 1973, p 16)

Unit-linked insurance also circumvented the problem of new business strain. Conventional with-profits insurers typically spread the charges for the companies' expenses over the entire life cycle of a policy. However, because insurers incurred most expenses at the start of the contract, their capital base would deplete rather quickly with growing business volumes. Unit-linked insurers, however, deduced most, if not all, of the expenses from the first premium paid. This left a rather small amount for investment in units but allowed the insurers to avoid the problems of new business strain. This practice, known as 'front loading', enabled unit-linked insurance to write large volumes of new business at once. In the freedom with publicity regime, moreover, capital requirements were rather low. Regulators required insurers to put up a minimum of £50,000 in starting capital. For conventional insurers, this was rather low. If they wanted to attract significant volumes of new business, they would require more capital. For the less capital-intensive unit-linked insurers, however, £50,000 already implied a significant capacity to do business. Abbey Life, for instance, managed to grow significantly without attracting any new capital over and above the £50,000 starting capital (Weinberg, 1973, p 6).

Finally, challenger firms like Abbey Life and Hambro Life undermined incumbent insurers' control over distribution channels by the adoption of commission-based 'direct sales forces', a costly but effective means quickly to gain market share. Challenger firms also benefitted from their ties to banking and investment. Some banks, for instance, prohibited local branch managers from selling policies from competing offices, restricting incumbent insurers' access to the branch networks of banks and building societies (Gupta and Westall, 1993). The 1986 Financial Services Act took the competition over sales channels even further by introducing the concept of 'polarization'. From then on, sales agents either had to be tied to specific companies, solely selling the policies of those companies, or to be fully independent, offering the whole range of policies available in the market (Black and Nobles, 1998). The Act, which significantly reduced the number of agents selling policies from multiple companies, put insurers into direct competition over 'tied agents', and many insurers in response either developed in-house sales forces or merged with banks (Gupta and Westall, 1993; Carter and Falush, 2009, pp 68–71).

The peculiar structure of unit-linked insurance enabled newly established insurers to challenge the dominant position of the longstanding incumbents. In so doing, however, unit-linked insurance also posed a challenge to traditional forms of actuarial expertise. In the next section, I focus on this dimension of the unit-linked challenge.

'Nothing to lose but the chains of actuarial thinking'

Perhaps nowhere was the challenge of unit-linked insurance for the actuarial profession posed as clearly as in Weinberg's 1973 lecture at the Institute of Actuaries Students Society. Weinberg set the stage for his talk by joking that he was 'not sure whether I am brave to be here or whether you are brave to invite me here' (Weinberg, 1973, p 1). Weinberg, after all, had made a career of challenging conventional life insurance, which he associated with the actuarial profession. Unit-linked insurance, he claimed, eliminated 'virtually all the conflicts and rigidities of traditional actuarial forms', even if they were 'mathematically less elegant' (Weinberg, 1973, p 19). The rise of unit-linked insurance, in Weinberg's view, would thus have important jurisdictional implications for the actuarial profession:

> I see unit-linked assurance not as a vehicle for making the Actuary obsolete, but rather as an opportunity to use his unique qualities

- through an opportunity for him to employ himself in weighing up complicated mathematical relationships, rather than to use his time attempting to resolve conflicts of interest of his own making or exercising social judgments which he is no more qualified to assess than a layman. (Weinberg, 1973, p 20)

The core competence of actuaries, Weinberg argued, was mathematics, not management. Yet, conventional insurance arrangements relied on actuaries making judgements that in Weinberg's view had little to do with mathematics. When it came to analysing mortality, most, including Weinberg, recognized that some degree of actuarial discretion was warranted to account for the mismatch between the population from which mortality statistics derived and the insured population. When it came to the management of with-profits funds, however, actuaries also claimed jurisdiction over decisions for which, in Weinberg's view, they were no better placed than well-informed laymen. As noted in the introductory chapter, since the late 18th century life insurers typically sold a mixture of 'non-profit' and 'with-profits' policies. The financial management of this 'conventional' style of insurance relied on actuarial prudence and discretion. To ensure that insurers could meet future claims, actuaries made conservative predictions not just of mortality but also of investment income. In so doing, however, with-profits insurers tended to accumulate large surpluses, which they sought to return to policyholders. To release these surpluses, insurers typically adopted a bonus system in which with-profits policyholders participated in the profits and losses of the company. *How* the accumulated surpluses should be distributed, however, remained an open question, a question that, according to Weinberg, would lead to a 'long dispute' out of which 'the actuarial profession was born' (Weinberg, 1973, p 9). Unit-linked insurance, Weinberg now claimed, resolved the need to answer this question and, in so doing, challenged not just the dominance of incumbent insurers but also the jurisdictional claims of the actuarial profession, especially with respect to with-profits bonuses.

The task of distributing surpluses among different groups of policyholders was certainly not easy. Conflicts of interest may emerge among policyholders, between policyholders and shareholders (in the case of proprietary companies), between offices and their policyholders, and between agents and policyholders. 'One of the considerable achievements of the actuarial profession over the years', according to Weinberg, 'has been to find ways of coping with and living with these various conflicts of interest' (Weinberg, 1973, p 10). Crucial, in this respect, were reversionary bonuses. To distribute their surpluses, insurers would periodically announce an increase in policyholders' sum assured. These bonus announcements were based on rather laborious calculations and occurred at best every five years. Thanks to their infrequency, the announcements acquired a dramatic quality and became 'a potent marketing device'. This, however, also created a tension 'between the prudent social practice of well-regulated investment and the choreographed drama of public spectacle' (Alborn, 2002, p 69), putting additional strain on the conflicts of interests baked into with-profits arrangements.

In the 1930s and '40s, the tensions in insurers' bonus practices became increasingly visible. Within the context of wild fluctuations in the level of inflation and interest rates, it was difficult to estimate the size of insurers' financial surpluses, estimations of which could be substantially different from year to year. Insurers, moreover, had increased their equity investments, which further exacerbated the problem of estimating surplus. With equity investments, at least part of the profits may come in the form of capital gains rather than dividends, which further complicates the evaluation of surplus. As capital gains surged, various companies rapidly accumulated large undistributed surpluses, which posed a problem: on the one hand, there was the perceived need to increase bonuses, bringing actual benefits in line with what was perceived as policyholders' 'equitable' share of surplus. On the other hand, however, insurers also wanted to make sure that in a period of financial decline, they would not be stuck with irreversible bonuses from the past.

To resolve this tension, life insurers started using 'terminal' or 'final' bonuses. The size of a terminal bonus would be determined at the contract's maturity. Terminal bonuses gave companies increased 'elbow room' to see 'that each policyholder obtained a fair return as he went out' (Blunt in Benz, 1960, p 11). What it meant to receive a 'fair share', however, was not so obvious. Although the market value of insurers' investments provided some indication of what this share should be, market values were also seen as rather volatile, making policyholder benefits overly dependent on financial markets. Policyholders, actuaries typically maintained, expected 'something more stable than market values' (Turnbull, 2017, p 132). Actuaries therefore sought to use their 'elbow room' to 'smooth' policyholder benefits across financial cycles. An 'equitable' bonus distribution, in other words, smoothened policyholder benefits across market fluctuations.

For much of the 20th century, bonus smoothing was common practice. More controversial was the question of *how* policyholder benefits should be smoothened. How, after all, would actuaries know whether capital markets were in a good or a bad state? And how long would financial cycles last for? 'The British approach', as Turnbull puts it, 'relied heavily on the judgement and expertise of the actuarial profession, and the public's trust in it' (Turnbull, 2017, p 143). From the 1960s onwards, however, some actuaries feared this trust had begun to dissipate, partly because 'there had been virtually no explanation, either by companies to their policyholders or within the profession as to how those bonuses were determined' (Barton in Melville,

1970, p 347). Suspicion of insurers' bonus policies and the actuarial rationality underpinning them also spilled into public discourse. In a 1969 article, for instance, *The Economist* wrote:

> The conventional policyholder gets no assurance that all the profits earned on his share of the fund will go to him, after a fair allowance for the cost of covering the risk that he might die early. True, he shares in the profits earned on the without-profits policies. True, he benefits from income on reserves built up in the past. But he is not told how much of these combined profits have been stacked away for the future, instead of being allocated to him. (*The Economist*, 1969, p 14)

In the view exposited by *The Economist*, actuarial discretion in surplus distribution made traditional with-profits insurance opaque. Policyholders relied on actuaries to distribute surpluses equitably, but they had no way of verifying what their 'fair' share was. This contrasted sharply with unit-linked insurance, according to *The Economist*. Unit-linked insurance promised 'the policyholder that he will get exactly his whack' (*The Economist*, 1969, p 14). Unit-linked insurance, in this view, was more equitable and fair precisely because it eliminated the intermediating role of the actuary, linking policyholders to capital markets. The actuary Galfrid Melville, who was instrumental in setting up the insurance subsidiary of the unit trust fund Save & Prosper, expressed a similar view:

> In effect, intending unit-linked policyholders are saying to the life office involved. 'We don't want your guarantees on investment. We don't want either you or your actuary to have to be bothered about the future of interest rates, nor about future capital appreciation (or depreciation), nor about short-term fluctuations in the market, in making your decisions about premium rates or surplus distribution. We just want you to credit the "savings elements" of the premiums we pay to your unit fund (or funds), invest these to the best of your ability, tell us exactly what you are doing and why, and give us exactly our share of whatever happens, good or bad, as determined in the market place. We want you to concentrate your thoughts on investment management rather than on its subsequent distribution.' (Melville, 1970, p 313)

Proponents of unit-linked insurance thus repudiated 'the traditional role of the actuary as the all-important and mysterious custodian of such surplus, distributing it in amount and in form according to his judgment alone' (Melville, 1970, p 313). Unit-linked insurance, in contrast, would take 'the market place to be the sole arbiter as to when and how interest and capital surplus should be distributed' (Melville, 1970, p 313). The 'reasoning' required by unit-linked insurance, Weinberg told his actuarial audience, was 'simplistic and mathematically unsophisticated' (Weinberg, 1973, p 18), well suited to the skills of accountants, who tended 'to be pretty hard-headed, straightforward chaps, with a solid knowledge of arithmetic but no algebra' (Weinberg, 1973, p 18).

Saving and investing for retirement

Unit-linked insurers thus not only challenged incumbent insurers' dominant position but also actuaries' jurisdictional claims on bonus policy. In unit-linked insurance, fairness was defined by the market not the actuary. To understand why unit-linked insurance became so popular, it is necessary to situate its emergence in a broader social and cultural context. The first thing to note here is that the rise of unit-linked insurance coincided with the increased importance of life insurance as a channel for retirement savings and the concomitant growth of the life insurance industry as a whole. From the 1950s onwards, life insurance gradually acquired a more prominent role in the UK's retirement income system. Prior to the 1950s, some insurers (for example, Legal & General) had already made a living of providing investment services and selling retirement annuities to occupational pension schemes, often benefitting from advantageous tax treatment (Hannah, 1986, p 37). In 1956, the government extended the right to tax relief on retirement annuities to the self-employed, such as solicitors, doctors and accountants, thus creating a market also for individual pension contracts. In 1986, the market for individual pensions expanded significantly with the implementation of the Social Security Act. While previous Conservative governments promoted occupational pension schemes, the Thatcher administration steered towards increased individual control over pensions and increased competition in the 'long-term savings' industry (Waine, 1992). The 1986 Social Security Act, for instance, incentivized opting out of the redistributive, government-led State Earnings Related Pension Scheme. It also gave workers the possibility to opt out of previously compulsory occupational pension schemes, introducing 'personal pensions' as an alternative. The emphasis of the retirement income system, in other words, shifted from collective saving vehicles to individualized saving (Langley, 2006; 2008), creating significant commercial opportunities for life insurers. Their premium income increasingly derived from pensions business (see Figure 3.2).

Within this context, unit-linked insurance fared well. As individuals became increasingly responsible for their own retirement income savings, they were also invited to make their own investment decisions (Langley and Leaver, 2012) and to 'embrace risk' (Baker and Simon, 2002). The notion of individual responsibility, however, sits uncomfortably with a model of insurance where actuaries operate as custodians of surplus. In

Figure 3.2: The share of total annual premium income per business segment

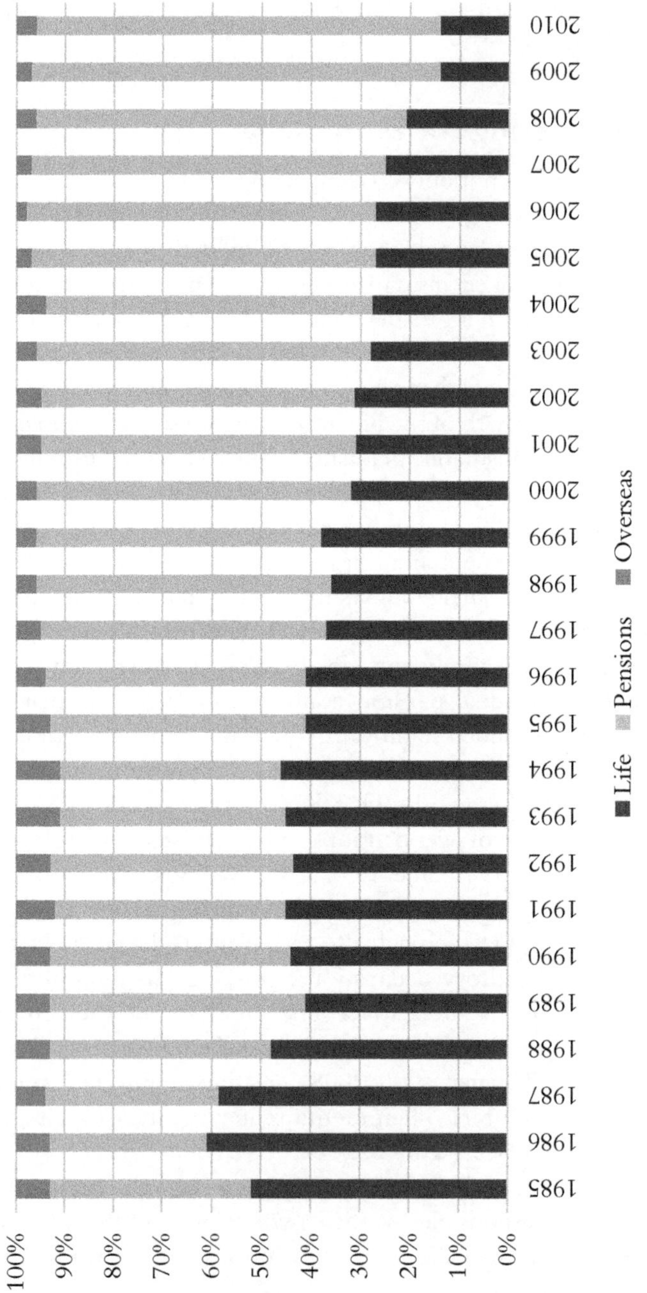

Source: Almezweq (2015)

contrast, by removing actuarial discretion from the issue of distribution, unit-linked insurance chimed well with the increased emphasis on individual responsibility in providing for retirement.

At least equally important was the increased cultural appeal of finance. As various authors have shown, throughout the 20th century the boundaries between finance and society were gradually redrawn. Representations of finance have become increasingly pervasive in the context of everyday life (Martin, 2002). Finance became more visible to a broader audience; and unit-linked insurance exuded the promise of being able to reap the fruits of finance. In itself, the appeal of investment and speculation was nothing new to insurance. In the early modern period, insurers had faced tremendous difficulties separating prudence from speculation (Clark, 1999). The investment dimension of insurance has also been prominent in the modern period. As noted earlier, for instance, insurers' reversionary bonuses became potent marketing devices, 'attracting customers' attention to a firm's underwriting efficiency and investment savvy' (Alborn, 2002a, p 67). Since the late 19th century, moreover, life insurers had competed with other savings institutions such as post offices and savings banks, yielding a flurry of innovations that emphasized the investment function of insurance (see, for example, Alborn, 2002b).

What was new about the investment appeal of unit-linked insurance, however, was that it provided savers relatively unmediated access to financial markets. Unit-linked insurers detracted the cost of the insurance component from policyholders' premiums and used what was left to purchase units of investment. This logic was quite different from the logic of with-profits insurance, where policyholders 'participate' in the profit of the firm as a whole. In with-profits insurance arrangements, policyholders have a stake in the company; in unit-linked insurance, policyholders have a stake in the market. Unit-linked insurance, in other words, turns a policyholder into an investor who 'can calculate the value of the policy himself, from day to day' (*The Economist*, 1969, p 14). Unit-linked insurance, in this sense, was not simply a symptom of the changing boundaries between finance and society but actively contributed to their remaking.

Unit-linked insurance thus likely benefitted from and contributed to the increased prevalence of stock markets in the public imagination. In so doing, however, it also made the success of unit-linked insurance contingent on the general financial cycle. The capacity of unit-linked insurers to attract new business, some suggested, was tied to the overall stock market trend (O'Neill and Froggatt, 1993). This suspicion indeed seems to be supported by the available data on business volumes. Plotting the share of overall new business going to unit-linked insurance against the FTSE 100 Index indeed appears to indicate that the long stock market surge of the 1980s contributed

Figure 3.3: Share of life insurers' premium income from unit-linked business

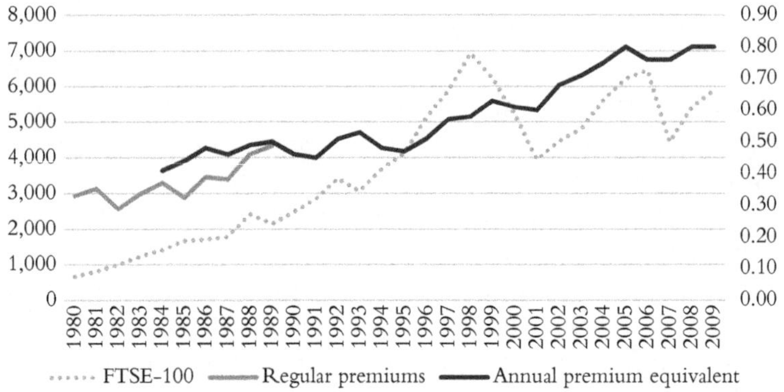

Note: Regular premiums exclude single premium business, while annual premium equivalent includes regular premium and single premium business.

Source: regular premiums are derived from O'Neill and Froggatt (1993); figures based on annual premium equivalent are taken from Almezweq (2015)

to the significant expansion of unit-linked business and that its subsequent rise was punctuated only by the stock market slumps and 'bear markets' of 1990, 1994, 1998–2003 (see Figure 3.3).

Converging models of insurance

Unit-linked insurance mounted a potent challenge on with-profits insurance, drawing on and fortifying the changing boundaries between finance and society. Yet the dominant model of insurance provision that emerged from this challenge was neither the conventional style of with-profits insurance, nor the style of unit-linked insurance as it was imagined by the likes of Weinberg and Melville in the late 1960s and 1970s. As DiMaggio and Powell (1983) argue, there are various processes that make organizations behave like one another, one of which is through imitation. Faced with uncertainty, for instance, DiMaggio and Powell suggest that it may be perfectly rational for actors to imitate each other, even if it is doubtful whether standard practice is optimal. A similar process occurred in the field of British life insurance. Faced with competition from unit-linked insurers, with-profits insurers started selling their own versions of unit-linked insurance. In the management of the more traditional with-profits insurance arrangements, moreover, insurers borrowed elements from unit-linked insurance that made the two arrangements morealike. Contracts sold by unit-linked insurers, in turn, typically contained elements traditionally associated with conventional with-profits insurance. Rather than one type of arrangement eclipsing the other, competition between the two types of insurance led to the convergence between the two ideal-types of insurance.

As noted, proponents of unit-linked insurance critiqued with-profits insurance for its lack of formalization. Unit-linked insurance, in contrast, explicitly linked policyholder benefits to the value of underlying investment units, and the policyholders' rights were contractually clearly defined. At any given moment, it was clear what the policyholder's benefits were *at that point in time*. Traditionally, with-profits insurers recorded no information on the value of investments made by each policyholder separately. The assets were put into a fund that was then to be distributed among different groups of policyholders. In the absence of efficient information processing machinery, calculating the share of the assets that was earned by each policyholder's premiums was very laborious and considered prohibitively costly. Indeed, bonus declarations, which occurred once every so many years, were hugely laborious exercises, even without the need to keep track of how much interest the investments made with policyholders' premiums had accrued:

> [E]very policy had to be separately valued based on age, policy size, and accumulated interest. Determining these individual policy values required massive work even in medium-sized offices – 'upwards of 75,000' calculations for the Clerical, Medical & General's 1867 valuation (IR 5: 3). Actuaries postponed their retirement, office cricket teams' scoring averages dipped, and clerks – armed with little more than inkwells, logarithm tables, and slide rules – put in countless hours of overtime (Norwich Union Board Minute Book, 11 May 1886; Ibis 15 [1892]: 251). The Prudential, already huge in 1886, 'had the whole of [its] staff on for double the usual office hours,' performing 32 million calculations on 7 million policies (Parliamentary Papers 1889 [10], q. 5195); the chair of the smaller Law Life office merely reported that his staff 'became elastic on occasions of this kind' (IR 13 [1875]: 149). (Alborn, 2002a, p 77)

Even after the introduction of information processing machinery, such as tabulating equipment and, somewhat later, computers, bonus declarations remained labour-intensive. Although these technologies sped up the required calculations, allowing bonuses to be declared more frequently, they also facilitated the production of 'what-if' scenarios to inform decision making about bonuses, multiplying the number of calculations that were to be made (Lewin et al, 1989).

By the late 1960s, however, information processing efficiency started to increase substantially, and it became easier and more straightforward to keep track retrospectively of what share of investment income and capital appreciation was generated by each policyholder's premiums. The availability of this information changed how with-profits insurers assessed the fairness and equitability of their bonus policies. The unit trust principle of challenger firms became an exemplar for the bonus distribution of with-profits insurers. With-profits insurers, for instance, started calculating policyholders' 'asset shares', a retrospective measure of policyholder benefits that is broadly equivalent to the value of units in a unit trust fund. For with-profits insurers, however, asset shares were an indicative measure and did not dictate bonus policy. After all, it was understood that with-profits insurance promised a degree of stability, smoothing benefits across the financial cycle. In good times, policyholders should receive less than their asset share; in bad times, they should receive more. This feature, which was widely understood as a core feature of with-profits insurance, divided opinions about the usefulness of asset shares in matters of bonus policy. Some argued that asset shares were of limited use if policyholders expected insurance benefits to be stable from year to year. Others suggested that customer expectations had changed and that 'policyholders ... expect rather less smoothing of with-profits payouts than in the past' (Eastwood et al, 1994, p 501). In such cases, asset shares, being loosely analogous to the unit-linked principle, could be useful in making decisions about terminal bonuses, while 'smoothing' could be achieved by limiting the annual change in terminal bonuses to a fixed percentage level threshold. Regardless, the introduction of asset shares provided new ways to think about the fairness and equitability of long-term life insurance arrangements.

With-profits insurers thus started to imitate unit-linked insurers. The obverse, however, was also true. Unit-linked insurers rarely sold the idealized version of unit-linked insurance envisioned by the likes of Weinberg. Ideal-typical constructions of unit-linked insurance, for instance, contained few guarantees other than the promise to return the cash value of investment units. In practice, though, guarantees were perceived as an important element for the marketing of insurance products, especially when compared to other saving and investment arrangements. They helped insurers weather the 'soft' and 'hard' cycles by making insurance contracts look relatively appealing in times of secular stock market decline. Events like the 1973–74 stock market slump and the 1987 crash hammered home the message that stock markets did not only go up, shifting policyholder demands in favour of security: 'For a number of years [policyholders'] concern had been to participate in the profits of equity investment, and the concomitant risk was generally ignored. Suddenly the risk was seen as more important than the potential gain, and the demand was for stability and guarantees' (Squires and O'Neill, 1990, p 281). To answer to the perceived demand for security, unit-linked insurers included various guarantees in their contracts. Many of the contracts written by Melville's office Save & Prosper, for instance, contained 'maturity guarantees', which set a lower limit to the value of units at a contract's maturity (Squires in Scott, 1977). Weinberg, who was well aware of the importance of guarantees, noted that 'if you must introduce guarantees into unit-linked policies, you should make sure that they are guarantees which are so remote that it is almost inconceivable that you will ever be called upon to pay out under them' (Weinberg, 1973, p 17).

The mutual imitation between unit-linked and with-profits insurance culminated in the introduction of 'unitized with-profits insurance' arrangements, which combined elements from both. While relying on the unit trust principle to measure policy values, unitized with-profits arrangements also contained a mechanism for 'smoothing', by allowing policy values to be adjusted upwards or downwards relative to unit values. Unitized with-profits insurance was sold neither just by challenger firms nor just by the incumbents but straddled the divide. Although challenger firms were the first to set up unitized with-profits arrangements, many conventional with-profits insurers started selling this type of contract too, driven inter alia by increased pressure on their capital reserves and bonus systems due to falling interest rates. From their inception in the late 1980s, unitized with-profits arrangements became rather popular (O'Neill and Froggatt, 1993). When regulatory returns included unitized with-profits arrangements as a category in 1996, many insurers classified what they formerly labelled as with-profits as unitized with-profits instead (see Figure 3.4).

Even if incumbent insurers adopted the unitized insurance model, however, they couldn't stop the rise of the unit-linked challenger firms. The share of non-linked business, which includes both with-profits and unitized with-profits insurance, continued to dwindle throughout the late 1990s and noughties (see Figures 3.3 and 3.4). From the mid-2000s onwards, with-profits insurance had almost entirely disappeared, with over 80 per cent of new premium income deriving from linked pension contracts and the remaining 20 per cent from non-profit business. Although unit-linked insurance was thus hugely successful, the challenger firms that were instrumental in marketing it rarely survived as standalone companies. In 1998, for instance, Hambro Life became part of the Zurich Financial Services Group, while Municipal & General was acquired by Prudential in 1999. Save & Prosper was rebranded by its parent company Fleming in 2000, when Abbey Life stopped selling insurance altogether; the Phoenix Group, a holding company that hoovers up 'legacy' insurance companies, now owns the latter.

Conclusion

From the 1960s onwards, competition between incumbent insurance offices and newly emerging challenger firms gradually changed the dominant model of life insurance provision in the UK. Within this competitive environment, the challenger firms relied on the model of unit-linked insurance as a strategic resource to challenge the dominant position of incumbent insurers.

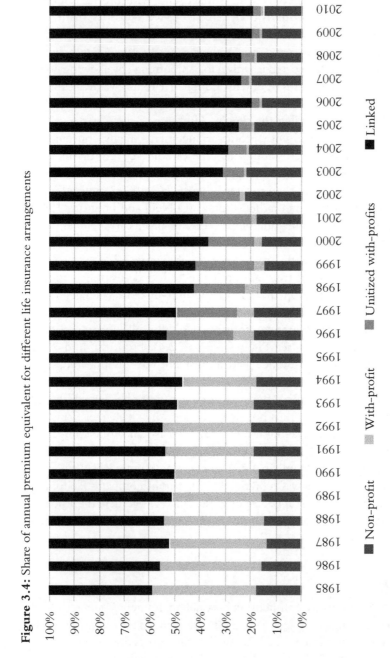

Figure 3.4: Share of annual premium equivalent for different life insurance arrangements

Note: The annual premium equivalent measure is designed to allow for comparisons across single premium and regular premium business and reflects the annual premium income that insurers will receive from new business written in a given year.

Source: Almezweq (2015)

This model enabled challenger firms to circumvent the rules of the game. In response, the incumbent with-profits insurers appropriated elements of the unit-linked model and acquired many of the challenger firms. Most challengers disappeared or were taken over. Their challenge, however, changed the nature of life insurance arrangements, albeit perhaps in different ways from those imagined by the early advocates of unit-linked insurance. Although unit-linked insurance promised to purge insurance arrangements from their conflicts of interest, in practice at least some of the conflicts remained. What it did achieve, however, was to raise new questions about the appropriate role of actuarial expertise in the business of life insurance and the extent to which important questions about the distribution of financial surplus should be left to actuarial discretion or whether and how policyholders' rights should be formalized, taking unit-linked insurance as the exemplar. In so doing, unit-linked insurers opened the gates not just for a new model of profit participation but also for a re-examination of financial risk. In the next chapter, I therefore examine how the unit-linked challenge to the jurisdictional claims of actuarial expertise reverberated within the field of actuarial science, reviewing the debates within the profession on how best to strengthen jurisdictional claims and address the problem of financial risk in the context of unit-linked insurance.

4

Actuaries Going on a Random Walk

> It is now over five years since Mr Benjamin's paper was discussed by the Institute. That discussion was by far the stormiest I have ever attended; I remember enjoying it very much. Although the paper was criticized from many angles, it highlighted a very real problem which could not be solved using traditional techniques and suggested a novel, alternative approach. (Smith in Corby, 1977, p 274)

In 1971, the actuary Sydney Benjamin, who was employed by the actuarial consulting firm Bacon & Woodrow, presented a paper at a sessional meeting of the Institute of Actuaries. In his paper, Benjamin proposed a novel approach to examining the financial risk of guarantees in unit-linked insurance. He argued that price movements in financial markets were random. Rather than relying on actuarial judgement, Benjamin proposed to quantify financial risk by drawing a random sample of historical stock price movements and projecting them into the future. In so doing, Benjamin drew – knowingly or not – on a quantification technique prevalent in modern finance theory: the modelling of stock market returns as a random or stochastic process, as following a 'random walk'.

As indicated by the quote opening this chapter, Benjamin's approach proved rather controversial. The future, most actuaries at the time agreed, could not be read from the past. It required expert knowledge of current stock market conditions and future economic developments, and it was folly to expect that the range of possible outcomes could be objectively captured by a random walk model. Against convention, Benjamin's paper was never published in the actuarial journals. Ronald Skerman, the President of the Institute of Actuaries at the time, decided to keep the meeting confidential. It marked the start of a long controversy within the actuarial profession about the nature of financial risk, the appropriateness of stochastic simulation techniques and the possibility of developing objective knowledge about the future of financial markets.

At core, the debate that followed the presentation of Benjamin's paper was a clash between two clusters of evaluation practices: one cluster revolving around the traditional actuarial practices of prudence and expert judgement to select an appropriate discount rate; the other cluster revolving around the practices of stochastic simulation and the modelling of the stock market as a random process, practices that belong to what Chiapello and Walter (2016) describe as the second age of financial quantification. In this chapter, I move my gaze from the market field of life insurance to the epistemic field of actuarial science to analyse how the rise of unit-linked insurance raised new questions about the nature of financial risk and the need to establish shared knowledge about financial risk. While the previous chapter dealt with the competitive dynamics of the life insurance field, this chapter takes up the task of studying the controversy that emerged from it within the epistemic field of actuarial science. I start the chapter with the question: what made Benjamin's paper so controversial?

Benjamin's challenge to conventional wisdom

To see why Benjamin's paper caused such a stir in the actuarial profession, its contents must be seen within the context of conventional actuarial practice at the time. Up to the 1970s, actuaries had not made any significant attempts at quantifying the financial risk embedded in insurance contracts. There was also little need to do so. In the 19th century, insurers were primarily invested in fixed-income assets such as government debt and mortgages (Scott, 2002), the major risk being 'roll-over' risk – the risk that they would not be able to invest incoming premiums at interest rates sufficiently high to match the interest rate assumed in the 'premium basis' (the set of assumptions used to determine premiums).[1] When held to maturity, however, the market price of assets hardly mattered once they were on insurers' books.

With-profits insurers also relied on the principle of prudence and actuarial discretion to deal with financial uncertainty. In deciding on a valuation basis, they would pick 'cautious' assumptions for estimating the return on investment and the mortality of the insured population.[2] The bonus system, moreover, gave actuaries additional leeway to adjust bonus levels according to the changing financial circumstances of the company. Although this mechanism was an imperfect one, for reducing bonuses may also mean that the company is less likely to attract new customers, it nevertheless provided a security mechanism that could be used in the face of financial turmoil.

As noted in the previous section, insurers increasingly moved away from fixed income investment into equities in the first half of the 20th century, which raised actuarial interest in the question of market value (Dodds, 1979;

Scott, 2002). Relative to fixed-income investments, the timing of returns from equity investments (dividends and capital gains) is more uncertain. In the context of with-profits insurance, this was not necessarily considered a problem, because the practice of actuarial prudence and discretion was considered to give sufficient room for manoeuvre to deal with this uncertainty. In the 1960s, moreover, it was also not considered a problem for unit-linked insurance, even if unit-linked insurers had only limited discretionary space in managing their funds. Most actuaries considered the likelihood that the guarantees on unit-linked products would bite so remote that only a relatively small reserve would suffice.

Benjamin's paper suggested otherwise. In contrast to actuarial convention, Benjamin proposed to assess the *degree of caution* in the valuation basis, noting that the typical actuarial approach of choosing an interest rate for valuation 'on a cautious basis' had its weaknesses when applied to guarantees. Although it was clear that a 'prudent' valuation basis would be strong if the likelihood that real interest rates would fall below the chosen discount rate was small and vice versa, Benjamin was concerned with the question of how to know whether the 'prudent' basis was strong or not. Indeed, he wrote, '[i]t is not so clear what is meant by a strong or weak basis of valuation in a situation where the benefit is sharply dependant [*sic*] upon a fluctuating situation' (Benjamin, 1971, p 5).

To assess the strength of actuarial assumptions, Benjamin suggested 'using the concept of a "probability of ruin" which is familiar from text-book examples of probability games and which is a central idea in "risk theory" as developed especially by continental actuaries' (Benjamin, 1971, p 5). Risk theory is a mathematical approach to evaluation that first emerged in some of the Nordic countries.[3] While British actuarial science had become relatively isolated from statistical theory in the 19th and 20th centuries (MacKenzie, 1981; Alborn, 1994), ties between insurance and academic mathematicians in most Nordic countries remained quite strong, particularly in the early 20th century. At this time, it was 'quite common for prominent university professors to work part-time as actuaries for life insurance companies' (Martin-Löf, 2014, p 8). Two of the most well-known mathematicians, Filip Lundberg and Harald Cramér, developed a modelling approach to evaluate surplus in general insurance business that pivoted on the calculation of a company's 'probability of ruin' – defined as the probability of a company's reserves dipping below zero at any given point over the timespan of the contract. They sought to do so by modelling the surplus of the company, subject to premium income and claims outgo, as a continuous random process, rather than relying on point-based estimates.

Similarly, Benjamin wanted to know what levels of reserve were needed to make the probability of a life insurer ending up with a shortfall (that is, the 'probability of ruin') less than 1/50. Up to 1971, however, 'the problem

of long-term business has not received much attention [in risk theory]'
(Benjamin, 1971, p 5). Benjamin therefore devised his own model, which
by today's standards seems rather crude. For his purposes, he reasoned,
future stock market returns could be adequately modelled as a random
projection of past annual returns into the future. Using the De Zoete stock
market index, he produced 50 simulations each projecting 20 years of future
stock market returns by randomly picking annualized return experiences
from a pool of 51 historic periods derived from stock market data over
the period 1920–70. Out of 50 different simulation paths, he then picked
the one that produced the worst result (corresponding to the 2 per cent
'probability of ruin' threshold), arguing that firms' reserves needed to be
large enough to cover such a shortfall. For a ten-year unit-linked policy
with a simple maturity guarantee, Benjamin concluded, 'a suitable reserve
[for the guarantee] … would be equal to approximately 25 percent of the
present value of all future basic premiums in force' (Benjamin, 1971, p 29).

To most actuaries, Benjamin's proposed level of reserves seemed excessive,
and his methodology was hitherto foreign to the British actuarial profession;
his claims were therefore easily dismissed. Although the precise arguments for
dismissing his claims are unknown – a transcript or summary of the meeting
was never published – future debates suggest that the combination of bad
news and Benjamin's unorthodox methodology provided the grounds for
scepticism among actuaries present at the meeting. Benjamin, however, did
not let go entirely of his paper, and he presented an updated version of it in
1976 at the International Actuarial Congress in Tokyo, which suggested an
even stronger 'starting reserve' of 30 per cent. Benjamin acknowledged that
the model's results seemed 'unexpectedly high'. Nevertheless, for Benjamin
the results indicated that the combination of unit-linked insurance and
maturity guarantees was 'probably not a commercial proposition' (Benjamin,
1976; Turnbull, 2017).[4] Many remained sceptical and sometimes even hostile
to Benjamin's approach; his paper, however, did raise significant doubt
about the adequacy of actuarial prudence in the management of unit-linked
insurance and succeeded in putting financial risk on the actuarial agenda.

'A drunken stagger around a random walk'

To address the concerns raised by Benjamin's paper, the Institute of Actuaries
set up two consecutive working parties on maturity guarantees both led
by Brian Corby, actuary of the influential company Prudential. The goal
of the first working party was to scrutinize Benjamin's assumption of
independence in stock market returns. The second working party was set
up to recommend appropriate reserving practices. Neither of these working
parties came to an agreement on these issues, and their reports were never
published. Nevertheless, the issues they were formed to address - how to

model long-term stock market returns and how to determine appropriate reserving levels – provide a good indication of the two major dividing lines within the profession on the topic of maturity guarantees.

The first issue revolved around the two-pronged question of the stock market's behaviour and the possibility of modelling it. Benjamin's suggestion that annual stock market returns were independent and thus followed a 'random walk' – an assumption that by the 1970s was hegemonic in modern financial economics – conflicted with prior actuarial beliefs. Although actuaries tended to have diverging beliefs about investments, most agreed that investment was more akin to arts than science (see, for example, discussion in Day, 1966). Perhaps the dominant intellectual tradition within the actuarial profession was 'fundamentals analysis' (Day, 1966). Fundamentals analysis maintains that the *value* of an investment should be analysed by looking at the company's business in detail. Because the *price* of an investment depends on other investors' judgements about *value*, price and value may diverge, and it is the task of the analyst to identify bargains. An emphasis on 'fundamentals' has important implications for the usefulness of historical information. Although in this view, past company performance may be considered a useful (though insufficient) guide for expectations about future profitability and estimations of value, historical prices are not. Indeed, as Day (1966, p 259) notes, actuaries 'find it very difficult to accept an approach depending on the past, for in so many instances the past can give no fair guide to the future, especially when Government policy and technical change can have such far-reaching effects'.

Occasionally, actuaries also drew on a different intellectual tradition: that of 'technical analysis' or 'chartism'. Rather than focusing on stocks' intrinsic values, technical analysts search for patterns and trends in stock price movements, typically with visual representations of the market, which can then guide predictions of future price movements (Preda, 2007). While fundamental analysts interrogate value by scrutinizing business fundamentals, technical analysts gauge value by scrutinizing price patterns (these types of investors, however, should be treated as ideal types because most analysts draw on multiple styles of reasoning). Most actuaries tended to draw on both forms of knowledge (see, for example, Pepper and Thomas, 1973).

Like technical analysts, Benjamin sought to analyse economic cycles, though he examined them with statistical techniques, not visual ones. In so doing, he concluded that there was no cyclical pattern to be found and that stock market returns followed a so-called random walk. This claim, however, failed to convince many actuaries. Members of the first working party tasked with interrogating Benjamin's assumption of statistical independence argued, for instance, that '[i]ndependence is not a meaningful concept. ... Statistical tests are essentially shades of probability, they cannot in general confirm or reject a hypothesis with certainty' (the working party as cited in Corby, 1977, p 260). For many, the hypothesis of independence did not match visual evidence provided by stock market charts. 'All we need', one actuary commented at a sessional meeting, 'is to look at a long-term chart of the equity price index. Traditionally ... the equity price index shows a cyclical formation ... with something like a four-yearly cycle between the peaks' (Plymen in Scott, 1977, p 401).

Some actuaries went ever further in their rebuttal of Benjamin's approach. They rejected not only his assumption of statistical independence but also questioned the more fundamental proposition that stock markets could usefully be modelled in the first place. Francis Wales, for example, commented that

> it is one thing to postulate a mathematical model of the stock market in an attempt to determine the extent of the risk exposure, but quite another to claim that it is possible to simulate future stock market price movements. ... [L]ike the first working party I am totally convinced that it is a fruitless exercise to attempt to find a satisfactory model of stock market behaviour. ... [S]tock markets operate in a constantly evolving environment. That means that the rules are always changing and thus the appropriate models must always be changing. (Wales in Corby, 1977, p 288)

Similarly, another actuary asked: 'Is it really right to use the history of 1920 to 1970 to assess future changes in prices? Or have things changed fundamentally during and since this period? I suspect that circumstances are different enough now in Britain to urge great caution in this' (Grant in Scott, 1977, p 394). In this perspective, stock markets were seen as open-ended social systems, which implied that past returns were a poor guide to future price movements.

To deal with this scepticism, alternative models were put forward in subsequent years. Two main approaches can be distinguished. The first accepted the need for a new approach to value maturity guarantees but rejected both the assumption of statistical independence and the probability of ruin approach. Dick Squires of Save & Prosper, for instance, said that 'it may well be impossible to define a model to the extent of giving numerical values to the parameters that underlie it'; he argued therefore that 'an extremely simple model' would give 'adequate results' (Squires, 1974, p 20). In his alternative model, not the unit price itself, but a 'trend line' was deterministically projected forward at an expected rate of return. At each point in time, the actual unit price would be equal to the expected unit price in 50 per cent of the cases and would be 30 per cent above or below the expected unit price in 25 per cent of the cases respectively.

A similar approach was put forward by Corby (1977), who decided to publish his own suggested approach after his two working parties failed to reach consensus. Corby similarly suggested using a trend-line approach, but with the additional assumption that units were bought at the top of the range and sold (at maturity) at the lower end. The results produced by the model strongly depended on the rate of return assumption as well as the size of the range within which the unit price was allowed to vary. The model was therefore rather flexible, allowing its user to adjust assumptions according to their expectations about economic fundamentals.

Both Squires and Corby thus suggested using a heuristic approach that did not aim to be realistic but that would be simple, flexible and transparent. The trend-line models, however, were vehemently opposed, although the reasons for this opposition varied considerably. Some noted that the assumption of 'buying high, selling low' was too conservative. Others argued that the model was based on the assumption of continued economic growth; when looking at economic fundamentals, however, it 'does not require much imagination to admit the possibility of negative growth' (Taylor in Corby, 1977, p 281). Most adamant in rejecting the trend-line approach was David Wilkie, who objected at a lack of correspondence to reality. A trend-line model, Wilkie argued, was 'a malevolent deterministic model'; it was 'as ludicrous a way of predicting share prices as to quote immediate annuity values on the assumption that everybody lives for precisely three score years and ten' (Wilkie in Corby, 1977, p 280). Elsewhere, he noted that with the trend-line approach, 'after some number of years ... the probability of the price being lower than the price at the outset was zero', which, according to Wilkie, was 'obviously nonsense' (Wilkie in Squires, 1974, p 44).

The second alternative, however, was not quite as radical in its rejection of Benjamin's model – it stuck to his 'probability of ruin' approach – but did divert from the independence assumption. William Scott conceded that 'chart studies of the type popular with financial journalists are of real value in detecting longer-term stock market trends' (Scott, 1977, p 373). Such charts were proof, for him, that stock market returns were not random, which he sought to corroborate using further statistical tests. Where Benjamin did not find any correlation between consecutive index values, Scott did find evidence for it and concluded that 'yearly stock market movements are *not* random, but negatively correlated' over a period of two years (Scott, 1977, p 366) – that is, the probability of an above average return diminished if the return two years earlier exceeded expectations. He noted, however, that a 'mathematical model' with negative correlation 'becomes so complicated as to be, in our view, of dubious practical worth' (Scott, 1977, p 375). While Scott's own model elaborated Benjamin's approach by fitting a lognormal distribution to the historically observed stock market returns (rather than drawing from a pool of historically experienced returns), he did not include negative autocorrelation in the model. Instead, he simply decided to lower the model's standard deviation to account for the difference between observed market values and the 'true price' of a stock, the latter 'very likely to be less erratic' (Scott, 1977, p 375). Rather than using a standard deviation of 19 per cent under the assumption of independence, Scott proposed using a standard deviation of 10 per cent.

Wilkie elaborated Scott's model. He criticized Scott's assumption that negative autocorrelation could be approximated by simply reducing the standard deviation of a lognormal model. Scott justified this by arguing that such dampened variation would be closer to 'true prices'. Wilkie dismissed this justification, suggesting that market prices should be taken as the best available indicator of value (a notion that was also dominant in modern finance theory at the time):

> Do any of the companies that issue these policies and pay out claims buy and sell units at true prices? I thought that they bought units at market price and sold units at market price and what true prices – whatever they may be – have got to do with this I don't know. (Wilkie in Scott, 1977, p 409)

In a brief research note published in response to Scott's paper, Wilkie updated the former's model to accommodate for autocorrelation. While Scott had claimed that autocorrelation was difficult to model, Wilkie proposed that its inclusion 'into the simulation program is a trivial exercise' (Wilkie, 1977, p 20). The inclusion of autocorrelation, which supported the view that markets were cyclical, made the stochastic modelling more palatable to the broader actuarial community.

The results produced by the different models diverged greatly. For an endowment policy with a maturity of ten years, Benjamin's model indicated required reserves at inception between 20 and 25 per cent (a later version of his paper presented at the International Actuarial Conference in Tokyo suggested reserves of 30 per cent). Both Squires' and Scott's model indicated somewhat lower reserves of around 15 per cent. Corby suggested using calibrations of his model that would bring it in line with Benjamin's 1971 paper. Even though Wilkie allowed for negative correlation of stock market returns, which would suggest reduced reserves, his model produced the strongest reserves, significantly in excess of those put forward by Benjamin: around 40 to 50 per cent.[5]

In 1977, the issue was far from settled. A new joint Institute and Faculty working party was set up to 'recommend bases of reserving' that would 'satisfy reasonable standards of caution and coherence' (Ford et al, 1980, p 114). The Maturity Guarantees Working Party made every attempt at tackling the approach as rigorously as possible, or, at least, convincing others they had done so. In its final report published in January 1980 (commissioned in August 1978), the working party noted that 'the amount of paper work produced, excluding enormous quantities of computer output, is well over a foot high' (Ford et al, 1980, p 103). The report itself was considered quite important and was published with some haste: it was published ahead of schedule in a dedicated issue of the *Journal of the Institute of Actuaries*.

The working party continued along the lines set out in Benjamin's, Scott's and Wilkie's earlier work, which is not surprising considering that both Wilkie and Benjamin took part in it.[6] Nevertheless, the working party's proposed model differed from earlier work in important ways. Instead of modelling stock market returns as a single stochastic process, the working party opted for a 'two-model approach', in which dividends would be modelled as a 'random walk' with a non-zero mean, and yields would be represented by an autoregressive model, fluctuating 'around a fixed mean'. The net result was a model that represented prices as "a drunken stagger around a random walk" (Wilkie interview).

Simulation modelling and actuarial science

Although the debate on financial risk focused on maturity guarantees in unit-linked insurance, it also involved arguments about the nature of actuarial expertise. In other words, participants' positions within the debate were determined not just by their epistemological beliefs but also by their opinions on the role of actuarial expertise in the insurance business and how best to strengthen the profession's jurisdictional claims. Two themes stand out: the relation between actuarial expertise and modern statistics, especially risk theory, and the role of computing power in actuarial work. Each are taken in turn.

Actuaries, risk theory and discretionary judgement

The early development of British actuarial theory was strongly tied to the emergence of statistical theory in Britain. By the late 19th century, however, actuarial work 'had become a fairly specialised line of work ... rather insulated from developments in statistical theory generally' (MacKenzie, 1981, p 250; Alborn, 1994). The connections between actuarial expertise and statistical theory allowed the former to make special claims on expertise in the insurance business. Towards the late 19th century, though, actuaries increasingly tended to emphasize the limited applicability of formalized knowledge, claiming more subjective forms of expertise that resisted formalization and thereby justified actuarial discretion. Statistical knowledge was the basis for actuarial expertise, but this knowledge could not be applied to insurance business without 'expert judgement'. In the late 19th century,

Porter (1995) reports, actuaries therefore tended to resist the protocolization of financial knowledge about insurers' finances, instead preferring individual actuaries to have the freedom to decide how a company's financial position should be calculated.

The divorce between mathematical theory and actuarial expertise was not as strong in some of the continental European countries, where mathematicians and actuaries had started quantifying not only diversifiable forms of risk, such as mortality or fire hazard, but also increasingly non-diversifiable forms of financial risk. Risk theory, which had emerged in the Nordic countries, sought to estimate the 'probability of ruin' of general insurance firms by modelling premium income, expenses and claims as continuous random process. An important question, however, was whether such random modelling was applicable to life insurance too, or whether variation in life insurance income, claims and expenses was a function of non-random processes best estimated using actuarial judgement. Bobby Beard, a general insurance actuary (this was rather uncommon at the time) from Pearl Assurance who had co-authored a textbook on risk theory, noted that the insistence on judgement implied that non-random variation was relatively important in the context of life insurance:

> Actuarial techniques, as developed for life insurance purposes, had been developed on the principle of making calculations on the basis of expected values of the various functions entering into the calculations and relying on judgment to allow for variables not specifically included in the underlying models. It had generally been considered that the non-random variation was considerably more significant than the random variation in the functions used, for instance, mortality, and thus judgment was a necessary part of an actuarial knowhow. (Beard in Benjamin, 1966, p 181)

The question now, though, was whether changes in the structure of insurance arrangements and insurers' changing investment behaviour justified a move away from actuarial judgement (implying non-random variation was more important) to formalized modelling of non-diversifiable risk (implying random variation was relatively more important). The debate over the quantification of financial risk, in other words, was also a debate on the appropriate role of actuarial expertise, and many actuaries perceived the insistence on the formalization of financial risk as a threat to the position of actuaries in the insurance business.

One strategy available to proponents of new forms of expertise is to reinterpret existing professional norms. Indeed, Benjamin and Wilkie sought to assuage sceptics of statistical modelling of random processes by arguing that it was not in conflict with actuarial expertise, but rather that it was the 'prudent' thing to do. In one of the debates, Benjamin argued for instance that the principle of prudence did not undermine random or stochastic modelling but rather justified it:

When doing research there is a duty to be cautious. The profession is faced with one model and method – that is to say the random walk approach – which has been written up, and other methods which have not been subjected to publication and which, from a brief description, do not sound coherent in the way that I have defined. The random model is apparently more cautious and hence it seems to me to be the only one which is professionally justifiable in this situation. Unfortunately, it leads to very large reserves and it is sometimes condemned as over-cautious, for that reason, but that of course is nonsense; it is inverted logic. (Benjamin in Corby, 1977, p 280)

Acceptance of stochastic modelling of non-diversifiable risk was further complicated by the fact that risk theory was relatively foreign to most British actuaries. In the 1970s, few actuaries were familiar with risk theory. The first English textbook on risk theory was published in 1969 and was co-authored by Beard and two Finnish colleagues, Teivo Pentikäinen and Erkki Pesonen. Risk theory was first discussed at the Faculty of Actuaries in 1970 when the statistician Robin Plackett exposed some of its elementary concepts in an address to the profession.[7] In response to Plackett's talk, one speaker expressed a feeling he suspected some of the other actuaries present would share with him: 'the feeling of being lost in this particular subject' (McKinnon in Plackett, 1970, p 352). The fact that the mathematics underpinning risk theory and the techniques required for its implementation through computer simulation were foreign to many actuaries also surfaced repeatedly in the sessional meetings at which the maturity guarantees were discussed. In response to Scott's paper, for instance, one actuary noted that 'mathematical concepts beyond my comprehension are used' (Russell in Scott, 1977, p 400). At the Institute, Colin Seymour recalled how in the early 1970s, the 'Scandinavians with their modern risk theories were an unheard-of mystery', and 'perhaps', he continued, 'many of us are still rather daunted by such high level statistics' (Seymour in Corby, 1977, p 284).

Risk theory was not the only development in statistical modelling that originated in the Nordic countries and would later emanate to other countries. Another important area was the modelling of mortality. In much of the 1980s, British actuaries continued to model mortality in much the same way as the actuaries of the late 19th century. In countries like Norway and Denmark, however, statisticians cum actuaries had started to develop new approaches to mortality that sought to model 'life histories in general', incorporating things like 'disability' and 'long-term care' in 'survival analyses'

(Macdonald interview). British actuaries had hardly picked up on these developments, relying instead on the more traditional approach to modelling mortality to the frustration of some. The actuary Angus Macdonald, for instance, who joined the actuarial science department of Heriot-Watt University in Edinburgh in 1989, feared that "the profession was falling way behind" (Macdonald interview). Although Macdonald previously "quite happily absorbed the traditional actuarial education" in his position at Scottish Amicable, he learned about the new modelling techniques when he joined Heriot-Watt University. Particularly influential there was Professor Howard Waters, who in 1981 had spent a year in Copenhagen and "came back with the latest thinking from Scandinavia. And literally from Howard in this department, this began to propagate through the UK and was eventually [put] into the [actuarial] educational syllabus" (Macdonald interview).

Proponents of stochastic simulation modelling joined forces with academic actuaries propagating new techniques to model mortality to make the case that there was a need to update the actuarial toolkit with new statistical concepts and techniques to strengthen the profession's claims of special expertise within the insurance business. Like Macdonald, Wilkie argued that adherence to deterministic techniques threatened the profession's credibility: 'We still teach life contingencies in a purely deterministic way', he noted, 'and if we continue to do so we shall be ridiculed by statisticians in every country' (Wilkie in Corby, 1977, p 280). Similarly, Benjamin noted that 'it would be very unfortunate if a statistician outside the profession were to come along with a solution which the profession would then examine in arrears' (Benjamin et al, 1980, p 229). In other words, the issue was not simply one of whether actuaries would be able to understand the mathematics involved: they were the experts whose task it was to translate general statistical theory into practical applications, not the statisticians. If statisticians beat them to it, Benjamin suggested, it would harm the profession's claims to special expertise.

Although few actuaries were familiar with risk theory, the scientific status it enjoyed by virtue of its connections to statistical theory endowed the stochastic simulation models with legitimacy that made resistance against the work of the Maturity Guarantees Working Party more difficult, especially considering Benjamin's assumption of complete randomness had already been softened.

Actuaries and computers

Another issue within the actuarial profession related to the debate on financial risk was the role of computing power in actuarial work. As documented in great detail for the US actuarial profession by JoAnne Yates (1999, 2004) and in slightly less detail for the UK's profession by Laurie Dennett (Dennett,

2004, pp 63–70) and Lewin et al (1989), life insurance companies were among the 'early adaptors' of computing technology. Actuaries played an active role in advocating the benefits of computing technology. In 1953, the Institute of Actuaries set up an Electronic Computers Committee chaired by Kenneth Usherwood, actuary at Prudential. While the committee sought to explore the potential capabilities of the various computer designs, it also 'sought to make the manufacturers aware of the needs of the actuarial profession with a view to influencing design' (Dennett, 2004, p 66). Two years later, the Institute set up seven separate study groups, one of which was tasked with maintaining links with British computer manufacturers. Yates (1999, 2004) explains this early interest in computing technology by looking at the conditions in which many companies found themselves in the post-war period. With the onset of industrial insurance and the rise of private pensions, insurers' business volumes grew significantly throughout the 20th century; yet in the post-war period, labour market conditions had grown increasingly tight, with surging labour costs as a result. Similar conditions prevailed in the UK. In the period 1937–53, annual premium incomes of both ordinary and industrial life assurance more than doubled (Johnston and Murphy, 1957, p 111). Within this context, computing technology was primarily perceived as a means to speed up work and reduce operational costs (Lewin et al, 1989; Yates, 2004).

Benjamin and Wilkie, who were among the most vocal proponents of simulation modelling, were also advocates of computing technology. Benjamin's professional career is particularly illustrative of the close ties between insurers and computing companies. Benjamin, who was employed by Prudential, went back to Cambridge (where he, like many fellows, had obtained his first degree in mathematics) at the insistence of his mentor Kenneth Usherwood to take a course in programming. He later briefly worked for Ferranti Computers as a contributor to the Cambridge University Atlas project to 'develop his knowledge of computing', before moving in 1962 to the actuarial consulting firm Bacon & Woodrow, where he would remain an active advocate of computing technology (Lever, 1992, p 383). In 1961, Benjamin set up and ran a programming course at the Institute's Students Society, consisting of '12 fortnightly lectures each of two hours, with several hours of homework between lectures, and a final practical of two sessions on a machine' (Benjamin, 1964, p viii). Hoping to 'fill perhaps 25 to 30 places', the course was oversubscribed with 'over 70 applications' (Benjamin, 1964, p viii).

Similarly, Wilkie had 'worked with programming on computers one way or another' ever since the company he worked for at the time, Scottish Widows, had purchased a computer in about 1960. A few years later, he would publish a rather bulky paper describing the 'procedures adopted by [his] company in setting up a computer system with magnetic tape files to provide valuation and other statistical information for ordinary assurances' (Wilkie, 1964, p 89). Although less active as an advocate of computing technology within the profession, Wilkie did have specialist knowledge of statistics, which aroused his interest in the affordances of the computer: he had taken "a specialist course on statistics" and had therefore done "a lot more statistics than most actuaries" (Wilkie interview). After having met Benjamin in the latter's employment at Ferranti, the two became friends. As Wilkie recalls, Benjamin "was very good at seeing what you could use the computer for", and Wilkie soon "started noticing" that you could "do a lot of mathematical things that were … obviously not impossible to do by hand, but that were not worth doing by hand" (Wilkie interview).

Initially, the impact of computing technology on life insurers' organizational practices remained limited. Pre-existing practices 'structured' how computers were adopted (Yates, 1999). In the early years, the costly and bulky mainframe computers were mainly used as 'data processing' devices. In so doing, computing technology often struggled to live up to the promise of reducing the cost of clerical work. As Benjamin noted: '[A]t any point of time a conventional costing has usually shown that a changeover to computers is at best only marginally worth while' (Benjamin, 1966, p 134). This raised questions about the usefulness of computing technology and encouraged advocates to find novel uses. In 1963, Benjamin published what he called 'a propaganda attempt to counterbalance the emphasis on data–processing applications which there has been in the past', which he regarded 'an unfortunate mistake'; indeed, he continued, '[c]omputers can be regarded as glorified desk calculators or high-speed punched–card machinery but this misses the real potential of the qualitative difference between computers and earlier machinery' (Benjamin, 1963, p 7). Wilkie similarly "started looking around for ways of using it [computing technology], rather than just replicating the previous clerical systems" (Wilkie interview).

Within this context, advocates of computing technology perceived computing as something that should be part of actuarial expertise, and the simulation modelling gave them a justification for its expenses; the maturity guarantees on unit-linked policies appeared as an important problem that could validate the need for simulation modelling. At the same time, this link between computing technology and simulation modelling also meant that as computers became more efficient and their use became widespread, the background conditions for simulation modelling also became more favourable, allowing a wider group of actuaries to gain familiarity with it.

The increased spread of computing power and actuaries' increased familiarity with risk theory lowered the threshold for stochastic stock market simulation, which by the 1980s was regarded as a legitimate actuarial technique. Few actuaries, however, had the knowhow to deploy this technique in practice. So what, then, was the impact of stochastic simulation modelling on the market field of life insurance and the epistemic field of actuarial science? This is the question I turn to in the next section.

Living in a stochastic world?

Most unit-linked insurance funds were heavily invested in equities and real estate. With the stock market slump of 1973–74, therefore, the riskiness of maturity guarantees suddenly appeared very real. Insurers that had sold 'guaranteed income bonds' got into significant trouble. The collapse of Nation Life, a mid-sized company, contributed to increasing public pressure on the actuarial profession to deal with the riskiness of guarantees. In an article entitled 'The Men Who Decide What Your Life Assurance Is Worth Should Wise Up', *The Economist* (1974, p 86), for instance, cited the 'absence of an actuarial code of practice' as an 'important reason why these companies boomed and bust'. Actuaries from the Government Actuary's Department, which carried out supervisory tasks on behalf of the Department of Trade and Industry, also started taking an active interest in the controversy, attending, for instance, the sessional meetings at which the issue of maturity guarantees were discussed. At one such meeting, at which Corby's paper was discussed, the Government Actuary Edward Johnston noted 'that there is no general agreement on the mechanical models which should be used for assessing … reserves'. Although he did not perceive active government interference with the substance of the debate as appropriate ('I am certainly not going to venture any opinion on which mathematical model is right'), he did emphasize the need for 'a practical answer … because companies do have to set up reserves of some size or other' (Johnston in Corby, 1977, p 284). By emphasizing the systemic impact of maturity guarantees, moreover, Wilkie also sought to enrol actuaries at non-linked offices. At one of the debates, for instance, he estimated that roughly £2,000 million worth of maturity guarantees had been written and that companies were 'short of around £1,000 million of reserves'. The maturity guarantees that had already been written, he continued to argue, therefore posed a 'practical problem' for the 'Department of Trade' as well as for 'other life assurance companies because … they are going to foot the bill when the companies writing this business – if they go bust – do go bust. So it is up to all life offices as well to think about how it should be done' (Wilkie in Corby, 1977, p 412).

Such pressures undoubtedly contributed to generating acceptance of the results produced by the Maturity Guarantees Working Party's modelling exercises. Maturity guarantees on unit-linked contracts were increasingly perceived as rather costly, and the volume of such policies quickly diminished. Although it is likely that the working party's model contributed to this perception among actuaries, it is less clear to what extent it also influenced decision making at the level of corporate management. Wilkie suspects, for instance, that the decisive moment for the decline of maturity guarantees was not the publication of the working party's report itself but would come later when Standard Life – Wilkie's employer after he left Scottish Widows – declined to participate in the underwriting of one of the major unit-linked offices founded by Weinberg, Hambro Life. At the time, Wilkie noted, it was common practice for institutional investors to take small stakes in a company when it could not sell all its shares to the public. When Standard Life's investment manager asked Wilkie for his opinion on Hambro Life, he replied: '"I think we shouldn't touch it", because Hambro had a lot of this [maturity guarantee] business, I knew that it was risky.' Wilkie suspects that 'since it was Standard Life' – a leading Scottish life office – 'those in the market thought that there might be something serious about it – one insurer not being sure about another' (Wilkie in personal communication).

Yet, even if the results produced by this modelling were accepted as legitimate, this did not necessarily imply that stochastic modelling had become part of actuarial expertise and had a major impact on the market field of life insurance. Most actuaries, after all, remained unfamiliar with risk theory and stochastic simulation modelling, and usage of the working party's model by company actuaries remained limited. Of the 22 companies whose regulatory returns the working party member Ben Rowe had seen in late 1980 – ten months after initial publication of the working party's report – only two companies had used the working party's model (Rowe in Benjamin et al, 1980). Many actuaries appeared to have been concerned with the limited practicality of the model – for instance because they had insufficient familiarity with programming or the model's underlying mathematics so that they could adjust it to the specific characteristics of different portfolios – and preferred some deterministic approximation of the model over the stochastic one.

So how, then, did the controversy over financial risk influence the epistemic field of actuarial science? First, a small group of actuaries continued doing research on stochastic simulation modelling of investment returns. Most notable, in this regard, was Wilkie himself, who continued to refine the working party's model in subsequent years (Wilkie, 1984, 1995) and developed what became known as the 'Wilkie model'. Although it is difficult to assess how widely the model was used in corporate decision making, interviews indicate that most life offices used the Wilkie model, or some alternative specification thereof, to get some "insight into how bad things might get" (Interviewee EA). What facilitated the model's uptake was that it was specifically designed for long-term actuarial applications, 'was relatively easy to apply - it could be coded into a spreadsheet' and was 'consistent' with the 'prior belief' that stock markets follow a mean-reverting process (Jakhria et al, 2019). In the 1990s, Wilkie's model was increasingly scrutinized within the profession (see, for example, Geoghegan et al, 1992;

Huber, 1997), and some practitioners developed alternative stochastic asset models (for example Yakoubov et al, 1999), which indicates widespread interest in stochastic asset models. Worries about the implications for actuarial judgement, however, remained. One of the working party reports on the Wilkie model noted for instance that a central topic of debate had been 'the extent to which "actuarial judgement" might comfortably override purely theoretical and statistical considerations' (Geoghegan et al, 1992, p 185). Usage of and familiarity with stochastic investment models thus significantly expanded throughout the 1980s and '90s, even if the extent to which it informed and constrained decision making seems to have been limited for most companies.

Second, with the report of the Maturity Guarantees Working Party, stochastic simulation modelling made inroads into the educational syllabus of the actuarial profession too. Initially, the report was listed as recommended reading under the chapter on the practice of life insurance funds, which in the latter half of the 1980s was replaced by an entry into the syllabus on stochastic methods. These were minimal changes in the structure of actuarial education, but they nonetheless had an impact as interview evidence indicates, because some of the newly trained actuaries had at least some basic familiarity with the concept of stochastic simulation modelling. More substantial reforms of the educational syllabus, however, came only towards the end of the 1990s, when stochastic modelling, financial mathematics, financial economics and an optional specialist certificate in derivatives were taught as distinct subjects.

Third, the now widely held belief that maturity guarantees on unit-linked funds invested in equities were expensive pushed actuaries to think about the relation between investment strategy and the riskiness of guarantees, which built on some early notable works in this regard and anticipated later developments in asset-liability modelling. Particularly noteworthy in this regard is a paper by the Irish actuary Colm Fagan (1977), who maintained close relationships with British colleagues, and who suggested that it was possible to adopt an investment strategy that would 'immunize' the risk embedded in the maturity guarantees. Fagan's approach, which some later argued replicated the option pricing theory developed by the financial economists Black, Scholes and Merton, was examined by the Maturity Guarantees Working Party too. Although the working party concluded that Fagan's immunization strategy 'does seem to have serious practical disadvantages because it depends upon several underlying assumptions', it also noted that it 'merits further investigation' (Ford et al, 1980, p 112). Fagan's immunization approach and option pricing remained a marginal topic in actuarial science, but actuaries like Wilkie nevertheless started to consider their potential actuarial applications in the years that followed (see, for example, Wilkie, 1987).

Conclusion

Within the epistemic field of actuarial science, debates about the nature of financial risk emerged at the intersection of unit-linked insurance (and especially the issue of maturity guarantees), the introduction of risk theory and the rise of computing technology in actuarial work. When the controversy settled, stochastic simulation modelling was accepted as a legitimate technique in the actuarial toolkit, albeit with a modified version of the random walk that included some degree of 'reversion to the mean' over longer periods. It thereby paved the way for the introduction of modern finance theory because its stochastic models could be seen as broadly similar to the stochastic models already present in the actuarial toolkit. There was also widespread agreement about the riskiness of maturity guarantees on unit-linked contracts, the underlying funds of which were invested in risky assets.

However, while stochastic modelling became a legitimate object of research in the epistemic field, the use of stochastic asset models in the field of life insurance remained voluntary and rather limited. Most actuaries working at the life offices remained unfamiliar with the statistical techniques and procedures of stochastic risk modelling at least until the early 2000s. A major factor in making stochastic modelling of financial risk a common feature of the life insurance business was the crisis in the British life insurance industry that ensued from the late 1990s onwards. Especially affected were those companies that had implemented mixed models of unit-linked and with-profits insurance. This crisis, I argue in the next chapter, led to the perception that traditional actuarial expertise had failed, thereby providing a window of opportunity for proponents of stochastic financial risk modelling and modern finance theory to redefine actuarial knowledge claims.

'Authors of Their Own Misfortune'

In an article published in *The Independent* on 18 December, 2000 David Hyman lamented the collapse of Equitable Life Assurance Society (or Equitable in short). Hyman is a retired stockbroker who had taken out several pension policies with Equitable. He told the reporter that:

> Equitable was a wonderful company with a cast-iron reputation. It has blown it through total incompetence (and) blown 238 years of history through one silly decision … The actuaries behaved stupidly and almost criminally. They did not believe it could happen. They should have cut bonuses and set aside provisions. But they wanted to be top of the table. (Hyman in Garfield, 2000)

Hyman's policies included attractive 'guaranteed annuity options' (GAOs). Hyman, in other words, could convert the benefits of his policies into a pension annuity – a contract that provides its policyholder with an income until death – at a predetermined rate of conversion. At the time Hyman had bought his policies, the guaranteed annuity rate was not very attractive. The annuity rates available in the market far exceeded those guaranteed by Equitable. During the 1980s and '90s, however, changing financial market conditions had depressed market annuity rates, to the extent that Equitable's guarantees had now started to 'bite'. Facing financial trouble, Equitable decided to lower the benefits of policyholders with GAOs, like Hyman. Hyman, who became representative of other policyholders too, took the case to court, accusing Equitable of unduly discriminating between different groups of policyholders. After several legal battles, the House of Lords ruled in his favour, precipitating the company's demise. The company's shortfall was later estimated at £4.1bn (HM Treasury, 2016). Hyman told a reporter that it was 'unfortunate for the non-guaranteed annuity rate members, but the fact is that we were made promises. It is not our fault that the company did not take account of the possible shortfall' (Hyman in Garfield, 2000).

Equitable's downfall brings together many of the themes of the previous chapters. For instance, Equitable sold policies that combined elements from unit-linked insurance with features of the more traditional 'with-profits' style of life insurance. The issue of guarantees, moreover, again highlighted the question of financial risk and the adequacy of financial reserves. In this chapter, I show how Equitable's failure was constructed as a failure of actuarial expertise, which was blamed for having failed to keep up with the changing reality of insurance. Although the mechanics of life insurance and the role of the actuarial profession therein had already been contested in prior decades, Equitable's failure provided a window of opportunity for outside professional groups to contest the profession's jurisdictional claims and marked the transition from one system of insurance governance to the next. If we are to understand what caused the company's collapse, however, I must first say a bit more about the changing landscape of regulation and supervision in insurance.

Protecting policyholder expectations

At least until the 1970s, the British insurance industry was exemplary of the liberal approach to regulation. Ever since the implementation of the 1870 Life Assurance Companies Act, life insurers have enjoyed a great degree of freedom in exchange for publicity. As noted in Chapter 3, this regime required life insurers to publish annual accounts and perform actuarial valuations of their liabilities every three or five years. Apart from a basic capital deposit, the Act did not impose any other capital requirements. Insurers, moreover, were allowed to invest their capital as they saw fit. The publicizing insurers' accounts, it was hoped, would give the more prudent and well-managed companies a competitive advantage and would provide policyholders with sufficient protection. The aim was not to eradicate insurance failures entirely – individual companies should still be able to fail – rather, it was to ensure that when companies failed, the failure should be orderly and the shortfall limited (Booth, 2007).

Within this system of 'freedom with publicity', as the regime was also called, actuaries enjoyed a privileged legal standing. The 1870 Act required liability valuations to be performed by an actuary. Actuaries were free to choose their methods and assumptions as they saw fit, as long as they made sure that their valuations included sufficient levels of prudence to safeguard the company's solvency. Actuaries, moreover, also played a key role in life insurers' bonus policies. As noted in Chapter 3, most life insurers traditionally sold a mixture of with-profits and non-profit insurance. The benefits of non-profit policyholders were guaranteed. The benefits of with-profits policyholders, however, depended partly on bonuses of two kinds, reversionary bonuses and terminal bonuses. Bonus systems like these give insurers additional flexibility. When the investments perform poorly, insurers can adjust their bonuses downwards; when they perform well, insurers can distribute some of the accumulated surplus to their policyholders. Insurers, however, typically aimed to keep their bonuses relatively stable, smoothing policyholder returns across financial cycles. Doing so required judgements on the state of financial markets, judgements that were often made by actuaries.

Although the basic features of the governance regime remained in place well into the 20th century, by the 1990s certain aspects had started to change. Two stand out. First, as noted in Chapter 3, incumbent insurers faced increased competitive pressure from unit-linked insurers and, in response, changed their bonus distribution methodology. Second, regulators and supervisors took up a more active role in the governance of insurance, with the aim of protecting policyholders. By the late 1990s, these two issues started to converge: what could policyholders reasonably expect from insurers' bonus policies?

Bonus methodology: from net premiums to asset shares

Actuarial evaluation traditionally revolved all around bonuses. Perhaps the single most important tool in the traditional actuarial toolkit was the net-premium valuation method, a method that was both loved and hated; it pitted different conceptions of life insurance against each other. Consider, for instance, the following description:

> The net premium method of valuation has been controversial ever since it was first advocated over a century and a quarter ago. Its merits and deficiencies have exercised the minds of actuaries whose names are legendary in actuarial science ... it has been tested in practice against almost every kind of experience; and its demise has repeatedly been predicted. Nevertheless, although it has been modified somewhat over time, in principle it remains today firmly entrenched in life office practice. Consideration of it, even in modern times, has divided actuaries in old ways – the artist from the scientist, the theoretician from the practical man. (Carroll, 1975, p 121)

The net-premium valuation method was not only controversial; it was also incredibly difficult to understand. At core, the net-premium valuation method is a peculiar instance of a discounted-cash flow model, which Chiapello and Walter (2016) argue belongs to the first age of financialization. The method seeks to ascribe a present value to insurers' liabilities, but it seeks to do so in a way that allows for the gradual release of profits. To get a sense of how this works, it is useful to compare it with the more straightforward 'gross-premium' method. A gross-premium valuation projects all future cash flows, both incoming (premiums) and outgoing (expenses and claims), which are then discounted to a present value.

Because insurers expect to make a profit on their policies, the liability value of a gross-premium valuation method will likely be negative at the inception of the contract; the present value of the income exceeds the present value of the outgoings. The contract, in other words, has a positive expected value for the company. Most actuaries, however, considered it 'inappropriate to immediately recognise the profit that was expected to be generated over the lifetime of the policy' (Turnbull, 2017, p 124). They preferred, therefore, to use net premiums rather than gross premiums. These net premiums were calculated by reducing the gross premiums so that the present value of expected premium income would be equal to the present value of the outgoing cash flows. The adjustment is sometimes referred to as the 'profit loading' or the 'bonus loading', which is the share of the premiums that goes into paying bonuses. Although the net premiums were explicitly recognized as 'artificial', they also nicely showed how much insurers should roughly pay in bonuses to their with-profits policyholders. Models don't need to be accurate to be useful (see: Millo and MacKenzie, 2009).

Although the net-premium method was well suited for bonus purposes, it was also perceived to have some major drawbacks. In his famous paper on the principles of life office valuation, Prudential's Chief Actuary Frank Redington (1952) argued for instance that a 'valuation has two main purposes, and the fundamental difficulty is that these two purposes are in conflict. The first and primary purpose is to ensure that the office is solvent. The second is to allow the surplus to emerge in an equitable way suited to the bonus system' (Redington, 1952, p 298). A net-premium valuation was well suited for bonus policy, but, Redington argued, this ideally required the valuation basis, that is, the assumptions that go into the valuation, such as the discount rate, to remain unchanged (otherwise the level of the bonus loadings would change too). The valuation basis, in this approach, was 'frozen to the original premium basis' (Carroll, 1975, p 125). To assess whether insurers would have enough assets to meet their liabilities, however, they should adapt their valuation basis to the changing circumstances as time went by. Particularly problematic was the fluctuation of interest rates, Redington argued, which had given rise to an 'expanding funnel of doubt' (Redington, 1952, p 287). With net-premium valuations, it was difficult to see the impact of changing economic conditions on insurers' balance sheets – a feature that became increasingly important with the surging financial market volatility in the 1970s and '80s.

As noted in Chapter 3, from the 1980s onwards insurers increasingly used policyholders' 'asset shares' to determine their bonuses, rather than the profit-loadings implied by the initial premium calculations. Faced with competition from unit-linked insurers, this asset share approach provided for a more fine-grained measure of the present value of premiums, both past and future; and allowed insurers to price their policies more competitively. The gradual uptake of the asset share methodology, however, led to a peculiar situation, as David Belsham remembered. Belsham started working as a junior actuary at a large office in the 1980s and recalls that:

'[Q]uite frankly, I found the net-premium valuation sort of difficult to understand … [I]t's trying to allow for profit emergence in a way that suits bonuses. And so you sort of shrug your shoulders and say, well, okay. But, you know, not long after I got there … asset shares were being used to decide what bonuses you wanted to pay, and then the net-premium valuation was just used to produce the answer and the surplus you needed to pay those bonuses. So, you know, I'm sure in the 1950s and '60s it was important that the net-premium valuation produced the surplus it did and then that was used to pay a bonus. Whereas by the time I got there it ran the other way. You use the asset shares to decide what bonuses you want and then adjusted the net-premium valuation to give you the right answer.' (Belsham interview)

Increased competitive pressures had pushed insurers to privilege competitive and individualized pricing over a stable bonus system, which reduced the usefulness of the net-premium valuation method. Insurers, however, continued to use this method to assess insurers' solvency – a task many had argued the net-premium valuation method was not very well suited for.

The question of policyholder reasonable expectations

Another important development involved the changing relations between insurers and their supervisors. Historically, supervisors have played only a marginal role in the governance of insurance. The 1870 Insurance Companies Amendment Act had placed responsibility for insurance supervision with the government's Board of Trade. The Board of Trade, however, lacked the in-house expertise to scrutinize companies' regulatory returns and sought actuarial advice, first from individual actuaries in government service, and from the 1920s onwards from the government's internal actuarial consultancy, the Government Actuary's Department. The Government Actuary's Department then became the de facto supervisor. For most of the 20th century, however, the resources dedicated to the supervision of insurance firms remained limited. By the 1960s, for instance, the Government Actuary's Department employed one full-time employee and one part-time senior employee tasked with insurance supervision (Daykin, 1992).

In the latter half of the 20th century, supervisors gained a more central role in the governance of insurance. After a series of insurance failures in the 1960s, the UK government expanded regulatory powers. The 1973 Insurance Companies Amendment Act, for instance, granted the Board of Trade the right to intervene in a company's affairs when it violated one of several conditions. The Act also required companies to appoint an appointed actuary who was a part of company management and was made responsible for protecting policyholders' rights. Appointed actuaries, as some put it, 'were expected to act "heroically" as the protectors of both individual and corporate interests' (Collins et al, 2009, p 251). The 1982 Insurance Companies Act further increased supervisory powers and brought UK regulations in line with the European Directives requiring insurers to maintain a regulatory solvency margin (Carter and Falush, 2009, pp 193–4). The margin was based either on a 'claims basis' or a 'premium basis', calculated as a percentage of recent claims experience or premium income. Insurers' actuaries, however, retained the freedom to determine the appropriate methods for calculating the balance sheet. Supervisors, moreover, started performing 'resilience tests', stressing insurers' balance sheets with equity shocks to gauge capital adequacy (Fine et al, 1988). In the same period, the Government Actuary's Department significantly increased its supervisory capacity. By 1992, for instance, the department employed 17 actuaries working full time on insurance supervision (Daykin, 1999, p 530).

Among the key ideas introduced in regulation was the notion of 'policyholder reasonable expectations'. The 1973 Act allowed the Secretary of State to intervene in a company's affairs when it threatened to fail on its contractual obligations, 'or, in the case of long term business, to fulfil the reasonable expectations of policyholders or potential policyholders' (Insurance Companies Amendment Act 1973). The Act, however, did not define what constituted reasonable expectations, and its meaning became subject to significant debate within the actuarial profession. In 1986, for instance, the then President of the Institute, Marshall Field, took the 'notorious phrase' as a central topic of his presidential address. Field suggested that there were 'perhaps two separate meanings of the phrase' (Field, 1987, p 2): one actuarial, and the other legal. The actuarial meaning, Field argued, referred to policyholders' expectations of future bonus declarations. In Field's view, these expectations were 'objectives' rather than hard promises because there were circumstances in which 'policyholders' expectations as regards the level of bonus declarations ought *not* to be realised' (Field, 1987, p 2). The legal definition of the term, however, referred to the level of benefits to which policyholders were reasonably entitled. Although this meaning was 'for the lawyers to determine', Field did not think that these expectations, over and beyond the 'sum assured', could adequately be captured in 'legal terms'. Bonuses, after all, were determined at the discretion of the insurer. The 'justifiable expectations of a policyholder', Field argued, should therefore not refer to any quantifiable amount, but rather to the fact that policyholders should be able to trust the actuary as custodian of a company's surplus.

The question of policyholder reasonable expectations became more prominent in the 1990s. By the early 1990s, several secular trends had started to erode insurers' capital bases, leading to a wave of demutualizations, mergers and acquisitions. Interest rates declined throughout the 1980s. Increased competition had pushed up insurers' marketing expenses and pressured their pricing. Supervisors, moreover, had set more demanding reserving requirements. All these developments created a field dynamic where proprietary insurers, which could more readily tap into capital markets to get additional capital, gained a competitive edge over mutual insurers (Dumbreck and Sanders, 1993). Economies of scale, moreover, were increasingly perceived as an important factor too (Needleman and Westall, 1991). In response to these developments, therefore, many mutual insurers demutualized, and many of the smaller insurers were acquired by some of the larger firms. This restructuring of insurance funds raised important questions about how the funds should be distributed among the various stakeholders: what, in other words, should policyholders reasonably expect?

In some cases, the distributional question was not so complicated. Some mutual insurers still had access to large estates or surplus funds. They demutualized from a "position of strength" (Eastwood interview). A demutualization, in this case, would have distinct advantages for current policyholders. A "disciplined application of a properly tested" asset share and bonus methodology, Eastwood argued, reduced a company's capital needs, and parts of the accumulated "orphan estates" (it wasn't clear to whom the estates belonged) could therefore be distributed to their policyholders. The demutualization of Scottish Provident, for instance, entailed an average £4,000 windfall payment to policyholders (Bachelor, 2001). Similarly, Scottish Widows made one-off payments to its policyholders of £5,500 on average, with the maximum windfall payment amounting to £116,000 (Jones, 1999). It is little surprise, therefore, that such demutualization transactions were strongly favoured by existing policyholders. In the case of Scottish Provident, for instance, 97 per cent of more than 200,000 voting policyholders voted in favour of the deal. Not everyone agreed demutualizations like these were desirable. Estates were considered an essential part of the traditional actuarial model of life insurance. They allowed companies to smooth benefits across financial cycles. In this view, estates were not at all 'orphaned'. They simply belonged to the company and its policyholders, past, present and future. The actuary David Forfar, for instance, considered demutualization a "fad". In his view, companies were demutualizing simply "because everybody was demutualizing at the time" (Forfar interview).

In other cases, a demutualization was considered a necessity. Without large estates to appease policyholders, however, the distributional question gained in importance. In an early discussion of the subject at the Institute of Actuaries, this question was framed around the notion of policyholders' reasonable expectations (Field et al, 1991). To get regulatory approval, after all, insurers had to show how the interests of existing policyholders would remain protected after the transaction. There was, in other words, a need for a practical interpretation of the term. The Institute set up a working party to this end, chaired by Bernard Brindley, which proposed that at the very minimum policyholders' reasonable expectations should refer to the guaranteed benefits (including any reversionary bonuses already rewarded), and, more vaguely, that the company would be managed 'ethically and competently' (Penrose, 2004, p 436). In the context of a demutualization, however, many actuaries agreed that with-profits policyholders could reasonably expect more. With-profits policyholders, after all, expected compensation (through bonuses) for paying premiums in excess of equivalent non-profit premiums and accepting a degree of uncertainty. The working party noted that 'in the normal day-to-day actuarial management of a life policy, policyholders' reasonable expectations are 'synonymous with equity and the almost universal method for measuring it is asset share calculation', though it also noted that 'it is, naturally, widely accepted that there are differing ways of calculating asset shares' (Brindley 1990 as quoted in Penrose, 2004, p 439). In their attempt to define the term, the working party had thus equivocated policyholders' reasonable expectations with the concept of asset shares; it was unclear, however, what those asset shares should be, leaving the actuarial discretion characteristic of with-profits insurance unscathed.

Equitable's demise: from pioneer to pariah

Equitable Life is often credited with having pioneered modern life insurance in the 19th century. By the 1960s, however, Equitable ran a modest with-profits life insurance fund, mainly selling pensions. Its biggest customer was the Federated Superannuation Scheme for Universities, which comprised more than half of Equitable's business (Penrose, 2004, p 69). In the 1960s, the Federated Superannuation Scheme for Universities was restructured, and, as a consequence, Equitable lost a large chunk of its business. Its management changed tack and decided to embark 'on a programme of branch expansion, … revised its marketing policy and adopted a more aggressive approach to sales' (Penrose, 2004, p 69). The company grew substantially. Equitable managed £39mn in assets in 1960; £113mln in 1970, £534mln in 1980, £5,786mln in 1990 and, eventually, a whopping £33,553mln in 2000 (Penrose, 2004, p 70).

While Equitable managed to sustain high growth in consecutive decades, interest rates declined throughout most of the 1980s and '90s. With the bursting of the Dotcom bubble in 2000, moreover, stock markets slumped. The FTSE-100 Index, which contained the 100 largest companies listed on the London Stock Exchange, nearly halved. Many insurers got into significant financial trouble, and some of them, like Pearl Assurance, Royal Life and Sun Alliance, stopped writing new business. None, however, were so hard hit as Equitable, which, after the court ruling mentioned at the start of this chapter, was forced to close its doors. In many ways, the story of Equitable is exemplary of the developments discussed in this book. To enhance its competitive position, for instance, the company had drawn on various concepts and techniques borrowed from unit-linked insurance to manage its with-profits funds. Nevertheless, as many of my interviewees pointed out, the company's practices were also somewhat idiosyncratic. I will therefore first examine how Equitable's actuaries rationalized their approach to with-profits insurance and then move to the more specific issue of GAOs.

'With profits, without mystery'

In 1989 and 1990, the actuaries Roy Ranson and Chris Headdon presented a paper to the Institute and Faculty of Actuaries entitled 'With Profits, Without Mystery' (Ranson and Headdon, 1989, 1990). Ranson and Headdon were Equitable's Chief Executive and the Appointed Actuary. In their paper, Ranson and Headdon presented their strategy for managing Equitable's with-profits funds. The occasion was somewhat unusual: although company actuaries often presented papers on general themes relevant to the management of life offices, they rarely gave detailed descriptions of individual offices. This, though, was what Ranson and Headdon were doing. 'Within our office', they wrote, 'we had begun to feel a growing frustration with the fairly prevalent obfuscation within the industry regarding with-profits business compared with our tendency to view it in a simple straightforward way' (Ranson and Headdon, 1989, p 301).

Equitable's approach, the two actuaries explained, was 'to regard each with-profits policy holder as having a specific stake in that fund':

> The premiums they pay, after meeting expenses and the cost of life cover and other benefits and options, are invested in the managed fund. The benefits a policyholder ultimately receives will reflect the value of the assets in the fund attributable to his policy, i.e. that policyholder's asset share. Viewed like that, the analogy with linked business is clear although, in the case of with-profits business, results will not follow asset values with the precision that applies with linked business. The mechanics are, of course, different because with a linked contract a

specified proportion of the premium invested at a specified price and benefits emerge calculated on a specified basis. With with-profits, the price at which a policyholder buys into the managed fund and the value placed on the underlying 'asset share' when the policy benefits become payable are bound up in the premium basis and the various bonuses added; those are within the control of the actuary and directors. (Ranson and Headdon, 1989, p 303)

Equitable's 'managed fund' approach, as Ranson and Headdon called it, closely resembled the unitized with-profits funds discussed in Chapter 3. Reactions to the paper were divided. Although some praised Equitable's approach for its simplicity and flexibility, there were also many critical responses. One concern involved the assumption of full discretion over bonus policy. As noted earlier, the then President of the Institute, Marshall Field, had expressed concerns about how much leeway companies actually had in setting bonuses. With respect to Equitable's approach, Field wondered 'what controls are there on the discretion that I was so concerned about?' (Ranson and Headdon, 1989). Others questioned the company's 'full distribution policy', which entailed a full distribution of financial surplus. One actuary, for instance, argued that having an 'estate' as a risk buffer allowed insurers to invest in riskier and more profitable assets. Another actuary claimed that an estate was even necessary to support the risks implied by the guarantees on policies. Still others suggested that the approach wasn't as clear as Ranson and Headdon had made it out to be. Although Ranson and Headdon posited that policyholders 'expect a return broadly commensurate with a unit-linked approach', unlike unit-linked insurance their approach also implied smoothing. It was thus unclear what was meant by the policyholder's asset share. 'Is the asset share regarded as including the smoothing element, or is it a figure which then has the smoothing process applied to it?' (Jenkins in Ranson and Headdon, 1989, p 327). Even though some considered the managed fund approach to offer a simpler and more flexible alternative to conventional business (and they suspected that some other offices were running on a similar approach), many agreed there was a tension between the 'equity' approach to asset shares, which implied full distribution and reduced actuarial discretion, and the smoothing logic of conventional insurance, which required at least some degree of discretion.

The managed fund approach, as presented by Ranson and Headdon, appears to be a rationalization of the strategic choices Equitable's directors had made in prior years. An investigation into Equitable's demise, for instance, showed that the managed fund approach had precipitated from a desire to offer more competitive pricing and to expand market share. In the period 1973–6, Equitable had already boosted its policyholder benefits to attract new business, exhausting its estate. It then rebuilt a 'significant estate by 1982', which from then onwards was again used to boost benefits. Throughout the 1980s, as the company relinquished the idea of maintaining an estate, Equitable's surpluses continued to shrink to such an extent that it 'entered the 1990s with a negative estate accordingly' (Penrose, 2004, p 117). 'Thus', the Penrose report found, 'it was only in the middle to late 1980s that there came to be a positive assertion of a full distribution policy, when the Society ... related the terminal bonus allotment to the whole of the investment reserve' (Penrose, 2004, p 119). The competitive pressure to sustain high bonuses had thus led Equitable to conceive its full distribution bonus policy in the 1980s – an approach that used future policyholder premiums as a contingency reserve. This approach had put Equitable in a vulnerable financial position.

Guaranteed annuity options and the legal limits to actuarial discretion

By the 1990s, Equitable had already exhausted its reserves. When in 2000 the House of Lords ruling came, the company's finances deteriorated even further. At core, the case revolved around the meaning of 'policyholder reasonable expectations' and the limits to companies' discretion in setting bonuses. The High Court of Justice, which dealt with the case in the first instance, had initially ruled in Equitable's favour. The company subsequently wrote to its policyholders that the court had confirmed that its 'directors have discretion "well wide enough" to grant final bonus of an amount depending on how the benefits are taken by a policyholder' (Penrose, 2004, p 26). The ruling of the High Court of Justice, however, was then overturned by the Court of Appeal, a decision that was then upheld by the House of Lords (which, at the time, still functioned as the court of last resort). How, then, did the court envision the limits on insurers' bonus policies?

To be able to answer this question, it is first necessary to examine the issue of GAOs, a feature that Equitable – like some other insurers – had included on a substantial share of its business. As noted at the start of this chapter, a GAO gives a policyholder the right (but not the obligation) to convert cash benefits into an annuity (a regular stream of payments until death) at a predetermined rate. A guaranteed annuity rate of 10 per cent, for instance, would guarantee that a policyholder, given a certain age, would receive £100 per annum until death for every £1,000 cash at maturity of the savings policy. The value of this promise depends on the expected mortality as well as the expected investment returns. If the expected investment returns or the expected mortality decline, the value of the annuity increases. GAOs thus provide additional security for retirement income under changing investment conditions. GAO policyholders may, of course, also decide to buy an annuity in the open market.

From 1957 to 1988, Equitable had sold around 116,000 policies with GAOs. At the time Equitable issued its GAO policies, market annuity rates were more attractive than the guaranteed rates. In the 1990s, however, this gradually changed. Most problematic were the contracts Equitable had sold between 1975 and 1988, when rising interest rates had led the company's actuaries to assume higher investment returns (Corley, 2001; Penrose, 2004). In the 1980s and '90s, however, interest rates declined persistently, while life expectancy continued to increase above expectation. The GAOs on Equitable's policies started to bite. Already in 1982, market rates dipped below the guaranteed annuity rates, and in the early 1990s, they did so again. Finally, from 1997 onwards, they continued doing so even more (O'Brien, 2006). Among insurers, however, there was significant uncertainty about the value of GAO policies. Actuaries' deterministic models, for instance, relied on point-based estimates of key variables, allowing for assessments of 'single' scenarios. This method, however, did not yield any measure of the *degree of uncertainty*. Even if actuaries understood that GAOs were risky and required reserving, they did not have a quantitative measure of *how risky* they were.[1]

The case of Equitable versus Hyman was not the first time the problem of GAOs was discussed. Nick Dumbreck remembers that the issue of annuity guarantees had also come up during demutualizations. When Provident Mutual demutualized, for instance, Dumbreck remembers that the company had "some quite onerous guarantees" on its books (Dumbreck interview). In the late 1990s, moreover, the Faculty and Institute of Actuaries set up a joint working party to compare insurers' reserving practices. In a survey, the working party found that of the 66 respondents, 41 had sold annuity guarantees. In aggregate, nearly 12 per cent of the business of these companies contained annuity guarantees (Bolton et al, 1997, p 5).[2]

As the GAO issue became more urgent, insurers faced the following questions: how should they obtain the funds to meet the increasingly valuable guarantees? And who should pay for that? Should insurers pay for the guarantees by reducing the bonuses of all with-profits policyholders? Or just those whose policies benefitted from annuity guarantees? In the former case, policyholders without annuity guarantees would be affected by policies other than their own. In the latter case, which was also called a 'differential terminal bonus policy', the benefit of having a guarantee seemed to be defeated. After all, if exercising the guarantee meant that the contract's benefits were reduced, what was the point of having the guarantee in the first place?

Already in the early 1980s, Equitable's actuaries settled on a differential terminus bonus policy. This policy was defined as follows (Penrose, 2004, p 6): 'The income available to the policyholders is the higher of: (i) Fund (including final bonus) x current annuity rates; (ii) Fund (excluding final bonus) x GAR [Guaranteed Annuity Rate].' Starting in 1998, however,

Equitable received complaints from policyholders, who disagreed with the differential terminal bonus policy. The policyholders, among whom David Hyman, argued that the differential bonus policy unduly discriminated between different types of policyholders. As members of the same fund, with-profits policyholders should receive the same treatment, regardless of what other conditions their contracts entailed. Unable to come to an agreement, Equitable's management – confident it had a strong case – then took the case to court.

As noted earlier, the High Court of Justice initially deemed Equitable's approach legitimate. This decision was subsequently overturned by the Court of Appeal and the House of Lords, who ultimately ruled in Hyman's favour, respectively with a 2–1 and a 5–0 majority. Although the Lords recognized that '[b]onuses are determined by directors in the exercise of a discretion conferred upon them', they also argued that a differential terminal bonus policy undermined policyholders' reasonable expectations:

> [F]inal bonuses are not bounty. They are a significant part of the consideration for the premiums paid. And the directors' discretions as to the amount and distribution of bonuses are conferred for the benefit of policyholders. In this context the self-evident commercial object of the inclusion of guaranteed rates in the policy is to protect the policyholder against a fall in market annuity rates by ensuring that if the fall occurs he will be better off than he would have been with market rates. The choice is given to the GAR [guaranteed annuity rate] policyholder and not to the Society. It cannot be seriously doubted that the provision for guaranteed annuity rates was a good selling point in the marketing by the Society of the GAR policies. It is also obvious that it would have been a significant attraction for purchasers of GAR policies. The Society points out that no special charge was made for the inclusion in the policy of GAR provisions. So be it. This factor does not alter the reasonable expectations of the parties. (House of Lords, 2000)

It is not within the purview of this chapter to explain exhaustively why the decision fell one way or other (that would require another chapter). It is important nonetheless to note that the conformity of Equitable's practices with legal terms such as 'policyholder reasonable expectations' could not simply be deduced from the existing rules. After all, the meaning of terms like 'policyholder reasonable expectations' and 'asset shares' was open-ended. Whatever interpretation one chose appeared defensible in theory. What the ruling achieved, however, was to establish a shared understanding of a new set of rules of the with-profits game. The case of Equitable was central in this shared understanding: it provided an exemplary case, which indicated where the limits of actuarial discretion were.

'Fallen heroes': constructing a failure of actuarial expertise

The courts had set limits to actuarial discretion. They had made clear that henceforth actuaries were required to rationalize their decisions through the concept of policyholder reasonable expectations. As noted earlier, the constraint on discretion was not inherent to any specific interpretation of the term but was constituted by the threat that, if decisions were poorly rationalized, the courts may well rule against insurers' actions in the name of protecting policyholders' reasonable expectations. This raised some thorny questions about the adequacy of actuarial expertise: did the tools that actuaries used previously to rationalize decision making still suit their purposes?

Investigations into Equitable's collapse suggested they did not. The Penrose Inquiry, for instance, proved highly critical of the actuarial profession and suggested that actuaries had been 'the authors of their own misfortune' (Penrose, 2004, p 439). They had shown a 'reluctance to indulge in mutual criticism', the report noted, and they had failed to set adequate standards for actuarial practice (Penrose, 2004, p 121). Traditional actuarial methods had obfuscated insurers' 'real' liabilities to the extent that the 'regulatory returns and measures of solvency applied by the regulators did not keep pace with developments in the industry', the Inquiry claimed. '[R]egulatory solvency became an increasingly irrelevant measure of the realistic financial position of the Society' (Penrose, 2004, p 727). The profession had also failed to confront the question of policyholder reasonable expectations as a *legal* question; instead, they had perceived the issue exclusively in actuarial terms, assuming full discretion in setting bonuses. 'Actuaries', however, 'were not competent to adjudicate on the issues that emerged' (Penrose, 2004, p 39). The issue of policyholder reasonable expectations could thus have been resolved, the Inquiry suggested, if actuaries had sought external advice regarding its legal interpretation.

The Penrose Inquiry also triggered a more formal review of the actuarial profession, which was commissioned by the government and led by Sir Derek Morris. The Review provided a platform for competing professions and bodies of expertise to contest the jurisdictional claims of the actuarial profession. It published a consultation, on which it received over 100 responses, mostly from actors outside the actuarial profession. It fielded questionnaires to pension scheme trustees, pension scheme sponsors and non-executive directors. And it appointed an external advisory panel, which counted among its seven members two accountants, one director of a large investment bank, and a Canadian actuary. Based on these sources of information, the Review published an interim assessment that was highly critical of the actuarial profession. The profession had been 'too insular … and has been slow to adopt new approaches and techniques'. The profession had neglected to communicate uncertainty in their advice. The profession had allowed for insufficient transparency in their advice, black-boxing their analyses with opaque methodology. The profession's jurisdictional claims were too strong and included areas of work that may have been better served by other bodies of expertise. And, finally, the profession had been 'too slow to adjust to the changing [macroeconomic] circumstances', failing to account for declining inflation and interest rates and tumbling stock markets (Morris, 2005, p 14). The interim assessment, in other words, questioned the legitimacy of the profession's jurisdictional claims in the insurance and pensions business, as well as the techniques and methods they used to carry out their work. In its final report, the Review recommended increased external oversight over the profession, a strengthening of internal standards and accountability, and a loosening of actuarial jurisdictional claims to facilitate increased competition among actuaries and between the actuarial profession and other professional groups.

Apart from external critique, there was also a growing body of actuaries that critiqued the profession from within. By the mid-1990s, Turnbull writes, a group of predominantly younger actuaries had emerged (of which Turnbull himself was part), 'who had independently developed expertise in financial economics and who worried that the British actuarial profession was dangerously behind other financial professionals' (Turnbull, 2017, p 216). These actuaries often worked for actuarial consulting firms, where they sometimes interacted with other professional groups. Among the most vocal members was a consulting actuary at Bacon & Woodrow, Andrew Smith. Having been "seconded to an investment bank" in the early '90s, Smith had become familiar with modern finance theory and its approach to valuation, which, as Smith remembers, was "completely different from the way that actuaries did it" (Smith interview). Other members included David Dullaway, who, rather unusually, had a background in economics, Malcolm Kemp, Jon Exley, Shyam Mehta, Cliff Speed, David Bowie, and the academic actuaries Andrew Cairns and Angus Macdonald, both at Heriot-Watt University's actuarial department.

In the 1990s, the proponents of modern finance theory gradually started propagating its benefits. They presented various papers in the sessional meetings outlining its possible applications in the context of pensions and insurance (Mehta, 1992; Dyson and Exley, 1995; Smith, 1996; Kemp, 1997), and they wrote opinion pieces in the profession's monthly magazine *The Actuary*. These opinion pieces were oftentimes rather provocative. Exley et al (2000), for instance, wrote that 'the questioning of actuarial judgement risks exposing an "emperor's new clothes"-type scam'. They suggested, moreover, that any resistance was due to the fact that 'a switch would entail radical retraining. Consultants would be selected more on the basis of technical skill in their area of expertise ... The result might be greater involvement by non-actuaries in areas where previously it was believed that there was some special actuarial skill' (Exley et al, 2000).

Anecdotal evidence suggests that proponents of modern finance theory indeed encountered significant opposition, sometimes bordering on hostility. Dullaway, for instance, remembers "one public meeting ... where somebody actually stood up and called me a traitor to my profession". The issue, Dullaway acknowledged, was a sensitive one:

> 'There's a lot of people here who have senior positions, it's a very well-respected profession, and I'm saying: everything you've been doing for the last ten, twenty years has simply been wrong. At least that's what they felt I was saying. And people like Andrew Smith were getting the same responses. There was a real backlash of: "you can't say that, because if you're right everything that we're doing is wrong."' (Dullaway interview)

With Equitable's downfall, however, opposition against modern finance theory subsided. Equitable's failure was interpreted as a failure of actuarial expertise. Outside the profession, many perceived actuaries' outdated valuation methods as culprits. Using these methods, actuaries had struggled to account for the optionality in insurance contracts and the changing economic circumstances. The actuarial profession thus faced external demands to update its technical repertoire and increased pressure to defend its jurisdictional claims. With the integration of insurance and banking supervision, moreover, the actuarial profession met with a new supervisory agent, the Financial Services Authority (FSA), that was less attached to actuarial expertise. Within the profession, there was already a faction that had sought reform of the 'professional project' by propagating the benefits of modern finance theory. In the early 2000s, then, the process of paradigmatic change gained significant traction.

Observing the increased contestation of actuaries' jurisdictional claims post-Equitable, Collins et al (2009) describe actuaries as 'fallen heroes'. Prior to Equitable's demise, they argue, actuaries held a 'heroic' position in the insurance business. In the role of the Appointed Actuary, actuaries were responsible for protecting both policyholder and commercial interests. This strengthened their jurisdictional claims but also gave them a powerful position within the insurance business, providing little incentive to produce 'transparent' knowledge about insurers' financial position. This worked as long as insurers continued to generate profit. With Equitable's downfall, however, it also exposed the actuarial profession to significant jurisdictional contestation. The case of the actuarial profession thus seems to confirm

Abbott's (2005) claim that 'dominant professions often destroy themselves by a ruinous exercise of domination'.

Conclusion

Equitable's demise was one of those rare moments marking a rupture from one way of doing life insurance to the next. The company's demise was the culmination of several trends: the challenge of unit-linked insurers, which pushed with-profits insurers to alter the management of their funds; increasing competition among insurers; increasing financial market volatility and a secular decline in interest rates; and expanding regulatory powers. The case of Equitable was not just symptomatic but also generative. The court ruling on Equitable's bonus policy established new limits to actuarial discretion. The company's demise, moreover, was widely perceived as a failure of actuarial expertise. Actuaries did engage with techniques allowing for the quantification of financial risk, as seen in Chapter 4, but the uptake was limited, remaining mostly confined to some of the larger offices and unit-linked business. The perceived failure of actuarial expertise provided a window of opportunity for outside groups to contest the profession's jurisdictional claims and strengthened the position of proponents of modern finance theory within it. In the next two chapters of this book, I examine more closely what happened in the period after the collapse of Equitable. How was the system of insurance governance remade? And how did the shift towards the paradigm of modern finance theory unfold in practice?

6

'Taking Account of What the Market Has to Say'

'[I]t's like a Kuhnian paradigm shift had to happen before people would say: okay, yes, maybe you're right, now let's look at the details. … It was exactly like one of those shifts, like, you know, when Newton came along or when Einstein came along and the whole world changed.' (Dullaway interview)

In this quote, David Dullaway describes the appropriation of market-consistent quantification techniques as a paradigm shift, techniques that belong to what Chiapello and Walter (2016) refer to as the third age of financialization. At least two other interviewees also referred to the transition from traditional actuarial modelling to market-consistent modelling as a paradigm shift, and the term was also used to make sense of the events at the time the paradigm shift allegedly happened (for example Clarkson, 1997). Kuhn's notion of the paradigm shift has become a convenient shorthand in public discourse for describing a period of rapid cultural change in knowledge practices both within and outside of scientific fields. The notion of paradigm shift tends to be accompanied in popular usage by an understanding of cultural change that is somewhat non-sociological. It assumes that paradigm shifts follow an internal logic, where new paradigms emerge as unsolvable anomalies proliferate. A more sociological reading of Kuhn's work, however, proposes that paradigms can be understood as exemplary problem solutions that are central in the organization of research fields (for example Barnes, 1982). What Kuhn refers to as 'normal science' then involves the analogical extension of already existing problem solutions to new problems, a creative endeavour that already implies change or shifting practices. In this view, paradigms co-exist even in highly specialized fields of research, and paradigm shifts occur with the diffusion, institutionalization and analogical extension of exemplary problem solutions and may be either gradual or abrupt, in which case they may be experienced as significant discontinuities.

The paradigm shift my interviewees referred to, from traditional actuarial modelling to market-consistent modelling, had already started in the 1990s, if only in a very limited way. Especially in the context of mergers and acquisitions, consulting actuaries increasingly drew on key exemplars from modern finance theory to estimate the economic value of insurers' liabilities, even if the calculations were somewhat indicative and the models rather crude. When the regulatory regime started to change in the early 2000s, market-consistent valuation became increasingly institutionalized, and the exemplary models of modern finance theory were extended and adapted to a variety of insurance-specific valuation problems (when writing about insurance-specific valuation problems in this chapter, it refers specifically to those valuation problems central in life insurance). What my interviewees referred to as a paradigm shift, in other words, had already been in the making for quite some time but gained momentum in the early 2000s.

In this chapter, I investigate the appropriation of modern finance theory, focusing on how and why the core models of modern finance theory were used as exemplars for the modelling of insurers' liabilities. First, I describe the emergence of modern finance theory and its impact on financial market practice. Second, I trace the process of appropriation from early discussions about the utility of modern finance theory in actuarial practice to the implementation of the new regulatory regime in the mid-2000s. Third, I briefly examine how insurers' market-consistent models diverge from more traditional actuarial models. Some readers may wish to skip this section, which may be a rather challenging read for those less familiar with modern finance theory. Finally, I review what the paradigm shift towards market-consistent modelling entailed.

No-arbitrage modelling and modern finance theory

Since the 1950s, modern finance theory has gradually established itself as a distinct field in academic economics (Whitley, 1986; MacKenzie, 2006). What 'had started as separate streams [of research]' from the 1950s onwards, was in the 1970s increasingly 'seen as parts of a largely coherent view of financial markets' (MacKenzie, 2006, p 66). One stream revolved around the efficient market hypothesis and focused on the analysis of movements in stock prices. The efficient market hypothesis, which had famously been formulated by Eugene Fama (1965, 1970) and built upon an earlier claim that stock prices follow a 'random walk' (a topic that was also discussed in Chapter 4), put forward the suggestion that markets were efficient and at all times would reflect all available information in prices. Following this proposition, it would be impossible to predict whether prices would move up or down over time. Another stream centred on modern portfolio theory (Markowitz, 1952; Treynor, 1961; Sharpe, 1964; Lintner, 1965), focusing on the analysis of optimal investment strategies given the expected returns and risks of individual stocks and on questions such as whether capital structures mattered for companies' market value (Modigliani and Miller, 1958). Important in this stream of research is Chiapello and Walter's (2016) second financial quantification convention: the mean-variance approach, which links an asset's discount rate to its expected return and expected variance.

The third, and arguably most influential stream of research, has yielded what Chiapello and Walter (2016) refer to as the third financial quantification convention. This convention finds its roots in options pricing theory and its key exemplar of the Black–Scholes–Merton model for pricing financial options. Options pricing had been a longstanding puzzle in finance research. Options are derivatives, which derive their value from the price movements of an underlying asset and are therefore notoriously difficult to value. An owner of a stock option has the right but not the obligation to purchase (or, in the case of a 'put option', to sell) the underlying stock at a predetermined price. An option's payoff thus depends on the price of the underlying stock, but how exactly the price of the derivative should relate to the characteristics of the underlying stock was difficult to know. Practitioners had therefore historically relied mostly on rules of thumb (MacKenzie, 2006, chapter 5). The Black–Scholes–Merton model, in contrast, drew on arbitrage arguments, similar to the work of Modigliani and Miller, to give mathematical expression to the relation between the characteristics of the stock and the price of a stock option. The Black–Scholes–Merton model suggests that an option's payoff can be replicated by a portfolio of shares in the underlying stock and 'risk-free' bonds in continuously adjusted proportions.[1] Following the arbitrage logic (and some simplifying assumptions), the price of the option should then be equal to the price of the 'replicating portfolio', for if not, arbitrageurs could potentially make a 'riskless profit' by buying or selling the option and 'hedging' their risk by buying or selling the replicating portfolio, depending on their relative prices. The model's solution to the problem, the Black–Scholes equation, expressed the price of a stock option in terms of time, a risk-free interest rate and the volatility and price of the underlying stock.

The Black–Scholes equation gave a solution for the pricing of European call options and ignored dividends.[2] The model, however, provided an exemplary problem solution that in subsequent years was extended and reformulated to solve a wide variety of other derivative valuation problems (MacKenzie, 2006, p 139). The Black–Scholes–Merton model, in other words, 'became the central paradigm … of financial economics' (MacKenzie and Millo, 2003, p 109). In subsequent years, a host of 'no-arbitrage' models were developed, some of which were intended to express the intuition behind the Black–Scholes–Merton model in more general theoretical and mathematical terms. A good example of this is the work of Stephen Ross and John Cox, who 'showed that the determination of option prices in [the way suggested by the Black–Scholes–Merton model] was equivalent to the principle of "risk-neutral valuation"' (MacKenzie, 2006, pp 139–40), a principle that could be applied not just to options but to all asset classes.

No-arbitrage theory found an even more general mathematical expression in the work of the operations researcher Michael Harrison, the economist David Kreps, both at Stanford University, and Stanley Pliska, an operations researcher at Northwestern University. The papers by Harrison and Kreps (1979) and Harrison and Pliska (1981) proved mathematically that if a market is 'frictionless' and free from arbitrage, it is possible to assign a probability measure – an 'equivalent martingale measure' in mathematical terms – describing the likelihood of future price developments such that the price of a derivative on that asset is simply the expected payoff discounted to a present value using the appropriate discount rate. Moreover, in a complete market, that is, a market in which all risks can be hedged, there is a *unique* probability measure for which the appropriate discount rate is the risk-free rate of interest: the *risk-neutral* measure implied in the work of Cox and Ross (MacKenzie, 2006, pp 140–1). Harrison and Kreps had shown, in other words, that in a 'frictionless' and 'complete' market, and in the absence of opportunities for arbitrage, every asset could be assigned a price by assuming that all assets provided the same expected rate of return, the risk-free rate, a complicated proposition that nonetheless proved useful in a wide variety of settings (Chiapello and Walter, 2016). As MacKenzie argues, with the publication of Harrison and Kreps's propositions, 'the basic structure of "orthodox" modern finance theory was essentially complete' (MacKenzie, 2006, p 141). The papers by Harrison, Kreps and Pliska 'turned financial economics into mathematical finance' (Davis and Etheridge, 2006, p 114).

What makes no-arbitrage models like the Black–Scholes equation distinctive is that they seek to calculate value 'synchronically'. The Black–Scholes equation 'posits the existence of a specific socially imagined totality, *the market*' (LiPuma, 2017, p 2; emphasis in original). The model, which requires a number of auxiliary assumptions to make the problem mathematically tractable, 'exteriorizes the social structuring of the market, setting aside both the objective structures of the financial market and the motivating structures embodied in its agents' (LiPuma, 2017, p 3). In so doing, the model does not provide an accurate description of real financial markets but constructs an idealized image of their underpinning 'objective structures', an image that allows the formulation of useful practical devices such as the Black–Scholes equation. It allows, in other words, the relation between prices and volatility of different assets, enforced through arbitrage, to be expressed in mathematical terms. Those who use the Black–Scholes equation in practice rarely believe that it describes financial markets accurately but tend to argue that it helps to perceive, orientate and structure financial action – perhaps in ways that make markets more 'rational' (MacKenzie, 2006; Millo and MacKenzie, 2009; Svetlova, 2009). Risk-neutral valuation circumvents the problem of arbitrarily having to pick a discount rate, and it does not rely on the modelers' expectations about the asset's real returns. It is therefore perceived to be more 'objective' and constraining relative to the first and second financial quantification conventions.

No-arbitrage models, for these reasons, are often imputed with a certain 'ontological dignity' (Van der Heide, 2020). Apart from the 'real world', there is also the 'world contained within the model' where all assets are expected to generate returns equal to the risk-free rate of interest. Chiapello and Walter write for instance that '[f]or calculative purposes the "new finance" has imagined a new world, the risk-neutral world, in which all invested assets are assumed to provide the same expected rate of return, namely the risk-free rate, regardless of the risk of each specific asset' (Chiapello and Walter, 2016, pp 163–4). Similar distinctions surface in the language of practitioners. Kemp, for instance, writes about the 'Black–Scholes world' and the 'no-arbitrage world', a world that satisfies assumptions underpinning no-arbitrage models and in which opportunities for arbitrage are absent (Kemp, 2009).

The construction of a model world allows no-arbitrage modellers to see things that others cannot see. '[K]ey to the ontology of no-arbitrage models', as MacKenzie and Spears (2014b, p 399) point out, are the martingale or risk-neutral probabilities referred to earlier. These are central in the derivatives quant culture studied by Spears (2014). No-arbitrage modellers do not assign 'real-world' probabilities (again, not to be confused with 'realistic' estimations of value) to the possible future price trajectories of an asset (probabilities that are based, for example, in archival-statistical analysis), but rather describe such price trajectories with a probability distribution that reflects the expectation that future prices will on average be equal to today's price. Risk-neutral probabilities 'are simultaneously less real and more real than actual probabilities' (MacKenzie and Spears, 2014b, p 400). They are less real in the sense that they do not describe true expectations; they are more real, because they provide access to the 'objective' value of an asset. No-arbitrage models thus posit a specific ontology or a particular way of viewing the economic world, which sees the world of finance as an objective totality held together by the logic of arbitrage and in which martingale probabilities apply.[3]

Although finance practitioners initially tended to be sceptical or even hostile towards early financial economics, a 'significant body of practitioner opinion came gradually to embrace at least some of [its] conclusions' (MacKenzie, 2006, p 87). Particularly influential was the Black–Scholes equation, which entered the trading floor of the Chicago Board Options Exchange in the form of paper sheets as early as 1973. The sheets described the relation between the volatility of the underlying stock, an option's strike price and its value, and made the prices of options of different strike prices and maturities comparable by expressing them in a single commensurable variable – the 'implied volatility' (MacKenzie and Millo, 2003; MacKenzie, 2006). In so doing, the paper sheets greatly facilitated the development of novel trading strategies (Beunza and Stark, 2004, 2012).

By allowing the 'backing out' of assets' implied volatility (deriving the implied volatility from an observed 'market price' of a particular derivative), no-arbitrage models also contributed to developments in risk analysis and management (Millo and MacKenzie, 2009). This backing out facilitated the calculation of risk for large portfolios. Quantitative risk management, moreover, helped justify economic capital allocation decisions (Lockwood, 2015) by making the risk–reward trade-off of different portfolios comparable (Holton, 2002; Kavanagh, 2003; Rosen, 2003). These uses enhanced the legitimacy of derivatives. Without any clear economic rationale for their pricing, derivatives were often regarded as a form of gambling. No-arbitrage models, in contrast, endowed derivatives with a clear economic rationale; when used appropriately, they could be used to manage risk and reduce financial uncertainty (MacKenzie and Millo, 2003; de Goede, 2005b); and they rationalized and justified the proliferation of derivatives and structured products (Dionne, 2013). An early practical example of this is portfolio insurance, a dynamic trading strategy using insights from the Black–Scholes–Merton model to create a 'synthetic put option' on a market portfolio (Leland and Rubinstein, 1988; MacKenzie, 2006). Other innovations included credit derivatives, interest rate swaps, caps and floors, and collateralized debt obligations (see Dionne, 2013).

Finally, the cultural authority of financial economics and the concomitant proliferation of derivatives influenced accounting practice too, manifested by the ascendancy of 'fair value' accounting. In the second half of the 20th century, accounting standards both in the UK and globally increasingly emphasized the economic meaning of corporate balance sheets, rather than their legal meaning (Power, 2012). This shift is most clearly manifested by the emergence of 'fair value accounting' standards, which define value as 'the price that would be received to sell an asset or paid to transfer a liability in an orderly transaction between market participants at the measurement date' (Laux and Leuz, 2009, p 827). Most kinds of derivatives are traded 'over the counter' and therefore have no observable 'market value'. No-arbitrage models, however, allow for the calculation of market-consistent prices, that is, prices that are consistent with a Black–Scholes world in which (theoretically) no arbitrage opportunities are available. These practices are not without critique: some argue that 'market values' for assets that are not actually easily tradable give accounting representations somewhat of an imaginative character (Laux and Leuz, 2009; Müller, 2014; Zhang and Andrew, 2014), potentially compromising the 'reliability' of the accounting representation

(Ronen, 2008). Fair value accounting, moreover, may strengthen procyclical tendencies, inflating the value of a firm in good times and thereby allowing it to become more highly leveraged (or to take on relatively more debt), while deflating it in poor ones (compare: Laux and Leuz, 2009, pp 829–30). These issues surfaced in the context of insurance valuation too.

From no-arbitrage to market-consistency

Sometime in 2003, Barrie & Hibbert, a small company based in Edinburgh, received a phone call from a life insurer asking for an "economic scenario generator". Although John Hibbert, who picked up the phone, recalls he "had to ask them what they meant", it was essentially what the company had already been doing since the late 1990s; they simply had "never used that terminology before" (Hibbert interview). After the first company had called, the "phone rang again and somebody wanted the same thing, and then the phone rang [again]" (Hibbert interview). In subsequent years, economic scenario generators became a pivotal piece of technology in the knowledge machinery of British life insurers. Barrie & Hibbert, whose scenario generator became widely used, grew to become one of the main model providers to the industry, covering most of the market for outsourced modelling capacity. "When you get to the end of the month", a former modeller at Barrie & Hibbert reflected back on that period in the late 2000s, and early 2010s,

> '30th of the month or 31st, depending on which quarter it is – they've got people in there at midnight. And so 24 hours after … there's a model and calibration files being sent off to clients. You should walk past there at midnight, or walk past at six in the morning on the first of July and see if there's a bunch of folk in there … eating pizza and coffee and cranking through their models.' (Interviewee CB)

Barrie & Hibbert started as a relative outsider to the market for actuarial advice. Both its founders were former investment bankers who, for personal reasons, returned from London to Edinburgh. Unable to find a job as "quantitative analysts" in Edinburgh's financial sector (because there were very few to none), they decided "to try and create an advisory research business" (Hibbert interview). Founded in 1995, Barrie & Hibbert helped asset managers manage market risk and understand structured financial products. The company also did some asset-liability management, helping companies in their investment strategy while taking account of the characteristics of their liabilities. When in the early 2000s the UK's FSA asked insurers to report what they called the 'realistic' value of their assets and liabilities (that is, their 'market-consistent' value), requiring insurers to measure their liabilities using techniques similar to those used in the derivatives departments of investment banks, few insurers had access to the relevant expertise in-house. Barrie & Hibbert filled the 'structural hole' (Burt, 1992). The expertise of Barrie & Hibbert in 'state of the art' financial modelling techniques and the work they had done on asset-liability management formed the basis for their economic scenario generator – a piece of software that allowed insurers to calculate the market-consistent value of their liabilities.

In this section, I examine how and why regulators preferred to build the evaluation machinery using the models of modern finance theory as key exemplars and why Barrie & Hibbert became the main supplier of models in the industry. The first thing to note here is that actuaries had already deliberated on the merits of the Black–Scholes equation in particular and modern finance theory more generally when the issue of unit-linked guarantees came to the fore (see Chapter 4). The Irish actuary Colm Fagan (Fagan, 1977) had suggested an approach to managing the risk of maturity guarantees that was very similar to the replicating portfolio logic of option pricing theory (see Chapter 4). Moreover, a former colleague of Scholes and Merton at MIT, Michael Brennan, his doctoral student Eduardo Schwartz, and the Irish actuary and economist Phelim Boyle, all at the University of British Columbia, had published papers in finance journals indicating how option pricing theory could be used to price such guarantees (Brennan and Schwartz, 1976; Boyle and Schwartz, 1977).[4] The Maturity Guarantees Working Party had also examined the possibility of using option pricing theory, though reaching a negative verdict about its utility; option pricing theory, the working party concluded, seemed 'to have serious practical disadvantages because it depends upon several underlying assumptions', which were seen as unrealistic (Ford et al, 1980, p 112).[5] Two years later, the actuary Thomas Collins reached a similar conclusion, arguing 'that the theory … is not practical enough' (Collins, 1982, pp 281–2). Although actuaries acknowledged that option pricing theory could in principle be extended analogically to maturity guarantees on unit-linked contracts, doing so would be of limited practicality because of the unrealistic assumptions and the perceived incommensurability between insurers' long-term perspective and the short-term perspective of modern finance theory. With-profits liabilities were entirely out of the question.

In the 1990s, however, the status quo in the epistemic field of actuarial science started to change. A first factor was that, as noted in Chapter 4, a group of predominantly younger actuaries had emerged who became increasingly vocal in their advocacy for the benefits of modern finance theory, often meeting with fierce opposition. Many of the most brazen proponents of modern finance theory were actuarial consultants and increasingly drew on the exemplars of modern finance theory to estimate the economic value of insurers' liabilities, for instance to advise on the takeover of insurance companies. Proponents of modern finance theory, moreover, published various papers in the *British Actuarial Journal*, outlining how modern finance theory could be used in the insurance business. These papers outlined for instance how financial economics could be applied in an actuarial context (Smith, 1996), how modern finance theory could be used to value pension funds (Exley et al, 1997; Head et al, 2000), and how derivatives could be used to manage financial risk (Kemp, 1997).

The tensions between the proponents of modern finance theory and traditional actuarial approaches came to the fore perhaps nowhere as clear as in the discussions following the actuary Robert Clarkson's papers. Clarkson was one of the most vocal opponents of the market-consistent approach, and his papers (and the discussion thereof) laid bare a divide between actuaries concerned mostly with the management of uncertainty through imprecise but prudent judgements about economic value and risk and actuaries favouring the mathematical precision of modern finance theory. Proponents of modern finance theory responded to Clarkson's paper, for instance, by suggesting that Clarkson (and many other actuaries with him) had 'no desire to allow the precision of mathematical argument to stand in the way of his assaults on his chosen targets' (Macdonald in Clarkson, 1996, p 959). Wilkie, whose earlier contributions to actuarial science had led both the Institute and Faculty of Actuaries to award him a gold medal and whose embrace of modern finance theory was less wholesale than that of some of the younger actuaries, also criticized Clarkson's use of mathematics. 'I have been depressed by the discussion', Wilkie said in response to Clarkson's paper. 'It is, I am afraid, a dialogue of the deaf, between those who know something about statistics, about financial economics and about mathematics, and those who do not' (Wilkie in Clarkson, 1996, p 961).

The changes in the regulation of the market field in the early 2000s were another important factor. Not long after its establishment in the late 1990s, the FSA decided to overhaul its regulatory approach, adopting what it called a system of 'realistic reporting' (that is, market-consistent reporting). In the words of the FSA's chairman at the time, Howard Davies, this system would require insurers to use 'the same techniques as are used by banks and other participants in the capital markets' to calculate capital requirements (Davies, 2002). The immediate cause for the FSA's adoption of a market-consistent and risk-based regime was the widely shared perception that the previous system of insurance governance had failed and that capital requirements should be raised. However, while some insurers found their reserves had dwindled after the bursting of the Dotcom bubble and the persistent decline of interest rates, others remained relatively well capitalized. This put the FSA in a difficult conundrum. On the one hand, there was a perceived need for more stringent capital requirements. On the other hand, however, the newly established regulator did not want to unduly punish those companies with relatively high capital requirements. A risk-based approach offered a way out of this conundrum, enhancing the capital requirements of companies pursuing the riskier strategies while relaxing the requirements for the more 'prudent' ones.

The fact that the FSA was an *integrated* financial services supervisor made its decision towards a market-consistent and risk-based capital regime seem more logical. The merger of insurance supervision with banking supervision had made the boundary between the fields of banking and insurance more porous, allowing some supervisors to travel between the two largely distinct fields, gaining familiarity with different approaches to supervision. With few exceptions, the direction of travel between both fields mostly occurred from banking to insurance. Banking supervisors had in previous years implemented the Basel regime for banking capital regulation and, in so doing, had already gained experience with a capital regime partly operating on banks' internal models, making it more likely that they would prefer a similar system of governance in the insurance business. Another factor favouring the adoption of a market-consistent capital regime can be found in broader international developments in financial governance, which exhibited an increased tendency towards market-consistent regimes across all financial services. International accounting standard setters, for instance, had started work on 'fair value' accounting standards, and the European Commission had started developing a market-based regulatory regime. The FSA reckoned that moving in a market-consistent and risk-based capital direction in advance of international developments would later easethe transition of British life insurers into the new transnational capital regime.

Market-consistency, moreover, had a major advantage from the perspective of supervisors: market-consistent valuation was considered a more objective affair than traditional actuarial methods relying on actuarial discretion and judgement. Craig Turnbull noted, for instance, that

> 'one of the fundamental attractions to adopting these approaches, for the regulator in particular, and maybe for the accountants and others, was this idea that you could get to an objective measure of these costs in a way that removed actuarial judgement or actuarial judgement or strange actuarial assumptions that no one else understood. You know, you mark-to-market and there's market prices. You use them. And that was your price, and it would be this objective single answer.' (Turnbull interview)

A market-consistent regime thus articulated well with the changing regulatory environment in the UK, which moved away from self-regulation towards a system of principles-based regulation with closer regulatory oversight (Black et al, 2007). As a supervisor put it: "[I]f you're producing a standard that has got to be audited, you've got to reduce the discretion available for firms" (Interviewee BB).

Although there were various factors that made the transition towards a market-consistent and risk-based capital regime in the early 2000s more likely, there were also circumstances that made the timing of the transition somewhat surprising. Some actuarial consultants had already developed nascent forms of market-consistent modelling, but on the whole, the life insurance industry was ill prepared for a market-consistent and risk-based capital regime. The FSA acknowledged this and explicitly perceived realistic reporting as 'a developing art' (FSA, 2003). The models of modern finance theory cannot simply be transplanted to the context of life insurance but have to be adapted and adjusted to the specific features of insurance arrangements. "[A] lot of the stuff that … comes out of finance and banking", as Dullaway put it, "isn't directly applicable, you know, because the products are different" (Dullaway interview). As Macdonald explained:

> We are not dealing with a market in which all the instruments are traded both ways. You cannot decide arbitrarily to buy or sell a life insurance policy. Also, the very notion of doing so only considers the pure investment part of the risk, and ignores all other aspects of a with-profits policy, such as the pooling across generations and the smoothing. (Macdonald in Hare et al, 2000, p 208)

The prices of insurance guarantees cannot in practice be enforced by arbitrage, and the 'no-arbitrage' prices that could be assigned to insurance guarantees only considered investment risk, not life insurance-related risk. Moreover, the value of insurance guarantees on with-profits policies typically depends on multiple random variables at once (including, for example, interest rates, inflation, equity prices and real-estate prices) and, crucially, the *correlation* or *dependency* between them. The valuation of life insurance guarantees, in other words, is an *imperfect market problem* in the sense that not all assets required to hedge those guarantees are available. Modellers referred to insurers' valuation models not as 'no-arbitrage' models but as 'market-consistent' models, a concept that in the words of Kemp (2009, p 1) is 'a catch-all for the activity of taking account of "what the market has to say"'.

The complexity of modelling insurance liabilities and the fact that most actuaries directly employed by life insurers had not gained any formal training in modern finance theory gave the 'knowledge brokers' (Burt, 2007) – the actuaries with expertise spanning actuarial science *and* modern finance theory – a pivotal position in the development of life insurers' evaluation machinery. With the notable exception of Prudential, most life insurers outsourced the modelling of their liabilities. As indicated at the start of this section, the modelling firm Barrie & Hibbert became the dominant modelling firm supplying economic scenario generators (or sometimes even simply economic scenarios) to more than half of the British life insurance industry.[6]

Building models, shifting between worlds

The Black–Scholes equation is an analytical, closed form solution for pricing a European call option. The market-consistent models life insurers ended up using were not. If the valuation "was completely simple", the actuary Parit Jakhria explained, "you could try and use a closed form solution like Black and Scholes. Trouble is, none of these [insurance guarantees] were simple, and hence you had to use a Monte Carlo [simulation]" (Jakhria interview). In contrast to a single stock option, the value of insurance liabilities typically depends on multiple stochastic processes at once. Their value is influenced, for instance, by movements in the interest rate, the stock market index and real-estate prices. Monte Carlo simulation allows for the production of scenarios by randomly sampling from multiple probability distributions and enables modellers to find numerical solutions to problems that are difficult to calculate analytically. This is what an economic scenario generator does: it produces a set of scenarios, which can then be used to calculate the value of an insurance liability by averaging the value of the liability in each scenario.

The main problem in valuing financial instruments is to find the appropriate, risk-adjusted discount factor. The riskier an instrument is, the higher the discount factor (and the lower the value of the instrument) should be (Jarvis et al, 2001). There are different approaches to solving this problem, and the differences between them seem rather technical. One approach, which is the one that the Edinburgh-based Barrie & Hibbert adopted from the start, is to produce a set of risk-neutral economic scenarios, in which the probability measures of the stochastic processes are adjusted so that all assets generate an expected return equal to the risk-free rate. Another approach is to produce a set of 'real-world' scenarios – scenarios that reflect the actual expectations of the modeller about the returns that assets generate – and to have a 'stochastic' discount factor, or a state-price deflator, which accounts for the varying levels of riskiness in each of the scenarios. Put simpler, a risk-neutral economic scenario generator produces 'unrealistic' scenarios, which allows the value of all financial instruments, including insurance liabilities, to be calculated simply using the risk-free rate of return; the real-world economic scenario generator produces 'realistic' scenarios but requires the discount factor to be modelled stochastically, changing according to the state of financial markets.

The two approaches are 'mathematically equivalent', but they each have different advantages. The difference between the two approaches, Smith said, "was actually more a cosmetic difference than anything else. Those two models calibrated the same way would produce pretty much the same answer" (Smith interview). The cosmetics of the real-world model were more intuitive to grasp. At the time, Smith suggested, "not many actuaries understood risk-neutrality" (Smith interview). In contrast, Smith said, "the deflator was a way of explaining, well, this is how you get from a realistic-looking model to something that replicates market prices" (Smith interview). The risk-neutral approach, however, was easier to implement in practice. Modellers described risk-neutral valuation as 'a neat trick' and likened risk-neutral probabilities to 'pseudo-probabilities' that provide 'a neat short cut to the correct answer every time' (Whelan et al, 2002, pp 57–9). Financial mathematicians, moreover, had primarily built models of the latter type, which meant there was a rich repository of exemplars from which insurance modellers could borrow. The construction of a risk-neutral economic scenario generator consisted primarily of bricolage. Steven Morrison was trained as a physicist and was one of the modellers at Barrie & Hibbert who worked on the development of their economic scenario generator. "What we were basically doing", Morrison explained, "was picking up those models that were already used for valuation problems [in banking] and ... putting them all together in one large model ... almost sort of glue them together into one model" (Morrison interview). Barrie & Hibbert, in other words, "patched together off-the-shelf banking models that you could get from textbooks" (Interviewee CJ). Its main competitor, the Smith model, which was developed by Andrew Smith at Deloitte, similarly started "out of things that were out there in the public domain" (Smith interview).

The main aim of both risk-neutral and real-world models is to find the discount rate that reflects the 'market risk premium' for an insurance liability. In the real-world model, this is done by modelling a stochastic discount factor that can reproduce the appropriate discount rate for every single asset traded in financial markets. In the risk-neutral model, this is done by adjusting the probability measures of the stochastic factors so that all assets can be discounted at the risk-free rate. The key point here is that both models aim to identify a discount factor independent from modellers' expectations about returns on investment. This is what is characteristic about the market-consistent convention: an attempt to eradicate modellers' discretion in picking the discount rate.. They create a world in which uncertainty is reduced to a single factor, 'risk', which has a unique price, the 'risk premium', which is held together by the logic of arbitrage. Although risk-neutral and real-world models are mathematically equivalent, the choice of method nonetheless matters for the outcome. Risk-neutral models were simply calibrated to reproduce observable market prices by 'back-solving' for the volatility of the underlying asset, yielding a 'market implied volatility'. "[I]n theory", Smith explained, "that volatility ought to be consistent with historic volatility, but in practice it never is." Subsequently, he continued, "we discovered ... that a model which would replicate market prices was not, in mathematical terms, absolutely continuous with respect to any credible model of real worlds" (Smith interview). This is because the "change of measure argument relies on all sorts of assumptions that don't actually hold true in the real world" (Morrison interview). No-arbitrage models, for instance, assume trading to be 'frictionless', a condition that few would argue holds true in practice. The no-arbitrage world within the model, in other words, can only be constructed by smoothing and paving over some real-world 'inconsistencies'.

One of the inconsistencies pertains to the calibration method of the model – that is, the method to calibrate the volatility – riskiness – of the model's various stochastic factors. Modellers can choose to calibrate their models to either a market-implied volatility or a real-world volatility derived from, for example, historical data. The calibration method matters. It is well known among modellers, for instance, that "historically option implied volatility has been higher than the corresponding real-world volatility" (Morrison interview), which is another way of saying that market prices exceed the prices produced by a model calibrated to real-world parameters. This leaves modellers with a choice, Morrison explained:

'If you use the option implied volatility, you'd probably be overstating ... the real-world volatility. If you use the real-world volatility, you would under-price options. So if you want to use the same model for two different things, constraining yourself by the theoretical straitjacket means you're actually doing neither of those things particularly well.' (Morrison interview)

For some "sizeable problems", Smith said, whether you calibrated to historic volatility or market implied volatility "really mattered". For instance:

'[I]f you are an insurer and you've written some liabilities that had guarantees and you were considering whether to hedge or not, if you use ... [a] model calibrated to market prices of options, then hedging always looked like a fantastic idea, because you got rid of all these risks of things going wrong, and you would just pay a fair price for the option, whereas if you used the historic calibration it's much more a trade-off, because you think the volatility is going to be 15 per cent, the market is charging 20 per cent, but ... when you've paid that 20, you've got some peace of mind ... you're no longer exposed to your model being wrong.' (Smith interview)

While real-world modelling is limited by the availability of relevant data, the calibration of risk-neutral models is limited by the availability of relevant market prices. Take for instance the calibration of a stock market model, which requires stock-index option prices going as far out into the future as, say, 20 years. Prices for such options are not readily available, which leads to the blending of market-implied and real-world views:

'When we look at the longer-term options, we're essentially extrapolating towards something which is informed by our real-world views. Because we don't have … market information … you're sort of constructing a pseudo option-implied vol[atility] in the long term … using real-world assumptions to inform what an implied volatility might look like.' (Morrison interview)

In the early years, a former regulator explained, a "vast number of insurance liabilities [were] being valued on the back of a handful of [market] transactions" (Chamberlain interview). To enhance the availability of market information, modelling firms such as Barrie & Hibbert and Deloitte had set up panels of investment banks who would supply them with over-the-counter quotes for longer-term derivatives. But when banks realized they were not obliged to sell options contracts at those prices, "regulators started to worry those prices were artificial" (Chamberlain interview). Regulators pushed for companies to show that they "could actually deal at that price", but banks were reluctant to facilitate the hedging of, say, equities 30 years out (Chamberlain interview). Calibrations of insurers' market-consistent models, especially in the long term, were necessary compromises between market-based estimates, on the one hand, and the real-world views and desire for profits of investment bankers, on the other hand; they were therefore less 'objective' and judgement-free than some perhaps initially hoped.

To sum up, the appropriation of no-arbitrage models in insurance was not simply a case of straightforward application of already existing models to new domains. Rather, modern finance theory served as a repository of exemplary problem solutions and modelling techniques insurers could use to construct an economic 'model world' that allowed them to calculate a hypothetical economic value of their liabilities. This model world seeks to replicate or mimic real-world stochastic processes and to constrain actuarial discretion in picking discount rates by anchoring models in market expectations.

Making insurers' evaluation machinery market-consistent

So far, in this chapter, we have seen that the institutionalization of market-consistent evaluation machinery was accompanied by the appropriation of modern finance as a repository of exemplary problem solutions for the valuation of insurance liabilities. Actuaries' usage of the term paradigm shift implies that the new way of doing things differed substantially from the old way of actuarial knowledge production, organized around a clearly identifiable set of exemplary problem solutions – the traditional actuarial approach. It is, however, not so easy to identify what constitutes the actuarial paradigm that was replaced. Exley et al (2000), for instance, have suggested that there is no overarching actuarial theory. They distinguish modern finance theory from traditional actuarial practice by arguing that 'much of UK actuarial "science" is in fact no science at all, but rather a collection of ad hoc techniques evolving over time to suit the business objectives of clients and consultants'.[7] Actuarial science had drawn on theory, like statistical theory or risk theory, but none of the exemplary problem solutions had remained a central point of reference in the actuarial field. One example of this is the Wilkie model, discussed in Chapter 4, which had been developed through analogical extension of risk theoretical models used in general insurance to the problem of investment risk. The model was widely used, but it did not gain the status of central exemplary problem solution around which the field of actuarial science was organized.

Another exemplary problem solution was Redington's (1952) 'immunization theory', developed in the mid-20th century (Shedden, 1977; see Hare, 1989). Redington was chief actuary at Prudential, whose works addressed the typical problems of with-profits insurance: reserving, bonus policy and valuation (Turnbull, 2017, p 106). Concerned with the volatility of interest rates and its potentially devastating impact on insurers' financial position, Redington wondered whether such risk could be mitigated or 'immunized' by 'matching' the characteristics of an insurer's assets with those of its liabilities. Redington postulated that if the sensitivity of the value of an insurer's assets to the interest rate was equal to the sensitivity of the value of its liabilities to that same interest rate (which he both expressed mathematically as the first derivative of the respective values with respect to the interest rate) and the rate of change in the former was at least as great as the latter, then the total portfolio would be 'immunized' against interest rate risk. Although Redington's immunization theory may have 'delivered a thunderbolt of much-needed clarity to the management of interest rate risk', as Turnbull (2017, p 109) suggests, its concrete practical applications remained limited. 'For life offices ... it did not resolve the question of *which* liabilities it ought to be applied to' (2017, p 109). While Redington's model of immunization depended on the assumption that an insurer's liabilities were non-arbitrary, with-profits insurance arrangements relied on actuarial discretion for the distribution of surplus, making it more difficult to predict how valuable the liabilities actually were.

Even though Redington's theory was quite influential in actuarial thought and sparked some debate about investment strategy, it wasn't considered an exemplary problem solution proper because it did not seem to give any straightforward solutions.[8] Once insurers had adopted market-consistent modelling, some actuaries perceived the Black–Scholes–Merton model as an analogical extension of Redington's immunization theory. Crucial in this respect was the fact that the Irish actuary Colm Fagan had independently developed a concept for a dynamic investment strategy similar to that underpinning the Black–Scholes–Merton model. He presented his model as a generalization of Redington's immunization, 'both being dynamic investment strategies designed to keep the market value of the assets and liabilities equal at all times by imposing certain constraints on the assets' (Whelan, 2002, pp 34–5). In the early days of the paradigm shift, 'dynamic hedging' was often referred to as a form of immunization and was considered of the same family as Redington's concept of 'duration matching' (Ford et al, 1980; for example Collins, 1982).

While the exemplary problem solutions central in 20th-century actuarial science remained somewhat diffuse – they did not form part of a single coherent theory – this changed with the FSA's imposition of realistic reporting. Actuaries now had a clearly defined set of problems (the valuation of liabilities containing guarantees that were *similar* to financial options), for which a repository of exemplary problem solutions was available. The paradigm shift towards market-consistent modelling also demanded that actuaries gained familiarity with the exemplary problem solutions of modern finance theory. It was only in 1999 that the actuarial profession required prospective actuaries to do a basic exam in financial economics, with the additional possibility to take an advanced exam in derivatives pricing. Consultancy firms played an important role in familiarizing actuaries with modern finance theory too, especially those who had already done their exam before 1999. Turnbull, who worked at Barrie & Hibbert at the time, remembers for instance that "a lot of our work, as well as doing all the modelling and [writing] papers … was actually more education" (Turnbull interview 1). "You were going along to clients", Dullaway said, "explaining what a market-consistent valuation was, doing these simple examples" (Dullaway interview). The shifting demand of expertise was not only reflected in actuarial training but also in the hiring patterns of the firms that built the modelling machinery. As John Hibbert recalls, "we employed actuaries, we had economists, we had probably more physicists than any other background among our technical professional staff, but I think that was a bit of a departure for the profession" (Hibbert interview 1).[9]

The institutionalization of market-consistent modelling was a period of rapid cultural change that also had a significant impact on the careers of those active in the field of actuarial science and life insurance more generally. In the previous chapter, I suggested that market-consistent modelling was at the core of the professional project propagated by mostly younger actuaries who had gained familiarity with modern finance theory. They perceived the adoption of market-consistent modelling as a necessary condition for the sustenance of the profession's jurisdictional claims. Many actuaries, however, also feared that the introduction of market-consistent modelling, and the concomitant loss of discretion in setting modelling assumptions, would weaken actuarial jurisdictional claims on reserving practices. If the valuation of insurance liabilities and reserving was simply a technical matter of getting the models right – a matter of what Porter (1995) calls 'mechanical objectivity' – then what claims to special expertise did actuaries have? Porter suggests that professions are more likely to abandon their claims on expert judgement in a climate of suspicion, amid calls for improved public oversight over a given domain of practice. Historically, the actuarial profession had been quite successful in fending off public demands for greater precision and enhanced transparency in valuation and reserving practices (Alborn, 1994; Porter, 1995). The downfall of Equitable Life, the rise of an integrated financial services supervisor and broader changes in global financial governance, however, had raised a climate of suspicion around actuaries' claims on the need for expert judgement in dealing with uncertainty.

Conclusion

The shift towards market-consistent modelling of insurance liabilities was a shift towards a culture of exactitude and precision. In the wake of Equitable's downfall, the discretionary elements in the traditional approach to dealing with uncertainty met with increased suspicion, which contributed to a favourable environment for the institutionalization of modern finance theory. Within this environment, modern finance theory offered a repository of exemplary problem solutions that could be drawn upon to model insurance liabilities more 'objectively'. What interviewees described as a paradigm shift required the analogical extension of these exemplary problem solutions to the insurance context, which was done by a relatively small group of modellers employed by consultancy firms that built the modelling infrastructure, as well as the retraining and education of actuaries to enhance their familiarity with modern finance theory. The modelling infrastructure, and the newly acquired financial expertise of actuaries, enabled the transformation of financial uncertainty into financial risk: financial uncertainty was increasingly seen as something that could be calculated and managed through the appropriate investment strategy.

Although the adoption of market-consistent modelling implied a triumph of mechanical objectivity and risk management in the business of life insurance, this is not to say that the introduction of market-consistent modelling has eradicated financial uncertainty. The extension of financial models to insurance-specific problems creates additional forms of uncertainty. As financial history has shown, the use of no-arbitrage models may create unexpected effects that 'overflow' the boundaries of the idealized world within the model (Callon, 1998a; MacKenzie, 2003). In the idealized world of market-consistent modelling, precision and exactitude reigns, but how this idealized world interacts with the economic processes that this world purports to describe remains uncertain. The extension of these models to the world of insurance, moreover, itself involved significant uncertainty about how the models should be extended. The arbitrage logic that is at the core of modern finance theory cannot easily be transposed to insurance contracts because the latter are further removed from financial markets. No-arbitrage models are assumed to work well as descriptions of price patterns in financial markets because they posit a mechanism through which prices converge towards their predictions, namely via actors' exploitation of arbitrage opportunities. In life insurance, no such arbitrage opportunities exist because there is no active secondary market in insurance liabilities (besides the runoff and buyout markets discussed in Chapter 9). Insurance contracts are not financial instruments. The primary aim of insurers' market-consistent models is to estimate the value of insurance contracts in a way that reflects the uncertainty around investment income to assess the adequacy of financial reserves. To the extent insurers don't or can't fully hedge their liabilities, then, uncertainty reigns, not just because the model's framing may potentially overflow (Callon, 1998a), but also because without the arbitrage rationale, market-consistent models remain firmly in the business of uncertain predictions and expectations about the future.

7

Managing Risk in Insurance

Market-consistent modelling was not just attractive to supervisors because it would lead to more objective and exact valuations of insurers' balance sheets. It also came with the promise of rationalizing insurers' management of financial risk. Risk management is a somewhat elusive concept that can refer to a wide variety of practices. Historically, risk management has been primarily about the identification, categorization and quantification of risk in the context of finance and insurance (Baud and Chiapello, 2017). In life insurance, for instance, risk management involved the collection of mortality statistics and the calculation of individual risk. As the rich body of historical literature on insurance has shown, however, risk management is not just about the quantification of risk. It also involves various organizational processes through which 'risks' are selected, assessed and contained – that is to say, through which risks are 'made' (Van Hoyweghen, 2007). Risk management, in other words, is a mode of governance that involves both the analysis and organization of risk. This mode of governance has become increasingly prevalent in a wide variety of domains since the 1990s (Power, 2007).

The history of *financial* risk management is intimately intertwined with the rise of modern finance theory (especially options pricing theory) and the rapid development of markets for financial derivatives from the 1970s onwards. Options pricing theory legitimized the use of derivatives as instruments for managing financial risk and facilitated the organizational cognition of and communication about risk (Millo and MacKenzie, 2009). The Black–Scholes equation, for instance, allowed for the 'backing out' of instruments' market-implied volatility, allowing managers to put a concrete number on the riskiness of internal portfolios. In the 1990s, moreover, large financial institutions developed internal risk management systems, adopting 'value-at-risk' (VaR) as a universal measure of risk, which aided the rationalization of capital allocation across the organization as a whole (Holton, 2002). This development was accompanied by the rise of the Chief Risk Officer, which signalled the increased importance of the risk control function within large financial services groups (Power, 2005).

From the late 1990s onwards, moreover, banks' internal risk management systems also became the basis for capital regulation standards, which further institutionalized the VaR models as core elements of governance in banking (Baud and Chiapello, 2017; Coombs and Van der Heide, 2020). Risk-based capital regulation chimed well with shareholder demands because it incentivizes rationalized decision making and the optimization of return on capital (Kavanagh, 2003; Rosen, 2003).

In this chapter, I examine how financial risk management became organizationally embedded in the field of life insurance from the early 2000s onwards. Like in the banking sector, regulation played a key part in institutionalizing risk management in the insurance sector. The transition towards realistic reporting and market-consistent valuation, discussed in the previous chapter, is one aspect of this. Another is the introduction of the Individual Capital Adequacy Standards (ICAS), which, like the Basel capital standards for banks, require the calculation of regulatory capital through VaR models. The chapter starts with a section on risk management as a mode of governance, pointing to the power relations that are involved in the ascendancy of risk capital as a dominant governing principle. The chapter then moves on to the practice of risk management in the life insurance business, describing the methods and techniques that insurers use to quantify new forms of risk that had remained hitherto outside the purview of insurers' risk management practices, and the management of financial uncertainty through financial instruments.

Financial risk management

The concept of risk is inextricably tied to the concept of risk *management*. 'When uncertainty is organized', Power (2007) argues, 'it becomes a risk to be managed' (p 6). This is not to say that 'all risks are manageable', he adds, but rather that risks are treated 'as if' they are manageable. Understood in this way, the history of risk management is closely associated with the history of insurance, where the collection and processing of statistical knowledge has contributed to the perception that risks can be managed, and uncertainty – at least at the level of aggregate collectives – can be reduced. The management of insurance risk relies on the principle of diversification and the law of large numbers, which reduces what appears to be extreme uncertainty at the level of individual cases to a high degree of predictability at the level of the aggregate, or at least in theory (Hacking, 1990). Although this mode of statistical reasoning has increasingly underpinned insurance practice since the late 18th century, it is also complicated by a series of phenomena that limit the applicability of risk knowledge, including what is now known as moral hazard, adverse selection and a general discrepancy between the population based on which risks are calculated and the population taking out insurance. Insurers, therefore, may do various things to create populations of policyholders with characteristics similar to the characteristics of the population based on which risks are calculated, including, for instance, risk selection and contractual arrangements intended to undermine moral hazard and adverse selection. Risk management is not just about the quantification of risk – it is also about the organization of the world in such a way that risk can be quantified in the first place (Baker, 1996, 2003; Porter, 2000; Ericson et al, 2003).

A similar observation can be made about the world of finance and the rise of financial risk management. As noted, the history of modern financial risk management is intricately entangled with the rise of modern finance theory and the proliferation of markets for derivatives. While there is some overlap between financial risk management and insurers' traditional risk management practices, there are notable differences too. Modern portfolio theory, which was one of the three key strands of research culminating in modern finance theory (see Chapter 6), still took an approach to financial risk that is reminiscent of insurance risk. The key problem in this line of research was how to optimize investment returns relative to risk by diversifying away the idiosyncratic risks of individual stocks. In modern portfolio theory, risk was still something to be managed by diversification. This changed with the rise of options pricing theory, which moved away from the problem of diversification and instead focused on the question of how to manage risk by 'hedging' exposures with instruments that offset movements in the price of an investment or a portfolio of investments. Options pricing theory suggested that it was possible to construct 'replicating portfolios' of investments that mimic the payoff structure of a derivative instrument. In frictionless and complete markets, modern finance theory posited that derivative instruments could in turn be used to manage the non-diversifiable risk of investment portfolios, which legitimized derivatives as rational instruments of risk management. A world in which financial risk can be adequately managed, modern finance theory implies, is a world in which derivatives are widely available, allowing risks to be easily hedged (Wigan, 2009). The more the world of finance resembles the financial world assumed in the models of modern finance theory, the better risk can be managed (MacKenzie and Millo, 2003).

In the 1990s, financial risk management would become a core part of global financial governance, reflected for instance by the rise of the Chief Risk Officer. The emergent financial services colossi were increasingly concerned with the 'adequacy of risk-related returns on capital and [there was] a perceived need to manage and avoid sudden losses at point or origin' (Power, 2005, p 134). While the Chief Financial Officers, who had already taken up their seats at corporate boards in prior decades, represented the increased significance of shareholder value in corporate management

(Zorn, 2004), the rise of the Chief Risk Officer in financial services groups embodied the importance of risk management in the governance of value.

The increased importance of the risk management function was also underlined by regulatory reforms, most notably Basel II agreements on banking supervision. Although most regulators were initially sceptical about the promises of financial risk management, many later turned into enthusiasts (Goodhart, 2011). Notable, for instance, was the embrace of the then chairman of the Fed, Alan Greenspan (2003), who saw the 'growing array of derivatives and the related application of more sophisticated methods for measuring and managing risk' as 'key factors underpinning the enhanced resilience of our largest financial intermediaries':

> Derivatives have permitted financial risks to be unbundled in ways that have facilitated both their measurement and their management. Because risks can be unbundled, individual financial instruments now can be analyzed in terms of their common underlying risk factors, and risks can be managed on a portfolio basis. Concentrations of risk are more readily identified, and when such concentrations exceed the risk appetites of intermediaries, derivatives can be employed to transfer the underlying risks to other entities. (Greenspan, 2003)

For regulators, risk management promised to resolve the tension between the public demand for safety and the competitiveness of the domestic financial industry (Singer, 2007). Even if regulators remained sceptical of risk management, the internal risk models provided a powerful legitimating tool that banks could use to contest regulatory capital requirements (Power, 2007, p 75). Moreover, financial risk management and the concomitant ideas about derivatives as risk management instruments also chimed well with the deregulatory agenda of the 1980s and '90s, paving the way for the deregulation of derivatives markets in an effort to make markets more complete (Lockwood, 2020).

Not all risks can be diversified away or hedged (real-world markets, after all, are 'incomplete'), nor do financial actors hedge all the risks that they can hedge, either because they consider it too expensive to do so, or because they seek exposure to specific risks, expecting appropriate rewards in return. To protect against the remaining risk, regulators require banks to maintain capital reserves, which, since the late 1990s, are increasingly – though not entirely – calculated using banks' internal risk models, especially in the area of 'market risk'. These models estimate banks' VaR, the level of capital needed to withstand an adverse scenario in all but the worst scenarios, with a pre-specified level of confidence (Holton, 2002). VaR provides a convenient measure of risk that makes the riskiness of a wide variety of activities more readily comparable. VaR, moreover, allowed bank management to justify capital allocation as the outcome of rational decision making, skewing the internal balance of power in their favour (Lockwood, 2015), and contributed to what Power (2007) calls the 'financialisation of governance':

> It is an idea which represents a risk-capital based concept of organizational control presided over by a new class of chief risk officers who talk up the organizational value of risk management ... [I]ts appeal as a unifying, whole of entity approach aligned with the popular philosophy of shareholder value management. (p 75)

While financial risk management had become a core feature of banking governance by the mid-2000s, insurance governance lagged behind. Unlike banking, attempts at transatlantic alignment of capital regulation failed. The reason for this was not an innate aversion in the insurance sector to use internal models. Indeed, Interviewee BC suggested, internal models had already been a core element of insurance governance for a long time; and there was much more "resistance to internal models" in banking than in insurance. For three of their main risks – credit, liquidity and interest rate risk – banks had no internal models in the late 1990s to early 2000s. Insurers, in contrast, were quite used to working with formulae to calculate the adequacy of their reserves, even if these were imprecise measures of risk. "The main thing you had to do was quantify your liabilities" (Interviewee BC), which actuaries had been doing at least since the late 19th century with their traditional net-premium valuation models (see Chapter 5).

More likely, the absence of transatlantic alignment resulted from a dearth of transatlantic insurance partnerships other than in the reinsurance sector, and a concomitant lack of globally relevant 'soft law' (Posner and Newman, 2016). As will be discussed in the next chapter, harmonization efforts in Europe were therefore mainly driven by large European insurance groups in collaboration with the European Commission, which ultimately resulted in a regulatory framework similar to the Basel agreements for the regulation of banking capital. Even if this European project made the initial stride towards risk-based capital regulation, it was the British regulators who first implemented this model with the introduction of ICAS. Within this framework, risks were to be calculated and managed explicitly, not through the incorporation of invisible margins of prudence in actuarial calculations.

Like in banking, the explicit quantification and management of risk chimed well with the rise of shareholder value as the dominant conception of control in corporate governance (Fligstein, 1990). In the old system of governance, actuaries enjoyed significant leeway in calculating the adequacy of reserves and profitability of premium levels, relying in large measure on professional expertise. In the new governance regime, the actuarial role lost this discretionary leeway, enabling shareholders to take a more dominant role in the governance of insurance companies. The actuary Andrew Chamberlain captured this change in the following terms:

'In the old days … a lot of the [insurance] funds were with-profit funds, and the profits thrown off to shareholders from a with-profits fund properly run were fairly consistent. [Shareholders] bought life insurance companies for steady income that would grow at the time. And people didn't really understand anything about what went on underneath the bonnet of the car. They just knew that the car drove off at a fairly steady pace in the right direction. And that's why people would invest in … companies like Prudential … because they threw off this steady dividend string. Nowadays that isn't the way it works. With-profit is a much smaller part; it doesn't produce a consistent profit stream, because of the lower interest rate environment, and so forth. And they're now simply looking at reporting profits in the short term. And so the valuation methods take an excessive priority, because they drive investor sentiment … the world is being driven by the valuation practice rather than reflecting reality.' (Chamberlain interview)

The introduction of financial risk management thus changed the way uncertainty was organized in life insurance. From an opaque object that could be known only through some combination of experience and actuarial expertise, uncertainty became something to be measured and calculated through formalized models, the output of which could readily be scrutinized by shareholders. In what follows, I examine how this transition came about in practice.

Modelling life expectancy

The quantification of risk (or simply risk analysis) is a key part of risk management alongside the identification, mitigation and control of risk. Banks' quantification efforts initially focused on 'market risk', or the uncertainty about the performance of financial market instruments. After modern portfolio theory and options pricing theory had given banks the instruments to quantify this risk, banks also developed models to quantify credit and interest rate risk (Huault and Rainelli-Le Montagner, 2009; Spears, 2014). By the early 2000s, insurers could thus draw on an extensive repertoire of exemplary problem solutions for modelling their financial risks. However, insurance companies also face idiosyncratic risks that can neither be managed through diversification nor hedged against with financial instruments. One consequence then of the institutionalization of financial risk management was that insurers started modelling their insurance-specific risks explicitly too. In this section, I trace the development of longevity risk models, a type of risk that became especially important in the world of British life insurance.

Historically, actuaries approached the topic of mortality primarily through the lens of diversification. Within this frame, the quantification of mortality risk involved the collection of survival data, the construction of life tables and the making of additional adjustments to reflect the characteristics of the insured population. Initial actuarial work approached mortality as a static phenomenon that remains constant over time. Since the early 20th century, however, actuaries have also increasingly sought to examine mortality trends and generational effects in mortality improvement (for example Derrick, 1927). Actuaries, however, did not have the means to quantify the uncertainty around the rate of mortality improvement into a risk factor. Longevity risk – the risk that actually experienced mortality and life expectancies deviate from prior actuarial assumptions – became an object of actuarial quantification only from the 1990s onwards.

The first initiatives explicitly to quantify the uncertainty around increases in life expectancy originated outside the field of actuarial science. Notable, for instance, was the Lee–Carter model developed by the UCL Berkeley demography professor Ronald Lee and the sociology professor Lawrence Carter, from the University of Oregon. In their seminal paper, Lee and Carter noted that a simple extrapolation of average 20th-century mortality improvements of the US population might lead one to conclude that life expectancy would rise to 100 by 2065, a development, they noted, that would 'come as a nasty surprise to the Social Security Administration' (Lee and Carter, 1992). Drawing on recent developments in time series analysis and state-of-the-art extrapolation techniques, Lee and Carter examined how likely this extreme improvement in mortality would be and concluded that expected life expectancy in 2065 would be 86.05, not 100. Crucially, however, the Lee–Carter model also gave expression to the *degree* of uncertainty around life expectancy by providing 'probabilistic confidence regions for its forecasts' (Lee and Carter, 1992, p 659).

Within the British actuarial profession, improvements in life expectancy came on to the agenda around the turn of the millennium. In 1999, the actuary Richard Willets published a research paper entitled 'Mortality in the Next Millennium', which showed that while mortality improvements had been more or less constant for most of the 18th and 19th centuries, there had been a 'cohort effect' in the early 20th century. 'For the past four decades, people born between 1925 and 1945 have benefited from faster mortality improvements than those born in adjacent generations' (Willets, 1999, p 5). Following publication of Willets' paper, the Continuous Mortality Investigation (CMI), a bureau run by the Institute and Faculty of Actuaries to collect mortality data from insurers and pension funds and compiles mortality tables and projections based on this data. Ahead of schedule, the

CMI decided to update its mortality projections, publishing an influential working paper in 2002 authored among others by Willets. The paper was a "complete bombshell", Interviewee DB remembered. It found that recent improvements in mortality rates had indeed been 'significantly faster than anticipated in the projection factors' of its latest publication of mortality tables in 1992 (CMI, 2002, p 2), and that improvements in life expectancy had been structurally underestimated.

Past mortality projections were deterministic (that is, giving only point-based estimates of life expectancy). In its 2002 report, however, the CMI sought to 'give some impression of the uncertainty involved in projecting mortality' by reporting on three different scenarios with varying durations of the cohort effect. According to the previous projections of 1992, a male at the age of 60 was expected to live another 22 years; in the CMI's 2002 medium cohort scenario, which assumed the cohort effect would last until 2020, a 60-year-old male was expected to live another 27 years instead (Jones, 2003). The short cohort and long cohort scenarios extended the cohort effects until 2010 and 2040 respectively instead, showing significant implications for the annuity rates that would be appropriate for covering expenses (CMI, 2002). The inclusion of different scenarios, Interviewee DB said, "was purely to illustrate the range of results that might result". "We didn't have a stochastic model, which we would like to have had, but we couldn't develop one in time" (Interviewee DB).

Stochastic modelling of mortality improvements developed in subsequent years. Notable, for instance, is the work of Andrew Cairns, professor of actuarial science at Heriot-Watt University, who is regarded as a pioneer in the field of longevity modelling. Cairns spent the early years of his career on interest rate modelling, repurposing models from modern finance theory for actuarial use. When Cairns started modelling longevity risk, a direction that was suggested to him by the director of the Pensions Institute, David Blake, he "just blazed on" and did his "own model[ling] before reading about the more classic work from ten years earlier by Lee and Carter" (Cairns interview; on the Lee–Carter model, see Chapter 6). In his first longevity model, Cairns sought to project forward the 'instantaneous rate of mortality', or 'force of mortality', which, he argued, could 'be treated in a similar way to the short-term, risk-free rate of interest' (Cairns et al, 2004, p 1).[1] His longevity model, which derived from the analogical extension of his earlier work on interest rate modelling, "quickly got the attention of people in industry", Cairns recalled, "much more so than the interest rate model" (Cairns interview).

The stochastic modelling of longevity is just one approach to estimating longevity risk. This approach relies on the extrapolation of 'archival-statistical' knowledge (Collier, 2008) into the future and assumes that – subject to a degree of randomness – future patterns of mortality improvement can be deduced from the past. It assumes that even though we may not know what the average lifespan of people living today will be, we can still come up with a probability distribution reflecting the range of likely outcomes based on the study of past mortality improvements. It assumes, in other words, a degree of continuity. However, Smith said, in forecasting longevity, "there's a huge amount of really deep uncertainty" (Smith interview). This uncertainty arises partly from the fact that it is based on "an immensely complex data set", which is complicated, for instance, due to the existence of cohort effects. "[W]hen you're forecasting future longevity of people who are retiring now", Smith added, "you're forecasting the quality of care that they are gonna get ... the amount of exercise they are going to get, how good their diet is going to be. And all of these things are difficult socio-economic things to forecast" (Smith interview).

Forming expectations about the future is a fundamentally uncertain endeavour (Beckert, 2016). Of course, it is possible simply to extrapolate past results into the future and to take this as a placeholder for expectations, but in open systems the future will rarely be a straightforward replication of past patterns, and modellers may contest the extrapolated futures by propagating narratives about how the future will diverge from the past. In so doing, risk analysis increasingly revolves around 'storytelling' (see: Leins, 2018) and the use of 'expert judgement' in setting expectations about what a 1-in-200 scenario will look like, which is the level of confidence required by ICAS. For regulatory capital purposes, then, longevity risk may be quantified in one of various ways. On the one hand, longevity risk can be quantified simply through the construction of a scenario that roughly reflects the severity of the risk stress needed to obtain a 1-in-200 stress over a one-year period. Such a scenario, say, could be: what happens when life expectancy increases by two years relatively to the life expectancy assumed in insurers' valuation models? Though it informs the creation of a scenario, the VaR measure is not directly applied to a probability distribution in this approach. On the other hand, insurers can produce probability distributions based on historical data, from which insurers can read the VaR at the 99.5th percentile.

Modelling risk, calculating capital

In contrast to diversification and hedging, the management of risk through capital reserving requires quantification of ultimately uncertain risks. While the diversification and hedging strategies posit mechanisms through which uncertainty can be contained, the capital reserving approach does not. This is not to say that diversification and hedging makes uncertainty fully 'manageable' – they simply allow actors to behave 'as if' it is manageable (Power, 2007). As various financial crises have indicated, these approaches may well generate new forms of uncertainty, for instance in the form of second-order risks (MacKenzie, 2003, 2011). The point here is that risk management through capital reserving posits no mechanism of reducing uncertainty but simply seeks to estimate the buffers needed to withstand all but the worst of the imagined scenarios, and it is therefore highly dependent on how insurers form expectations about the future.

The fundamentally uncertain and contestable nature of risk forecasts needs not be an organizational problem when risk modellers have no incentive to skew their forecasts one way or the other and when they retain some scepticism towards the knowledge thus produced (Mikes, 2011). The coupling of firms' internal risk assessments to capital requirements, however, turns the arbitrary nature of risk projections into a problem, as Dullaway indicated:

> 'Before the realistic balance sheet [and ICAS regime], there were some companies that did economic capital calculations … But when [the calculations] were their own capital calculations and they didn't affect the capital you had to hold for the regulator, you tended to be very honest with yourself, because after all, *you chose* to do the calculation. … As soon as that model becomes your regulatory model, and you have to disclose it to the outside world, you suddenly have an incentive to get the numbers as low as possible. So, in some ways, making the regulatory model and the economic capital model the same thing, changed the way that companies thought about their economic capital models, from being a useful tool to being a number you wanted to minimize.' (Dullaway interview)

One solution to this problem of arbitrariness, which is discussed in more detail later in the chapter, is to construct a world in which longevity risk becomes hedgeable. Doing so not only provides an additional way to 'manage' this uncertainty; it also provides a 'non-arbitrary' means of establishing expectations by deriving them from the market price of risk.

Another, arguably simpler solution, is to arrive at an acceptable and more or less plausible estimation of risk, based on which actors act 'as if' this was their true expectation, at least for the purposes of calculating regulatory capital. The actuarial consultant Nick Dumbreck, for instance, noted that "some of the [modelling] assumptions were based on sort of almost a market consensus at the time rather than necessarily a lot of hard evidence" (Dumbreck interview). One mechanism for the establishment of shared expectations about risk involves firms observing what other firms are doing (White, 1981). Insurers, interviewees reported, compared their 1-in-200 stresses with one another. This mutual observation is typically mediated by consultancy firms: "Insurers", Smith said, for instance, "via consultancy talk to other insurers" (Smith interview). Dullaway said he had "a database of all the stresses" he had seen at his clients:

'So when somebody came along and said: what do you think this stress should be, I could say: "well, here's analysis we've done. But also, I think most of your competitors are in a range of this to this." So you know that would be equally important for somebody setting their stress because they didn't want to be too far out of the range.' (Dullaway interview)

Consultancies may also conduct surveys, such as the KPMG technical practices survey, that give some indication of what 'the market' is doing and help establish a market consensus about what plausible risk scenarios look like.

Supervisors played an important role in the establishment of shared expectations too. Supervisors review insurers' risk models and stresses and may push insurers to justify their choices. The issue here is not to produce correct estimations of risk but to produce credible ones. In reviewing insurers' risk models, supervisors focus 'upon whether the firm has used an appropriate approach to calculations and involved the people in the business in the best position to apply judgements. The more *credible* the approach, the more we can rely on the answer' (FSA, 2005, p 12, emphasis added). Under the UK's ICAS regime, this construction of credibility occurred in a dialogue between the regulator and the regulated (Thiemann and Lepoutre, 2017), which some interviewees described in rather combative terms. Dullaway, for instance, suggested that "there is actually a bit of a battle between companies and regulators because regulators clearly want the answer to be right in the round; companies want to say: 'where can I push it lower?'" (Dullaway interview). Consequentially, key decisions may be made during an extended approval process that takes the form more of a 'technical debate' between the regulator and regulated (Thiemann, 2018). This is, for instance, how a former chief actuary of one of the largest UK insurers experienced the ICAS approval process:

'I must have spent probably six months, you know, week by week negotiating with the regulators. We went through each element. They thought, no we disagree with this, this and this. And we think you should hold extra capital. And it was a genuine, not so much a negotiation, but a sort of a technical debate. And in the end, some things they agreed with us, some things we agreed with them. But you came to an agreed position on things, or even if it was just a gentlemen's agreement to disagree. You know, it was a proper dialogue around risk and what the company's view was, what the regulator's view was and what the balance in capital was … And I remember when we got our final ICG [individual capital guidance] I came back and told our executive committee, and there was a round of applause at the end of this six months of debate.' (Belsham interview)

The individual capital guidance is an important tool in the regulatory toolkit that allows firms and their supervisors to hold different views about risk without this affecting the regulatory capital requirement. If supervisors disagreed with insurers' modelling, they could simply impose 'capital add-ons'. The FSA made extensive use of this tool: of the first ten companies it reviewed, the individual capital guidance was between 110 and 170 per cent of firms' own estimations of capital requirements (Bruce, 2006, p 28). Although firm-specific information about the individual capital guidance remained private, any suspicion around large capital add-ons could reflect negatively on the analysis on a firm's reputation in the stock markets (Bruce, 2006). As a result, firms were keen to reduce capital add-ons by bringing their risk models in line with supervisory standards.

To scrutinize the credibility of insurers' risk models, supervisors benchmarked insurers' risk estimations against one another. The FSA, Dumbreck recalls, gradually "took a stronger line on assumptions that they didn't think were fully justifiable, and also maybe a stronger line on consistency between companies" (Dumbreck interview). The establishment of shared expectations involved various dynamics that had not so much to do with the epistemic question of what level of risk stresses would reflect 'true risk' (although considerations of this kind also played a role, of course) but rather around the question of having a shared understanding of what level of risk stresses was considered appropriate. This dimension of risk modelling sits somewhat uncomfortably with a system of risk management that relies on exact quantifications of risk and the establishment of concomitant reserves to face uncertainty. Although interviewees were well aware of the social dynamics of risk modelling, most public accounts of risk capital reserving will emphasize the technical rationalization of risk modelling choices instead.

Managing the balance sheet

Following the introduction of ICAS in the early 2000s, risk management rapidly gained influence in the British insurance business, which was manifested for instance by a proliferation of risk functions, increased use of derivatives to manage financial risk and an expansion of the actuarial education syllabus to include risk management. In 2003, for instance, insurers employed on average three people whose responsibilities were solely dedicated to the risk function, and only two out of 39 companies surveyed had appointed an executive level Chief Risk Officer (Dowd et al, 2008, p

9). By 2004, these figures had changed substantially. Insurers now employed on average five risk management specialists, and 21 of the 39 companies had an executive level chief risk officer on their boards. (Bartlett et al, 2005, p 7). Although, as Van der Graaf's (2018) ethnographic study of risk management in a continental European insurer shows, risk managers rarely see the 'precise' risk calculations as 'true' representations of risk (see also Mikes, 2011), risk nevertheless became an increasingly important object in shaping the field of life insurance.

The increased centrality of risk management in the life insurance business was not only the consequence of the regulatory injunction to perform risk calculations, but also by the legitimation of risk management as a profitable activity – a development that reflected changes in the broader corporate context of the 1980s and '90s (Power, 2007). In the early 2000s, insurers still appeared to conduct risk calculations primarily for compliance purposes or simply because it was considered 'good practice' to do so (Bartlett et al, 2005, p 3). Since then, however, insurers increasingly 'embraced the value adding aspects of risk management' to the extent that 'good risk management' was increasingly considered a 'competitive advantage' (Deighton et al, 2009, p 521). 'Ideally', Deighton et al wrote in the *British Actuarial Journal*, 'a company wishes to hold the minimum amount of capital required to meet its risk appetite, and create a win-win situation for shareholders and policyholders alike' (Deighton et al, 2009, p 521). Having appropriate risk management tools in place, in other words, would not only improve security but would also improve shareholder value by minimizing excess reserves given companies' risk appetite.

The introduction of financial risk management in the insurance business was accompanied by jurisdictional struggles (Abbott, 1988) among different professional groups with different claims to expertise. By the mid-2000s, in the words of two preeminent financial risk management experts, 'the stage was set for a classic turf war' (Dowd and Blake, 2006, p 221). While actuaries had 'been accustomed to thinking of themselves as "the" risk experts', they wrote, 'the FRM [financial risk management] profession had the advantage that it had a flagship, the VaR, that took center stage: VaR was the flavor, not just of the month, but of the entire decade, and everyone wanted a "VaR model"' (Dowd and Blake, 2006, p 221). Actuaries, in other words, had traditionally seen themselves as the risk managers of the insurance business. Their understanding of risk, however, had focused mostly on diversifiable risk. The new risk management practices, however, would require them also to quantify non-diversifiable risk, a task over which financial risk management professionals and their VaR models could challenge actuarial jurisdictional claims. In response to this challenge, the actuarial profession expanded its educational syllabus, also strengthening the actuarial claims over the management of non-diversifiable risk.

The centrality of risk as an object to be managed was also reflected by insurers' increased use of derivatives. In the 1990s, derivatives usage was only marginal. Paul Fulcher, who was an actuary at Friends Provident before he started working for various investment banks from 2001 onwards, remembers, for instance, that by the late 1990s he "would have had no idea what an interest rate swap or swaption was" (Fulcher interview). As mentioned earlier, the resilience reserve test was introduced to take the risk embedded in the guarantees into account when calculating reserves. Nevertheless, the resilience reserve test did rather little to push insurers to adopt derivative strategies. As Fulcher recalls,

'by the end of '93 we were holding a lot of money against interest rates falling another 100 basis points, say. But it wouldn't have occurred to you to go and get an interest rate swap or an interest rate swaption because you wouldn't have thought of it like that way.' (Fulcher interview)

The only sort of derivatives that were widely used, according to Fulcher, was for short-term equity protection:

'You might buy some equity protection pretty much every year-end, but it'd be very short-dated. It would almost be: look, we're going away, it's the start of December and we've already worked out what our bonus declarations are going to be. And we sort of worked out and are happy with our balance sheet. … Well, we better, sort of, lock that in. So you might buy some equity protection that would literally expire in two or three weeks, just to lock in the sort of balance sheet over year-end, almost on the grounds of, well, that way we can all go home and enjoy Christmas.' (Fulcher interview)

Other interviewees confirmed that in the pre-ICAS regime "the use of derivatives to meet balance sheet tests was relatively low" (Chamberlain interview).

This changed in the early 2000s, when investment banks like JP Morgan, UBS, RBS, Nomura, Deutsche Bank and Goldman Sachs started hiring actuaries to help sell derivatives. According to the actuary Paul Fulcher, who worked for various investment banks: "Investment banks suddenly realized that they could sell … interest rate derivatives. You know, they had these instruments – things like swaptions – that had a remarkably similar profile to the exposures that insurance companies had sold to their customers" (Fulcher interview).

Actuaries employed by the investment banks encountered quite a different environment, and they often faced a steep learning curve in gaining familiarity with derivatives market practice. "I spent my first six months at UBS just looking up things on the internet that all my colleagues took for granted", Fulcher remembers (Fulcher interview). Investment banks, however, hired actuaries not only for their expertise but also to benefit from actuaries' professional networks and cultural identification to engender trust (Granovetter, 1985). According to Fulcher,

> 'most of my clients perhaps … trust the bank I work for, because they trust me, if you see what I mean. That was part of the job in one sense. So, I trust him [the actuary], I don't trust the bloke he brings to meetings with him [the investment banker], but, you know, at least I trust him.' (Fulcher interview)

As the actuarial profession is rather small, individual members are likely to know each other or, if not, at least to have acquaintances in common.

Initially, the actuaries at investment banks spent much of their time modelling. The models used for valuation purposes – the economic scenario generators of Barrie & Hibbert and the likes (see Chapter 6) – were not necessarily well suited for risk management purposes. For solvency calculations, accuracy was considered key. economic scenario generators were designed to minimize statistical errors, Dullaway explained:

> 'If you're running only a thousand scenarios and average them, there's a good chance that you'll be out by 1 or 2 per cent either side. But 1 or 2 per cent either side when you're valuing a set of liabilities, which may be 50 billion, and you've got assets, which will maybe be 55 billion, okay, well, a one or two billion error can have a very big effect on your solvency.' (Dullaway interview)

For "hedge diagnosis", however, a model "wasn't supposed to particularly accurately model your balance sheet. It was supposed to be able to work out [for example] a replicating portfolio" (Fulcher interview). The models produced by the investment banking actuaries – so-called replicating portfolio models, or simply 'replios' – were "sort of quick and dirty", but "fit for purpose", as Fulcher put it.

It's not necessary to understand the intricacies of the differences between the two types of models. At this point, it suffices to say that market-consistent valuation models allow one to model the value of a liability at a specific point in time. It does not give any information about the sensitivity of the value of those liabilities to different 'stress factors'. Replios seek to infer the sensitivity of a book of liabilities to a set of different 'stress factors' (for example, a drop in the stock market index) by calculating how the value of liabilities changes in a subsample of economic scenarios. The model then attempts to optimize a portfolio of assets that replicate those sensitivities as closely as possible such that the value of the liabilities remains roughly equal to the value of the replicating portfolio in each of the stress scenarios.

Insurers paid investment banks for their modelling services by buying their derivatives. The business model of the derivatives departments of the investment banks, in other words, was "quid pro quo": "we'll sell you the insurance to do the financial management, but we'll help you with the modelling" (Fulcher interview). This model worked well for investment banks, who were keen on selling something that requires "a bit of analysis and intellectual value added", for it would mean that they would be "not just in competition on cheapest price", but could "charge a reasonable amount for it, because it's tailored" (Fulcher interview). Over time, however, modelling became a smaller part of the investment banking actuary's job. This was partly the result of insurers' expanding internal risk managing activities. As the ICAS and realistic balance sheet regimes were implemented, insurers increasingly "realized the importance of financial management" and "got the expertise themselves" (Fulcher interview). As a consequence, Fulcher noted, "there's people at insurers who understand the financial instruments better than I do … Quite commonly … they would actually understand investment banking products at least as well as I do, if not better" (Fulcher interview). This changed the business model of over-the-counter derivatives too. As Fulcher put it, "now it's much more, clients basically tell us, this is the derivative we need". "And so the model sort of 'we'll do some analysis, and then you'll pay us by doing the derivatives with us' has become quite hard" (Fulcher interview).

Financial risk management thus changed the way insurers dealt with financial risk. It also influenced how insurers dealt with more insurance-specific kinds of risk. Financial risk management, as noted earlier in this chapter, comes with the promise that all risks can be managed effectively when the appropriate markets for derivatives exist. In a risk-based capital regime, moreover, capital requirements can be reduced when risks are hedged against. Regulation, in this sense, may be a driver for financial innovation, turning the invention of new risk management instruments into a business opportunity. In life insurance, attempts were made to make risk manageable through the invention of derivative instruments that make longevity risk tradeable. Longevity risk was one of the largest contributors to life insurers' capital requirements, apart from financial market risk, motivating insurers to manage this risk, for instance by getting "rid of the tail risk … to just cool down the 99.5 per cent quantile a bit" (Cairns interview).

In the mid-2000s, banks, insurers and reinsurers engaged in various 'in-vivo market experiments' (Muniesa and Callon, 2007) to see if the commodification and marketization of longevity risk was viable (for an overview, see Blake et al, 2013; Blake et al, 2019). One experiment of this kind was conducted by the European Investment Bank (EIB) in cooperation with the French investment bank BNP Paribas, who issued longevity bonds. In exchange for a lump sum payment, bondholders would receive 25 annual coupon payments, the size of which was determined by a 'survivor index' based on a reference population. The higher the mortality in this reference population, the smaller the coupon payments would be (Brown, 2004). Another high-profile experiment was conducted by the American investment bank JP Morgan and the newly established insurance company Lucida (more on which in Chapter 9), who issued a 'q-forward' contract, the 'q' being the symbol used by actuaries for mortality (Coughlan et al, 2007). A q-forward contract involves the exchange of payments at a future date, the size of which is determined by predicted mortality (the 'fixed leg' of the transaction) and the actually experienced mortality in a reference population (the 'variable leg'). When the actually experienced mortality exceeds the predicted mortality, the buyer of the forward contract loses money; when the actually experienced mortality falls short of the predicted mortality, however, the buyer receives money.

Both experiments involved 'index-based' contracts, which required the construction and maintenance of mortality indexes such as JP Morgan's Life Metrics. The success of these instruments, however, remained rather limited. The EIB's longevity bond was discontinued due to a lack of buyers, and JP Morgan struggled to find investors for insurers' longevity risk. From the perspective of the potential buyers of protection, the risk commodity had become too detached from actual risk. Buyers remained stuck with 'basis risk' - the risk that mortality in the reference population would differ from the mortality of the population for which the buyer sought protection. For this reason, regulators were reluctant to allow for capital relief, which removed insurers' primary motivation for longevity risk management. For insurers, Cairns suggested, longevity protection is "all about managing down ... capital requirements" (Cairns interview). More successful was the 'longevity swap', a bespoke instrument that allowed two parties to swap payments based on predicted mortality and the mortality experience not of a mortality index but of a more specific reference population. In contrast to the index-based instruments, the longevity swaps did not contain any 'basis risk'. At the same time, however, these transactions require more specific knowledge about the characteristics of the reference population, making them less suited as general capital market instruments and narrowing the range of parties potentially interested in taking the other side of the trade to insurers seeking to shed longevity risk mostly to reinsurers.

Conclusion

The regulatory reforms of the early 2000s – that is, the introduction of the realistic balance sheet and ICAS – helped institutionalize financial risk management in the British life insurance business. The new kinds of risk management practices not only involved the identification, quantification and management of diversifiable forms of risk (as insurers had already done for over a century) but also of non-diversifiable forms of risk through 'hedging' against risk exposures in financial markets and maintaining capital reserves in proportion to the remaining risk exposures. As Power helpfully reminds us, the label of risk management should not mislead us into thinking that uncertainty is 'manageable' (Power, 2007). Uncertainty is a condition that actors have to live with. Risk refers to specific ways in which this uncertainty may be organized; in the case of financial risk management, through quantification and hedging, modes of governance that themselves involve substantial uncertainty about the feedback loops generated by risk calculations and the systemic risks produced through hedging transactions. Even if financial risk management exudes the promise of reducing uncertainty through quantification and hedging, insurance remains a thoroughly uncertain business (Ericson and Doyle, 2004; Baker, 2021).

The institutionalization of risk management in the life insurance industry had several implications for the boundaries between the field of life insurance and capital markets. First, the introduction of risk-based capital regulation created a business opportunity for the derivatives departments of investment banks, who could more easily sell their derivatives to insurance companies, not just as risk management solutions, but also as instruments that allowed for the management of regulatory capital. Through these derivative transactions, insurance companies became more tightly integrated in capital market circuits. Second, the institutionalization of risk management contributed to what Power (2007, p 75) calls the 'financialisation of governance', affecting the relative standing of different actor groups in the life insurance field. While the actuarial profession had previously occupied a position as gatekeeper to insurers' finances, keeping shareholders and supervisors at an arms' length of the insurance business, the institutionalization of risk management removed this actuarial privilege. Market-consistent valuation and risk-based capital calculation made insurers' financial condition more immediately 'knowable' to both shareholders and supervisors, favouring decisions that privilege short-term profit considerations and that contribute to the optimization of profits relative to risk.

The Long Road to Solvency II (and Back Again?)

In the previous two chapters, I described how in the first decade of the 21st century British regulators and supervisors overhauled life insurers' evaluation machinery. The decision made by the regulator to adopt a market-consistent approach was in part motivated by the anticipation of a European regulatory framework that would similarly be market-consistent and risk-based. However, even if the plans for the European regulatory reforms preceded the domestic reforms in the UK, the latter were implemented much earlier, which is why the previous chapter precedes this one. In this chapter, I examine the complicated relation of the British insurance industry to Solvency II. Even if British insurers and supervisors came to play a leading role in the design and implementation of the framework, they became highly critical of the rules soon after implementation in 2016, mostly because of a lack of flexibility restraining innovative investment practices. Within this context, Brexit was perceived as an opportunity to 'take back control' of insurance governance.

How to make sense of this change of hearts? At core, the implementation of Solvency II involved the translation of core concepts and models from modern finance theory into a set of detailed rules intended to fix their meaning. Even if the European Commission intended Solvency II as a principles-based framework – and this was indeed what the Solvency II directive adopted in 2009 was – the framework ultimately became highly prescriptive, with a large body of supporting guidelines and rules in addition to the original directive (including articles in another directive, the Omnibus II directive), which sought to define what it meant to conform to the principles of market-consistent valuation and risk-based capital. The implementation of Solvency II, moreover, was postponed several times, with the framework up and running only in 2016, seven years after the original directive was first adopted and nearly 20 years after the project had begun. The push towards detailed rules resulted from pressures to constrain the range of interpretation of the rules. While companies feared domestic supervisors would entertain relatively strict interpretations of the principles, supervisors feared that supervisors in other jurisdictions would be rather permissive.

The chapter makes these points in three parts. First, I provide a brief overview of the history and politics of Solvency II. Second, I describe some of the frictions and rough edges that emerged when supervisors sought to specify what it meant to perform market-consistent valuations. Third, I narrate how supervisors eventually dealt with the problems they encountered during implementation and how the resulting settlements caused unintended (and partially unforeseen) effects British insurers and ultimately their supervisors were increasingly unhappy with.

Towards a single market for insurance

Efforts to harmonize insurance regulation in Europe date back to the 1950s, when a subcommittee of the Organisation for European Economic Co-operation sought to facilitate debate about the integration of the market for insurance services and the harmonization of supervisory rules. The EU's harmonization agenda began in earnest with the adoption of 'an ambitious programme' envisaging the 'freedom of establishment' and the 'freedom of services' in an integrated European insurance industry (Pool, 1990, p 7). The first concrete result of this programme was the 1964 Reinsurance Directive. This was low-hanging fruit. In contrast to direct insurance, the market for reinsurance was already relatively well integrated across the six participating countries (Belgium, France, Italy, Luxembourg, the Netherlands and West Germany). The integration of the other insurance markets, however, turned out to be more complicated than expected. Coming up with a single approach to insurance supervision was complicated for instance by the fact that across member states, 'different perceptions' prevailed 'of what life insurance is about' (Pool, 1990, p 33; see also Lengwiler, 2015). As in other parts of the financial sector, the differences in nationally specific models of insurance and the impossibility of coming to an agreement about whichever model worked best for all pushed the debate around the harmonization of supervisory rules towards the development of minimum standards (Story and Walter, 1997).

In subsequent decades, the EU adopted various other directives giving shape to the European regulation of the insurance business in three waves. The first non-life and life directives of 1973 and 1979 sought to institute the freedom of establishment.[1] They were not an undivided success. Bill Pool, the former head of the insurance division within the European Commission's Financial Institutions Directorate, for instance, later wrote that although the directives were intended to make it 'easier for an insurer having its head office in one Member State to open a branch in another Member State ... [they] tended, paradoxically, to emphasize the separateness of national markets through the stress they lay on the control to be exercised by national supervisory authorities' (Pool, 1990, pp 37–8). The second life and non-life directives of 1988 and 1990 set out some further conditions for the 'freedom of services' but made very little difference to cross-border business in practice (Sharma and Cadoni, 2010). By the beginning of the 1990s, then, the EU had made little headway with the creation of a single European market for insurance.

This changed with the adoption of the third life and non-life directives of 1992, which laid out minimum requirements for the assessment of solvency. One of the main problems with the harmonization of insurance supervision had been that different countries adopted significantly different methods for assessing insurers' solvency, and that they were not willing to let go of those. While the British system of governance relied on the actuarial profession to assess the adequacy of insurers' reserves, other countries, like Germany, imposed explicit solvency margins based on retrospective measurements of business volume and investments. Not willing to pick one side or the other, the European Commission defined minimum standards based on which insurers would be allowed to conduct cross-border business, while leaving their supervision to home country supervisors. The legislation was heavily influenced by the Groupe Consultatif des Associations d'Actuaires des Pays des Communautés Européennes (or simply Groupe Consultatif), a European association of professional bodies set up in 1978 to represent actuarial interests to European legislative bodies. Based on a survey conducted by the Dutch actuary Harry Horsmeier and the British actuary David Wilkie (whom we have already encountered in Chapter 3), Groupe Consultatif's Life Assurance Committee concluded that 'in spite of different methods and bases for calculating technical reserves ... each method provides ample protection for domestic policyholders' (Wilkie and Horsmeier, 1990, p 72). Hence, Groupe Consultatif argued there was no need to prescribe in great detail how solvency should be assessed. Indeed, Groupe Consultatif's report claimed, 'any attempt to introduce uniformity of methods or bases for calculating technical reserves ... would be inappropriate, unnecessary and harmful', and it recommended instead that 'the relevant directive should contain a statement of actuarial principles' (Wilkie and Horsmeier, 1990, p 72). The Commission agreed and asked its two actuaries to propose draft legislation. These actuaries, as Wilkie recalls, "felt that they needed a bit of help" and asked Groupe Consultatif "to draft a set of valuation standards" (Wilkie in personal communication). The Dutch actuary Theo Heiligenberg, who chaired the Groupe Consultatif's Life Assurance Committee, phoned up Wilkie and asked him whether he could come and see him in the Netherlands that weekend. Wilkie, who had already arranged to go to Switzerland that Saturday, arranged a stopover at Schiphol airport where he sat down with Heiligenberg and Horsmeier in a restaurant and "spent about three hours" drafting a set of valuation principles. "I never put my nose out of the building at all", Wilkie said. And although the directive had passed through various channels before being adopted in 1992, its text still resembled what the actuaries had written at the airport. "I still recognized in that third life directive sentences I wrote" (Wilkie interview).

Even if according to some of my interviewees the third life and non-life directives moved the harmonization debate significantly forward, it did not resolve the conflict between different approaches to assessing insurers' solvency. Although the directives clearly defined a set of minimum standards, they also allowed for significant leeway in the valuation of assets and liabilities. Wilkie favoured a 'bonus reserve valuation', which was essentially a type of gross-premium valuation that would also account for future bonuses. As noted in Chapter 3, many actuaries considered gross-premium valuations more adequate for solvency purposes. They were more transparent and could more easily be updated to changing economic circumstances. Most members of the Groupe Consultatif's Life Assurance Committee, however, preferred a more traditional, net-premium type of approach, which provided more stability over time but also created difficulties when for instance interest rates declined. One of the German members of the committee, Wilkie recalled, "did not like the idea of a 'breathing balance sheet'" (Wilkie interview), the assets and liabilities of which would go up or down as market conditions change. Other actuaries, including some of the British actuaries, also preferred the 'net-premium valuation' method. The legislation was drafted accordingly. Even if the text of the third life directive expressed a preference for Wilkie's bonus reserve valuation, it also allowed insurers to diverge from this standard and to use alternative valuation methods, such as the net-premium method, instead.

With the adoption of the Financial Services Action Plan in 1999, the European Commission changed tack and focused its efforts on positive harmonization. The new regulations adopted in the third life directive were already under review since 1997, but while the initial focus was on improving the provisions of the third life directive, the Commission now embarked on a fundamental review of insurance regulation, which would yield a new regulatory framework, designed from scratch, on a 'tabula rasa' (François, 2015; see also Quaglia, 2011; Van Hulle, 2019). In 2002, the EU adopted the so-called Solvency I directives, which "detached some early wins" from the 1997 review (Interviewee BC); these directives collated and to some degree strengthened the existing insurance capital regulations, paving the way for the long-term and more fundamental reforms of what would become the Solvency II directive. The Solvency II framework would in subsequent years be drafted according to the Lamfalussy procedure, leaving the directive to focus on the core principles of the framework, while the details would be worked out by expert committees, spearheaded by the Committeeof European Insurance and Occupational Pensions Supervisors (CEIOPS).

The design of the framework was strongly influenced by international developments in the private governance of finance (Underhill and Zhang, 2008). First, there were the Basel Accords for banking supervision, which pursued the international convergence of regulatory capital calculation. While the first Basel Accord published in 1988 was limited in scope and relied on a 'bucket approach' for weighting risk, the Basel Committee for Banking Supervision continued work throughout the 1990s on a new framework that would adopt a three-pillared structure and would more strongly rely on banks' internal risk modelling (Goodhart, 2011). Second, there was the International Accounting Standards Board, which worked on the development of a fair value accounting standard for insurance contracts from the late 1990s onwards. The European Commission commissioned several influential reports, one of which was produced by a group of European insurance supervisors (the predecessor of CEIOPS) led by Paul Sharma of the Financial Services Authority (FSA). This report suggested that the project's main aim should be to improve insurers' internal risk management practices (Conference of Insurance Supervisory Services of the Member States of the European Union, 2002). Another influential report, produced by KPMG, was remembered by one of its authors as "not strikingly original" (Interviewee FB): it recommended the adoption of a Basel-like three-pillared structure, as well as the use of fair value accounting and internal risk models (KPMG, 2002). That the international accounting standards for insurance contracts would take much longer than expected (they were finished only in 2017) hardly mattered in this regard. Fairly early on, the Commission had settled on a market-consistent and risk-based regime of Solvency II.

Once the framework's basic features were cast in a 'framework for consultation', the general principles were worked out in rather more detailed rules. Within this process, Dutch and especially British supervisors were among the 'pace setters' (Quaglia, 2011; François, 2015); as noted earlier, they chaired key working groups in CEIOPS and were generally considered key points of reference in the debates (Quaglia, 2011). There were two factors that enabled British supervisors to perform this role: first, the British were among the first to integrate insurance supervision with banking supervision, allowing for the exchange of expertise among supervisors of both sectors. Sharma, for instance, gained experience with banking supervision as a member of the Basel Committee of Banking Supervision. Second, the fact that the British had already decided to adopt a risk- and market-based framework for insurance supervision in the early 2000s meant that they gained significant experience with the methods and techniques that would also come to underpin Solvency II. The developments in British insurance supervision anticipated the development of Solvency II, and UK supervisors thereby gained significant influence over its design.

Even if British supervisors became important pace setters during the development of Solvency II, it was not originally the British advocating for a fundamental review of insurance regulation (François, 2021). The push for a fundamental review came from the European Commission, who aimed at furthering the integration of Europe's markets for financial services, and large insurance groups, who perceived a fundamental review of insurance regulation as an opportunity to make the supervision of large cross-border insurance groups more efficient. Insurers like Allianz, Axa, and Generali were active in many different countries and had to deal with as many different systems of supervision. Solvency II entailed the promise that could change. Initial drafts of the framework proposed making home supervisors responsible for the supervision of the entire group. This group supervision would yield significant benefits for insurers located in multiple countries: they would have to spend less resources on compliance, and they could more easily share capital resources across the group. However, some supervisors, especially those from countries with a large degree of foreign penetration, opposed group supervision, fearing that it would lead to a loss of influence (Tait and Felsted, 2008; Von Fürstenwerth, 2008). The politics of Solvency II, in other words, was not just a 'battle of the systems', but also pitched supervisors from insurance exporting countries against supervisors in insurance importing countries.

The directive that was ultimately passed by the EU's core institutions in 2009 compromised on group supervision, reneging on the idea of home country supervision and instead provided for the setting up of dedicated supervisory 'colleges', containing supervisors from all countries with a stake in a specific insurance group. The directive, moreover, contained a provision that the issue of home country supervision would again be examined in the future (Van Hulle, 2019). With respect to the calculative rules, the framework was kept deliberately at the level of principles. How those principles were to be determined in practice was to be worked out by the second and third level procedures of the Lamfalussy comitology. This turned out to be a rather difficult task. Work on it had begun well in advance of the directive's adoption in 2009. When the directive was finally adopted, however, several thorny problems still needed working out; the framework's implementation, which was originally planned for 2012, was postponed several times, and, before the framework finally went live in 2016, several additional amendments had been made with the adoption of the Omnibus II directive in 2014.

Frictions and 'rough edges'

One of the core principles of Solvency II is the economic balance sheet: insurers should calculate the 'true' economic value of their liabilities using market-consistent means. Based on this economic balance sheet, insurers should then calculate their capital requirements by performing various risk calculations, either by following a 'standard formula' defined by the regulators or using their own risk models (or indeed some combination thereof). The economic balance sheet, in the words of Karel van Hulle, who was responsible for the development of Solvency II as head of the Insurance and Pensions unit at the European Commission between 2004 and 2013, was a principle from which the Commission "was not willing to diverge" (Van Hulle interview). Coming up with rules about how insurers should calculate their economic balance sheets, however, proved more challenging. As noted in Chapter 6, by the early 2000s market-consistent valuation and risk-based capital calculations were still relatively new in the world of insurance. Actuarial consultants had started work on 'market-consistent embedded value calculations', yielding knowledge about the economic value of insurance portfolios to determine adequate pricing in mergers, acquisitions and demutualizations. By the early 2000s, however, there were no clear standards about how those calculations should be performed. Four aspects of the economic balance sheet were considered especially problematic: rules around risk-free discounting, the calibration of equity risk, the risk margin and liquidity risk. Each are taken in turn.

Simply put, models are deliberate simplifications of some phenomenon that serve a specific purpose or set of purposes. In making these simplifications – or 'idealizations' – modellers may seek to construct a world that is more readily knowable and that may be computationally tractable (Weisberg, 2013). In so doing, however, modellers also have to make decisions about what to take into account and what to leave out of the model. There is an infinite number of ways in which reality may be portrayed in a model, and choosing whichever way to follow inevitably involves trade-offs. The same holds for designing rules about how insurers should calculate and model their liabilities to arrive at an *economic* balance sheet. Take for instance the principle of risk-free discounting, which is a core feature of market-consistent valuation as noted in Chapter 6. The idea may seem simple (you discount future cash flows at an interest rate that you could earn on investments that bare no risk), but its application in practice requires one to make choices. "There is no such thing as a risk-free rate", Interviewee BC suggested. "It is a theoretical construct. It's not something that exists in reality" (Interviewee BC). To approximate a risk-free rate, modelers usually refer to the interest rates on government bonds, which are often seen as the 'safest' assets available (Boy, 2014). Yet, Interviewee BC noted, "even sovereigns have risk". In the context of a European regulatory framework, moreover, the use of government bonds as reference asset for risk-free rates came with complications. The government bonds of different sovereigns yield different interest rates. Discounting at government bond rates would thus cause the same liability to be valued differently across member states – an outcome that would clearly be unpalatable to countries whose interest rates on sovereign debt are lowest (Smith interview). An alternative was to use interest rate swaps, a derivative instrument that allows investors to exchange or 'swap' a variable interest rate for a fixed exchange rate. Although the 'fixed' leg of these swaps often yields slightly higher interest rates than government bonds (implying a lower value for future cash flows when used as a discount rate), they avoided the problem of inconsistent valuation of euro-denominated liabilities across countries. The interest rates implied by swaps with different maturities can then be used to construct a risk-free rate.

Another area where key decisions were to be made was how the risk-free curve should be extrapolated to maturities that were not readily available on swaps traded in financial markets. In some countries, the maturity of insurers' liabilities exceeded the maturity of actively traded ('liquid') interest rate swaps. In Germany, for instance, the actuary David Hare explained, some insurers "sell pension policies to 30-year-olds that look very similar to a deferred annuity to us" (Hare interview). These contracts contain guarantees that may well extend 60 to 70 years into the future and that in a market-consistent valuation framework should be discounted at the appropriate risk-free rate. What, then, should be the *market-consistent* discount rate? How should the risk-free curve be extended beyond the maturity of instruments available in the market? And when are swaps 'liquid' enough to provide useful information for valuation purposes? There are, again, many different ways to tackle this question. One is simply to use as much market information as available, regardless of how 'liquid' the underlying instruments are, and then to extrapolate the trend into the future when more information is needed. Another is to determine a 'last liquid point' and simply to extrapolate the discount curve beyond that point for longer maturities. Still another is to define an interest rate to which the discount curve will converge at infinite maturity, and then to interpolate between the last liquid point and the 'ultimate forward rate'. And within these approaches there are again different methods of extrapolation and interpolation. Though these might seem like minute details, even small differences in discount rates may yield significantly different estimates of the value of long-dated liabilities.

A second example of what one of my interviewees referred to as the "rough edges" of modelling concerns something known as the risk margin (Interviewee AD). The idea of an economic balance sheet was to report the value of assets and liabilities at the price at which they can be traded in a secondary market, or at which they could be traded in a secondary market were these markets to exist. The market-consistent models discussed in Chapter 6 only get you some way in this direction. They calculate the value of insurers' liabilities *as if* these liabilities were financial instruments; and, in so doing, they factor in only the financial risk of the insurance contract. Yet, insurance contracts are not financial instruments: they also have specific insurance-related risks. There is, for instance, lapse risk, the risk that policyholders cancel their contract before maturation. Or the risk that insurer's predictions about expected mortality were off. If an insurer wants to pass on its insurance liabilities to a third party, the price of these liabilities would thus likely exceed the price predicted by the market-consistent models because the party taking over the liabilities would also want to receive a risk premium for the insurance-related risks. This was what the risk margin was supposed to reflect: the additional risk premium required to make a measure of insurance liabilities truly reflect the economic price of those liabilities. What should be the risk premium over and above the market-consistent value of an insurer's liabilities if a third party would be willing to take them over? Even if modern finance theory seemed to indicate that the risk margin should exist, its exemplary problem solutions could not easily be extended to the insurance-related risks of insurers' liabilities.

A third friction between market-consistent valuation models and the reality of insurance concerns the issue of liquidity. Insurers are often said to have a unique capacity for 'patient' investment (Deeg and Hardie, 2016). Because their liabilities tend to be long term and fixed, insurers can commit to long-term investments without being forced to sell their assets in the meantime. Another way to put this is that insurers will often buy securities to hold. They buy securities not primarily for potential capital appreciation but for their dividend and interest payments to 'match' the payments they have to make to their policyholders. Applying the models of modern finance theory to this business model potentially causes frictions. When markets are assumed to be fully liquid, this should not be a problem. Any appreciation or depreciation in the market price of insurers' investments should reflect changing appraisals of credit risk: the risk that insurers will not be able to secure the payments they were promised. This is a real risk for insurers, even if they buy and hold. When markets cannot be said to be fully liquid, however, changing market prices may reflect what economists call changing liquidity conditions, at least partly. This, however, is not a 'real' risk for insurers that match their assets with their liabilities because they won't be selling their assets but rather holding on to them until they reach maturity. The relative fixity of insurers' liabilities, in other words, puts them in a good spot to benefit from premiums put on illiquidity. As we will see in the following section, like the risk margin and the risk-free discounting curve, the issue of liquidity became one of the problematic rough edges of the calculative framework of Solvency II.

Patching the rough edges

These issues were not immediately regarded as problematic at the start of the Solvency II project. As the rules were given shape throughout the regulatory process, actors learned about what they might mean for them in practice (François, 2015). As insurers learned about the possible implications of the Solvency II regulatory balance sheet, they sought to problematize specific aspects of the calculative framework that created uncertainty around the viability of their business models. Simply pointing out that a specific application of the economic balance sheet concept could cause solvency issues for some insurers, however, was not enough. Insurers lobbying for changes in the framework had to come up with arguments articulated in a language that is consistent with the vocabulary of modern finance theory and financial risk management. There are many different ways to produce an economic balance sheet, and insurers had to show that their preferred way was one of those ways.

Designing and testing the framework

To work out how the regulatory framework should operate in practice, CEIOPS set up various expert groups and permanent committees; the former tasked with specific assignments (designing the rules of the framework's three pillars), the latter with more general terms of reference. The Expert Group for Pillar I, which defines the framework's calculative rules, was led by Sharma and operated until 2008, when Sharma headed a new group to deal with internal models.[2] CEIOPS, moreover, issued various consultation papers and performed a series of quantitative impact studies (QIS), which would assess the framework's impact. Over the 2005–13 period, seven field studies were conducted first by CEIOPS and later by the European Insurance and Occupational Pensions Authority (EIOPA) – including a 'preparatory field study' – in which at its peak 68 per cent of the affected (re-)insurers participated.

Although the calculative framework underpinning the first pillar was ultimately worked out in quite a large number of rules, Solvency II was initially intended as a principles-based framework. Principles-based regulation is often touted as a British invention fashionable in the 2000s. Its benefits were perceived to be increased flexibility, fostering innovation among both supervisors and supervisees and increasing durability in a rapidly changing environment (Black, 2008, p 426). A principles-based regulatory framework defines only what the framework aims to do, leaving lots of space for the practical interpretation of those principles to supervisors and their supervisees. When the Solvency II directive was adopted in 2009, the framework indeed seemed rather principles-based. The directive contains 312 articles, most of which were collated from previous directives; the rules and regulations commonly associated with Solvency II are specified in 60 articles, containing rather generic prescriptions. About the best-estimate calculations of liabilities, for instance, the directive says the following: 'The best estimate shall correspond to the probability-weighted average of future cash-flows, taking account of the time value of money (expected present value of future cash-flows), using the relevant risk-free interest rate term structure' (p 46). The directive left the question of what the risk-free interest rate should look like in practice to be determined by CEIOPS in the so-called 'implementing measures' of level 2 of the Lamfalussy procedure.

Making principles-based regulation work, Black argues, requires 'the presence of a high degree of trust between participants within the regulatory regime ... there needs to be close engagement between regulator and regulated based on mutual trust' (Black, 2008, p 427). In the specific regulatory institutional constellation of European insurance regulation, this degree of trust seemed to be missing. Insurers feared that their domestic supervisors would impose relatively strict interpretations of the principles, leaving them at a competitive disadvantage relative to other European insurers. Supervisors, in turn, want to ensure that policyholders are well protected. Supervisors are caught, as Singer (2007) notes, between demands for the international competitiveness of the domestic industry and the protection of domestic policyholders. "The insurers didn't trust the supervisors", Van Hulle said. "And the supervisors themselves didn't trust the insurers" (Van Hulle interview). As Van Hulle remembers:

> 'The insurers came to me and asked me: what does this principle mean in this specific case? I often said to the insurers: don't ask me that question, because I will then have to write a rule. Use your common sense. Apply this principle in the spirit of Solvency II. But the insurers had difficulties with this, because they said, as long as the principles aren't clear, the supervisor is going to impose all sorts of things on me, because the supervisor is going to interpret the principles. I need something to hold on to. Similarly, insurance supervisors wanted more detail because they were afraid that this was the only way to enforce the principles in practice.' (Van Hulle interview)

Another complicating factor was the onset of the 2007–8 global financial crisis. The first draft of Solvency II was published in 2007. As the global financial crisis started to take the world of finance in its grips, however, new questions were raised about the desirability of Solvency II. The framework was alleged to introduce excessive volatility to insurers' balance sheets. Although the fifth quantitative impact study (QIS 5) performed in 2010 showed that insurers were generally well capitalized – insurers were reported to have a buffer of €110bn in excess of capital requirements (Davies, 2011) – an analysis by Eric Serant at Milliman suggested that French life insurers would have seen their capital ratio reduced from 179 per cent to 104 per cent if they had used their 2010 balance sheets rather than those of 2009.

Many British insurers experienced problems associated with the widening spreads between corporate bonds and the risk-free rate. British insurers specializing in annuity business tended to 'match' their long-term liabilities with investments in corporate bonds. After the collapse of Lehman Brothers, the 'excess spread' on corporate bonds over government bonds soared. In pre-crisis years, spreads had remained relatively stable in the UK around 40–50 basis points for the safest of corporate bonds (AAA-rated), while the spread for riskier bonds (BBB-rated) varied between 100 and 200 basis points. At the peak of the crisis, the spread for the AAA-rated bonds had increased to nearly 300 basis points, while the BBB-rated corporate bonds yielded an excess of more than 650 basis points over the risk-free yield on the UK's sovereign debt (FSA, 2009). If Solvency II's discounting regime had already been implemented, UK annuity providers would have been in trouble: while interest rates dropped and the market-consistent value of liabilities increased, the market value of their assets plunged. The widening spreads would have wreaked havoc on the market-consistent solvency position of annuity providers. Initially, they were an idiosyncratic British problem: when the spreads on peripheral eurozone government bonds started to increase, however, some of the larger European insurance groups were also affected.

A more general problem was the secular decline of interest rates on government bonds post-crisis. Especially for insurers with long-term interest rate guarantees on their books, this secular trend posed potential problems, drastically raising the present value of their liabilities. The declining interest rates also caused a proportional rise in risk margin requirements. The Solvency II directive prescribed a 'cost-of-capital' approach, requiring insurers to calculate the opportunity costs of capital required to back the insurance-related risks of their liabilities. In practice, this required insurers to discount future capital needs to a present value using the risk-free rate. Simply put: when the risk-free rate (closely associated with the interest rate on government bonds) declines, the value of the risk margin increases and so do capital requirements. Taken together, these issues meant that uncertainty about the impact of Solvency II increased drastically in the wake of the 2007–8 global financial crisis, which contributed to the creation of an environment in which it was difficult to establish trust between regulators and regulated. Both insurers and their supervisors demanded more specific rules about how the framework's principles should be applied in practice: insurers because they wanted certainty about how certain issues would be addressed; supervisors because they wanted to have a footing to stand on when enforcing the rules. This culminated in the adoption of the Omnibus II directive in 2014, which sought to resolve many of the issues raised earlier. Apart from laying down rules for risk-free discounting (and delegating the responsibility for the construction of the risk-free curve to EIOPA) for the calculation of the risk margin and some additional transitional measures, it also contained a package of adjustments intended to allow insurers to account for the 'illiquidity premium'.

The settlements

The economic balance sheet was one of the core features of Solvency II. It was calculated using market-consistent valuation methods on top of which the risk margin was added. The framework was strongly grounded in modern finance theory. Elsewhere, I argue that the framework institutionalizes modern finance theory, and the closely associated field of financial risk management, as the dominant 'vocabulary of motive' in the life insurance field.[3] That is to say, the postulates and prescriptions of modern finance theory provide the repertoire of legitimate motivations for choosing to do things one way or another. In this concrete case, it means that if insurers want to lobby for changes in the framework's calculative rules, they have to articulate their concerns in language compatible with modern finance theory and financial risk management. They need to show that specific enactments of the general principles outlined in the Solvency II directive are credible extensions of the core models of modern finance theory to insurance-specific problems.

This was most obvious in the case of the liquidity premium. One of the core assumptions of the exemplary models of modern finance theory had been that markets were fully liquid. In the idealized world of the paradigmatic Black–Scholes model, for instance, market participants can continuously buy and sell financial assets without their buying and selling having an effect on prices. Similarly, as Andrew Smith said:

> [T]he whole framework that we were looking at for market consistency just failed to have anything to say about liquidity effects. It was all in this theoretical world of perfect markets. And you buy and sell things, it doesn't move the price; you can observe the price, you can trade as much as you want for that price, and the price doesn't move as a result of your trading.

Before the financial crisis, the concept of the liquidity premium was rarely – if ever – used. "I think we all thought we understood how spreads worked", Interviewee BC said, "and we all understood that [you have the] risk-free rate and then you add on a bit for the credit risk, then there is a bit left … which you explain, it's the illiquidity risk." The illiquidity risk, however, was assumed to be immaterial. It just "made a few basis points difference here and there" (Interviewee BC). When spreads widened during the crisis, first on corporate bonds and later also on peripheral eurozone government bonds, the issue gained importance.

Modern finance theory did not preclude the possibility liquidity premia exist. Indeed, one of the authors of the Black–Scholes model, Myron Scholes, had suggested that the dramatic collapse of Long-Term Capital Management – a hedge fund employing both Merton and Scholes – in 1998 was due to surging liquidity premiums (Scholes, 2000; see also MacKenzie, 2003). Scholes, moreover, had suggested that investors' risk management systems, which did not account for liquidity risk, could affect liquidity and push financial markets into a liquidity spiral. Even if the liquidity premium was considered theoretically defensible, however, there was little consensus on how to measure it. A divergence from the idealized world of Black–Scholes also meant a divergence from the model's computational logic. The problem of liquidity had therefore remained a peripheral issue in modern finance theory. And, as Interviewee BC recalls, "we didn't have a methodology at that point to say to ourselves ... when a spread increases significantly in size, how much of that is the market reappraising credit risk? How much of that is actually liquidity?" (Interviewee BC).

What mattered most, however, was that the liquidity premium was considered theoretically defensible. The issue chimed well, moreover, with concerns about the regime's volatility. Insurers argued that the balance sheet volatility induced by Solvency II, and the related issue of illiquidity, prevented insurers from performing their stabilizing role in the European economy. In an opinion article in the financial press, for instance, Allianz's chief financial officer (CFO) said that 'insurers should be able to invest precisely when other investors don't want to. Future capital regulation, however, will prevent them from doing so' (List, 2011). In making this case, moreover, insurers mustered support from other financial actors, who expressed their concerns over the impact of the regulatory framework on the financial system as a whole (see François, 2019). EIOPA did not want to give in initially, and the issue devolved in a debate "with EIOPA on one side, and the industry on the other side" (Creedon interview). Nonetheless, the arguments proved successful, and the European Commission broke the stalemate. The Omnibus II directive allowed insurers to make either of two adjustments to the risk-free rate (a matching adjustment or a volatility adjustment) to discount their liabilities.

A very similar story holds for the construction of the risk-free curve, which was part of the same stand-off between insurers and supervisors (see also François, 2021). While the Solvency II directive merely prescribed that liabilities should be discounted at the 'relevant risk-free rate', the Omnibus II directive sought to specify in greater detail what this meant. The directive outlined an approach where the risk-free curve would be derived from market instruments up to a maturity of 20 years (the so-called 'last liquid point'), after which it would then be extrapolated to an 'ultimate forward rate'. What this ultimate forward rate should be was to be determined by

Figure 8.1: The risk-free curve as constructed by EIOPA (2016)

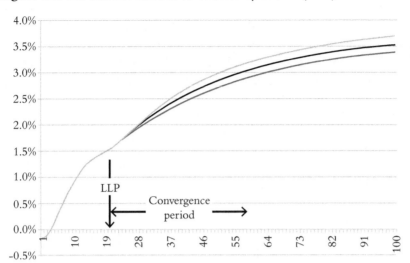

Note: The figure shows what the curve would look like for three different values of the ultimate forward rate. The size of the ultimate forward rate is respectively 4.4 per cent (light grey), 4.2 per cent (dark grey) and 4.0 per cent (grey).

EIOPA, who adopted an archival-statistical approach to calculating it. The approach proved convenient, especially for German insurers with very long-term liabilities. The discount curve EIOPA had produced showed a clear hump around the last liquid point, indicating that a simple extrapolation of market-interest rates (without an ultimate forward rate) would have produced a discount curve that was lower at the far ends (see Figure 8.1). The curve was widely recognized as having been influenced by political considerations for the viability of German life insurers. David Hare suggested that "[if] you extrapolate out constant spot rates ... then you could just create solvency issues for a number of foreign insurance companies – and potentially serious issues for some."

Some criticized the approach as theoretically indefensible because it created a wedge between the assets and the liabilities. Smith, for instance, asked: "Why are we kidding ourselves that the market prices beyond 20 years are perfectly relevant for valuing assets [valued at 'market value'], but not for valuing liabilities [when valued at an extrapolated rate of interest]? That doesn't really make any sense":

'You can observe [swap] prices out to about 50 years and in current market conditions, a 50-year rate is about 1.5 per cent. So insurers within the Eurozone will be discounting that liability at somewhere around 4 per cent. But if they held those 50-year swaps, they'd value them at 1.5 per cent. So you've got an inconsistency between the assets and liabilities.' (Smith interview)

Other approaches, however, could be argued to be equally arbitrary. This is the problem mentioned at the start of the chapter. In the absence of widely shared agreement about theoretically legitimated applications of 'risk-free discounting', political considerations and motivations may become an important factor determining how theories and concepts are applied in practice and thereby their meaning.

The issues around the framework's discounting regime, critics suggested, had compromised the idea of the economic balance sheet. "If you're trying to buy out [your] liabilities, are you going to find anybody who's going to give you credit for earning 4.2 per cent beyond 20 years?" Smith asked for instance. "Well of course you're not. Nobody is that stupid when they're actually buying the liabilities" (Smith interview). And with this, the point of having a risk margin was also defeated. The risk margin was intended to make insurers' liabilities equivalent to their exchange value. But if the exchange value was already compromised by other features of the liability calculations, then what was the purpose of having a risk margin in the first place? "[W]hen Solvency II first came out", Smith said, "I argued against including the risk margin, and said: 'the risk margin is going to end up being roughly proportional to your capital requirements. So why don't you just multiply the capital requirement by something and require people to hold 200 per cent rather than a 100 per cent?'" (Smith interview). Doing so "would have the same effect and be much simpler" (Smith interview).

Others reasoned that the risk margin was not needed. Belsham, a non-executive director of the Prudential Regulation Authority (PRA) and former Chief Actuary of Prudential, said for instance that "we liked not having a risk margin [in the regime prior to Solvency II]. It's not needed because you can run off the liabilities" (Belsham interview). Rather than passing on your liabilities to a third party, insurers could simply runoff their liabilities, for which the regulatory capital already provided enough protection, in Belsham's view, without adding an additional risk margin.

Along with some of the other features of Solvency II, the risk margin was heavily criticized by the British insurance sector. In early 2017, the House of Commons tasked the Treasury Committee with an investigation into Solvency II and its impact on the British insurance industry. Insurers argued that Solvency II was too capital intensive, erring too much on the side of policyholder protection. Legal & General's CEO, Nigel Wilson, for instance, argued that Solvency II is "a system that has way too much capital for all sorts of different reasons. In part it is because we have imported banking technology into the insurance industry and we are not banks."[4] Similarly, Sam Woods of the PRA said he "agreed with them [the insurers] that the risk margin is a problem".[5] Regardless of the veracity with which different actors repudiated Solvency II, scepticism towards the rules comfortably fitted within the Brexit narrative of 'taking back control'. This empowered a successful insurance lobby making the case for replacing what in the words of the Tory MP and Economic Secretary to the Treasury John Glen (2022)

> is an EU-focused, rules-driven, inflexible and burdensome body of regulation with one that is UK-focused, agile and easily adaptable. A body of regulation which facilitates, not hinders, market developments … which encourages the emergence of new types of assets … which supports the entry of new and innovative firms … and which, importantly, allows the release of meaningful amounts of capital for productive investment.

Conclusion

At the time of writing in the summer of 2022, it is still unclear what the British divergence from Solvency II will entail in practice. What is clear, however, is that the implementation of a principles-based framework for capital regulation in the context of European insurance induced sustained attempts to fix the meaning of core concepts in modern finance theory. Insurers feared their domestic supervisors would interpret the rules overly strictly, putting them at a comparative disadvantage. At the same time, supervisors feared that other supervisors would be too lenient in their interpretation of the rules. Within this environment, there was a tendency to delegate interpretation to the EIOPA and the European Commission. These attempts to fix the meaning of rules, however, also caused unintended side-effects, which could not easily be addressed and affected the different national insurance industries unevenly. In the UK, Brexit was therefore perceived in the words of the PRA's Sam Woods as an "opportunit[y] to improve things once we can emerge from our houses again into the brave new world of post-Brexit Britain".[6]

9

De-Risking Pensions, Managing Assets

The buyout transaction between the Vickers Group Pension Scheme and Legal & General was the largest of its kind in 2016.

> We look forward to welcoming the 11,000 members of the Vickers Group Pension Scheme to Legal & General. We are pleased to have worked closely with the Scheme Trustees, their advisers Mercer, and the Rolls-Royce Group to achieve a full buyout. … We are grateful for being able to play a part as the Trustees, with patient and careful management, steered their way through the financial crisis, recession, the consequences of QE [quantitative easing] and latterly the outcome of the EU referendum before reaching the point where buyout was appropriate and achievable for all Scheme members. (Legal & General, 2016)

The pension buyout market, or pension de-risking market, has existed for much longer than the 21st century. Since the mid-2000s, however, the market has started to take off, with volumes steadily increasing from a few billion pounds per year in 2007 to over £10 billion from 2014 onwards, peaking in 2019 with £43 billion of pension liabilities being transferred to insurance companies (see Figure 9.1). The pension buyout market is a 'runoff' market, which is a secondary insurance market in which insurers trade closed books of liabilities that they want to get rid of to free up capital for new lines of business. It is a market in 'legacy liabilities' or 'the bad bets on old insurance policies that tie up the insurer's capital' (Baker, 2021, p 78).

In many ways, the buyout market is exemplary for changes in the life insurance industry more generally. The insurers competing in the buyout market seek to profit from legacy pension liabilities by finding profitable investments for the funds that accompany them. In so doing, the buyout market exemplifies a more general trend in life insurers' business models: they

Figure 9.1: Transaction volume in the bulk annuity and longevity swap market, in billions (2006–20)

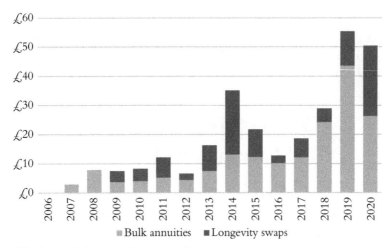

Note: The data excludes transactions among insurers.

Source: Willis Towers Watson (2021)

increasingly focus on their role as investment intermediaries and less so as the 'makers' of insurance risk. Life insurers, in other words, are increasingly in the business of taking risk rather than making risk. Of course, it has always been true that insurance is not just about the management of uncertainty by risk-spreading. Insurers have always been taking risk (Baker and Simon, 2002; Ericson and Doyle, 2004). Life insurers take risks by pooling resources and investing them in financial assets. In so doing, the insurance industry is a core part of modern financial systems. Compared with banks or most investment funds, though, insurers have several advantages. While banks have to fund their investments either by deposits or by short-term borrowing in money markets, life insurers' liabilities tend to be relatively fixed, providing a steady stream of funds that can be invested over the long term. For this reason, insurers have historically been key players in financing the war efforts of governments, funding housing booms and, more generally, supplying patient capital to the private economy (Scott, 2002; Haldane et al, 2014; Deeg and Hardie, 2016). Insurance liabilities, in other words, have always been an attractive source of funding for relatively illiquid, long-term financing needs. The development this chapter points to, however, is the increased importance of the investment function within insurance organizations. In the 21st century, insurers have significantly expanded their investment expertise, either in the form of internal asset managers that provide services to other departments within the organization and to outside clients, or in the form of outsourced asset management services.

In this chapter, I investigate the relation between the onset of market-consistent and risk-based capital calculation and the increased weight of the investment function in the insurance business by studying the emergence of the pension buyout market and the role of asset management therein. In so doing, the chapter picks up on a theme that often goes unnoticed in debates, on the one hand, about the rise of asset management capitalism (Braun, 2016) and, on the other hand, about processes of economization (Çalışkan and Callon, 2009) and assetization (Birch and Muniesa, 2020) that transform a broad variety of social and economic processes into tradable assets promising to generate predictable cash flows. These debates raise questions about the rise of passive investment and its implications for corporate governance and how an increasing number of social and economic processes are organized in such a way that they become investible. They have focused less on the question of what has created the increased demand for such investible assets. This increased demand, I suggest in this chapter, relates to the changing ways in which insurers evaluate the benefits and risks of both assets and liabilities, at least with respect to the insurance sector. First, I start with the question of how it is that legacy pension liabilities were increasingly considered a problem for which the insurance runoff market could provide a solution.

The pension crisis as business opportunity

In 2003, the UK government set up the Pensions Commission to investigate the adequacy of the British pension system and propose appropriate policy changes to improve the system's durability. In subsequent years, the Commission published two reports, the first diagnosing the system's ailments, the second offering recommendations to ameliorate them. The first report concluded that the UK's pension system faced significant challenges, both in the first pillar (state pensions) and the second pillar (occupational pensions). These challenges were posed against a background of continued increases in life expectancy. 'In the 1950s', the Commission reported, 'when many of the major corporate pension plans were put in place, with predominantly male members, male life expectancy at 65 was 12 years. Today it is 19' (Pensions Commission, 2004, p 121). The increased life expectancy raised important distributional questions. 'Pensioners will become poorer relative to the rest of society', the Commission suggested, or new funds should be made available to pensioners through taxation, increased saving or delaying retirement (Pensions Commission, 2004, p 1). Within this context, the specifics of the UK's pension system posed some additional challenges:

> The UK pensions system appeared in the past to work well because one of the least generous state pension systems in the developed world was complemented by the most developed system of voluntary private

funded pensions. This rosy picture always hid multiple inadequacies relating to specific groups of people, but on average the system worked, with the percentage of GDP transferred to pensioners comparable to other countries. But the state plans to provide decreasing support for many people in order to control expenditure in the face of an ageing population and the private system is not developing to offset the state's retreating role. Instead it is in significant decline. (Pensions Commission, 2004, p 57)

Although estimations of participation in occupational pension schemes varied, there was a consensus that the total contributions to occupational pension schemes declined, which was mainly due to falling employer contributions. Declining employer contributions correlated with the shift from relatively attractive defined benefit schemes to defined contribution schemes, which precipitated from a series of events starting in the '70s and running through the '90s. In the 1970s and '80s, several regulatory interventions had contributed to increasing the cost of defined benefit pensions. The 1973 and 1985 Social Security Acts, for instance, improved treatment of 'early leavers', and in the 1980s the government introduced mandatory indexation. Increased costs, however, remained hidden by exceptional returns on investment in the 1980s and '90s. High returns on investment, the Commission noted, 'had allowed many private sector defined benefit schemes to ignore the rapid rise in the underlying cost of their pension promises' (Pensions Commission, 2005, p 123). Many companies had even lowered their contribution rates. The 1990s, the Commission concluded, were a 'fool's paradise' (Pensions Commission, 2004, p 57), and as the fool's paradise came to an end, many of the defined benefit schemes were closed to new entrants. Some companies had already closed their defined benefit pension schemes in the 1980s, but the pace of closure picked up towards the late 1990s and early 2000s. In 1995, there were 5 million active members of open pension schemes, and another 0.2 million active members of closed schemes; in 2000, the numbers were respectively 4.1 million and 0.5 million; by 2005, there were fewer than 4 million active members, equally divided across open and closed schemes (Pensions Commission, 2005). Declines in saving rates were thus accompanied by 'a major shift in risk from the state, employers, and insurance companies to individuals' (Pensions Commission, 2004, p 104).

One reason the 'fool's paradise' had come to an end in the 1990s related to changes in the way that regulators and pension funds measured the adequacy of a fund's resources to meet its obligations. Pension finance had traditionally been thought of in terms of funding. It revolved around the question of what level of contributions were required to meet the outgoing cash flows with a certain degree of confidence. In this view, the value of the liabilities depended on the level of returns that a pension fund expected to receive on its investments. The higher the returns, the lower the value of the liabilities, the fewer assets needed to cover the pension promises. Throughout the 1990s, however, the emphasis was increasingly put on the *economic* value of liabilities, revolving around the question of what level of contributions were required to make sure that the liabilities could be passed on to a third party without requiring additional funds (Hibbert and Turnbull, 2003). The value of the liabilities, in this modern financial view, was independent from the actual investment strategy. Any excess return, after all, was compensation for additional risk. To have the same degree of certainty that liabilities will be met, a riskier investment strategy will require more reserves.

A first step towards the buyout logic was made with the 1995 Pensions Act. Two of its features are especially important here. First, the Act introduced a minimum funding requirement for pension funds, requiring companies to produce a 'recovery plan' when the value of the fund's assets dropped below 100 per cent (and an even quicker recovery plan if they dropped below 90 per cent) of the value of their liabilities (Pensions Commission, 2004; Bridgen and Meyer, 2009). Although the valuation of liabilities would still be done according to the traditional 'funding' logic, the funding requirement set a floor to funds' funding status, exposing employers to the risk that falling asset prices could lead to higher contribution requirements. Second, the Act posited that in case a company became insolvent, the trustee of the pension fund could claim the shortfall in pension assets as 'debt'. The analogy between a funding gap and debt articulated well with modern finance theory. "If you look at it from a finance point of view", the actuary Cliff Speed said, a pension scheme is "basically a collateralized loan" (Speed interview) – the loan being the future benefits and the collateral being the assets put up in the fund. Funding gaps, in this view, were loans that were not only collateralized but also incredibly cheap because the sponsor doesn't pay any interest on it. Viewed in these terms, companies had a structural incentive to underfund their pension schemes because it was essentially a cheap way of funding their activities. Giving funding gaps the status of debt reduced the incentive for shareholders to press for decreasing pension contributions.

By setting a floor to the funding of pension schemes and by framing funding gaps in terms of debt, the 1995 Pensions Act also contributed to a shift in the pension fund investment and valuation rationale towards asset liability management. Up until the 1980s and '90s, as Dullaway remembers, the actuarial profession still taught its students that equity was the most appropriate asset class for pension funds to invest in. Dullaway, whom we've already encountered in Chapters 6 and 7, was trained in economics and claimed that the equity imperative was "clearly nonsense from an economics perspective" (Dullaway interview). Since the first half of the 20th century, actuaries tended to believe that investments in equity were appropriate because they generated relatively high returns (making pension promises cheaper) and tended to be less sensitive to inflation than fixed-income instruments (the movement of share prices tends to correlate with inflation). In the 'economics view', however, pension liabilities were much more like inflation-linked government bonds. Pension payments, in other words, could be almost perfectly matched with investments in 'linkers', and the value of the liabilities should then be equal to the value of the bonds needed to replicate the pension payments. According to the actuaries propagating modern finance theory, investments in riskier assets effectively meant a subsidy from the pension scheme to the sponsoring company if they were not accompanied by additional capital to cover for the risk. The value of the liabilities should therefore be measured independently from the investment strategy that the pension fund actually pursued: "I don't care if I've got equities, if I've got bonds, or there's no assets there whatsoever. The liabilities are the liabilities" (Speed interview).

The transition from a funding logic to a buyout logic became more entrenched in 2004, when the government required pension funds to calculate their minimum funding requirements on a full 'buyout' basis (Coates and Lynam, 2005). This was around the same time as market-consistent valuation and risk-based capital calculation were introduced in the world of life insurance. To the extent that the new regulatory requirement did not specify in great detail how the full buyout value should be calculated, there was a lot of room for interpretation. The calculations, interviewees report, could easily be fudged. The relevance of such buyout calculations, moreover, remained contested, both within the actuarial profession and in the broader field of pension funds. Nevertheless, they helped establish the view that most defined benefit pension schemes found themselves in a dire financial situation by the 1990s, hastening the shift towards defined contribution schemes.

For the insurance industry, the pension crisis represented above all a business opportunity. First, the Association of British Insurers forecasted that increased emphasis of the UK's retirement income system on individual pensions and work-related defined contribution schemes enlarged the potential market for insurers' pension products. Data on insurers' premium income confirms this expectation. The share of premium income insurers generate from pension business has nearly doubled since the early 2000s (see Figure 1.1).

Second, the Pensions Commission predicted that the shift to defined contribution pensions would increase future demand for annuity products. The Commission, however, also warned that the annuity market could struggle to offer annuities at attractive prices in the future. Increased life expectancy meant that annuities would become relatively more expensive. Insurers' capacity to sell annuities at relatively attractive prices, moreover, depends on the investment returns that insurers can generate by investing the premiums. Annuity providers typically invest their premium income in fixed-income securities, the payments of which 'match' the outgoing payments to the beneficiaries of the annuities. Such investments include (index-linked) long-term government bonds and corporate bonds. Given declining interest rates and a 'limited supply of appropriate underlying instruments', the report raised questions 'about the capacity of the insurance industry to meet that demand at attractive prices' (Pensions Commission, 2004, p 108). Their worries proved justified. Although there was a gradual increase in annuity business in the years leading up to the global financial crisis, the post-crisis fall in interest rates inaugurated the decline of the annuity market, causing some insurers to stop selling annuities altogether.

Third, the shift towards defined contribution schemes would leave a vast landscape of 'legacy' defined benefit schemes. The Pensions Commission suggested that it was well possible that many of these schemes would be 'bought out' by private insurers, creating a new market for the 'de-risking' of the occupational pensions pillar (Pensions Commission, 2005). Transactions of this kind could be structured in various ways, ranging from products that would cover the risk inherent in the pension schemes while leaving the assets in the pension fund itself to complete buyouts where both assets and liabilities are transferred to a private insurer in exchange for a risk premium. The potential size of the market is huge, with over £1 trillion of pension assets locked into defined benefit schemes. In the years following publication of the Pensions Commissions reports, the de-risking market – also referred to as the 'new life market' (Blake et al, 2013) – has indeed seen substantial growth, peaking in 2019 at £43.8 billion of pension assets being transferred to insurance companies and an additional transfer of the 'longevity risk' embedded in the pension liabilities for another £11.8 billion (Willis Towers Watson, 2021; see also Figure 9.1).

The new life market

The transfer of assets and liabilities from a pension scheme to an insurance company can be a rather hectic affair. With the introduction of Solvency II, insurance companies were heavily regulated, more so than pension funds. These requirements, Speed suggested, were relatively demanding when a large book of assets and liabilities were transferred from a pension fund to an insurance company:

'In insurance, you have the case where you must be solvent, which includes having enough money and dealing with your value at risk on a continuous basis, at least every day. So you measure that. That's comparatively easy in the steady-state. But then imagine a transaction where you have a new liability that hits your balance sheet with a load of assets, which materially increases your asset-base and those assets aren't necessarily in the right shape. You've got one day to put that into the right position. That's pretty challenging. Getting all that executed, going through a process trying to make sure you're getting best value for money, you've got good execution, all that is consolidated, so that by the close of the play you can go and stand in front of the regulator and say: yep, that's all I executed. We've hedged our liabilities, we know where we are, and we can survive all those shocks.' (Speed interview)

Given the demanding regulatory requirements and the large efforts required to realize the transfer of liabilities from pension schemes to insurance companies, what is driving these transactions? What do both parties in the transaction gain from it? A simple (and perhaps simplistic) answer to these questions is of course profit. But how do actors profit from these transactions? Or better still, how do actors calculate the profitability of these transactions, even when this profitability materializes only in the long term?

Buying out pension funds

As noted, the emergence of the new life market had a lot to do with changes in regulation and in how the economic value and risk of pension promises were evaluated. The introduction of the minimum funding requirement had set a floor to pension funds' funding status, making pension liabilities seem riskier for companies. Changed views of how pensions should be evaluated, moreover, had made the pension promises seem more expensive than initially thought. Another crucial step in this regard was the introduction of a new financial accounting standard, FRS 17. According to Jon Exley (2002), who at the time was one of the main proponents of market-consistent valuation of pension liabilities, FRS 17 represented a 'spectacular improvement in pensions accounting' even if the accounting standard continued to have 'flaws that have the hallmarks of compromises with traditional actuarial arguments'. The pensions consultant Ronnie Bowie noted that the accounting standard had brought the pension problem 'to boardroom attention'.

I have been doing the job of a pensions consultant for nearly 30 years. I have never known such boardroom and finance director interest in pensions, nor have I ever been to so many full board meetings as in the past three or four years. Occasionally I have been told that I and all other actuaries are an entire waste of space, and that it is we who got them into this mess, but, more usually, to be invited to discuss how to manage the risks. (Bowie in Speed et al, 2008, p 239)

The regulatory initiatives in the 1990s increasingly created a level playing field between insurance companies and pension funds. Nonetheless, important differences between insurance companies and pension funds in the regulatory treatment of pension liabilities remained:

> 'In insurance, if you're holding safe assets, you need a certain amount. If I then want to move some of those assets, say, from gilts into equities, I need more capital. I need a higher capital buffer because there's more risk. Seems reasonable. Ask the question what happens in pensions, I'm holding bonds. If I go and hold equities, they say I need less capital.' (Speed interview)

As a consequence, Speed suggested, if you "imagine a pension scheme [becoming] a life insurance company, which, arguably, is the same thing, you'd say [in most cases] it's an insolvent life assurer" (Speed interview). Despite such differences, corporate sponsors were increasingly willing to shed the risk of increased future funding requirements from their balance sheets.

Another factor contributing to sponsors' willingness to transfer their pension liabilities to insurance companies, then, was the increased uncertainty around longevity risk. As noted earlier, life expectancy had increased significantly since the time occupational pension schemes had been set up. Willets' 1999 paper had suggested that improvements in life expectancy had significantly exceeded the historical average for the cohort born around 1926. Perceived uncertainty around life expectancy had increased too. The report published by the Continuous Mortality Investigation (CMI) in 2002, for instance, had shown that life expectancy could change drastically depending on how long the cohort effect was assumed to persist (see Chapter 7). In 2008, the Pensions Regulator initiated a further review of pension funds' mortality assumptions and noted that the CMI's medium cohort scenario had already become outdated; the regulator suggested that the long cohort scenario would be more realistic, implying a further two-year increase to the life expectancy of a 60-year-old male. Although supervisors acknowledged that different mortality tables might be appropriate for different schemes (as life expectancy may vary across occupations), they adopted the long cohort scenario as a benchmark that could trigger further investigations into schemes' mortality assumptions. The consequences for pension funds' balance sheets were severe. The value of pension promises increased by 3 to 4 per cent for each year that a worker was expected to live longer. For some companies, the liabilities could increase by as much as 15 to 20 per cent (Cohen, 2008).

By the mid-2000s, changes in the regulation and evaluation of pension liabilities had thus led to the perception that defined benefit pension promises were costly and risky. Corporate management increasingly perceived the buyout of pension schemes as an attractive option to get rid of a large risk on their balance sheets, which in their perception has little to do with their core business. Shareholders may perceive pension liabilities as rather risky while valuing companies without weighty pension liabilities more highly. Industry research indicates, for instance, that shareholders positively evaluate the transfer of pension risk to insurance companies, even if this requires paying a risk premium to insurance companies (Ellis et al, 2020). The decision to de-risk a pension fund, moreover, may also be a strategic choice to safeguard the careers of corporate management. As Baker (2021) points out with respect to the insurance runoff market, legacy insurance schemes may be regarded primarily as a burden for an insurance company, endangering the careers of those associated with it and providing an incentive to act proactively and sell the business to a third party in its entirety. The same likely holds for the legacy defined benefit schemes that, from the sponsor's perspective, pose a substantial risk.

For insurance companies, the buyout transactions provide an opportunity to capitalize on the risk premiums that sponsoring companies are willing to pay to remove the liabilities from their balance sheets. The transfer of pension funds' assets and liabilities to insurance companies also comes with new regulatory requirements. While pension funds tend to be heavily invested in equity, the risk-based capital requirements of Solvency II incentivize investment in fixed-income securities, which reduce financial risk (and capital requirements). Crucial in this regard is the matching adjustment (see Chapter 8), which enables insurers to capitalize on the risk premium of 'matching' assets. In 2018, for instance, three of the most specialized insurance groups (the Pension Insurance Corporation, Rothesay Life, and Just Group) had £13.7 billion of regulatory net assets including the matching adjustment and only £172 million without it (Ford, 2020). It is little surprise that insurers' asset allocation shows a clear predilection for fixed-income securities (see Figure 9.2). The transfer of pension liabilities thus involves a double de-risking: the company removes the pension risk from its balance sheets; the insurer reduces the investment risk, while profiting from an additional risk premium, largely made possible by the matching adjustment. What is frequently overlooked is that the transfer of pension liabilities from pension funds to insurance companies also implies a changing logic of security underpinning the pension promises. The security of pension promises in pension funds is backed by an 'employer covenant', which stipulates that employers are liable for any future shortfalls in pension funding. The security of pension promises in insurance companies relies on capital buffers. The degree of pension security thus depends on the evaluation machinery underpinning the assessment of capital adequacy. In pension funds, the degree of security relies mostly on the strength of the employer covenant and the solvency of the corporate entity as a whole. The transfer

Figure 9.2: Asset allocations of bulk annuity providers

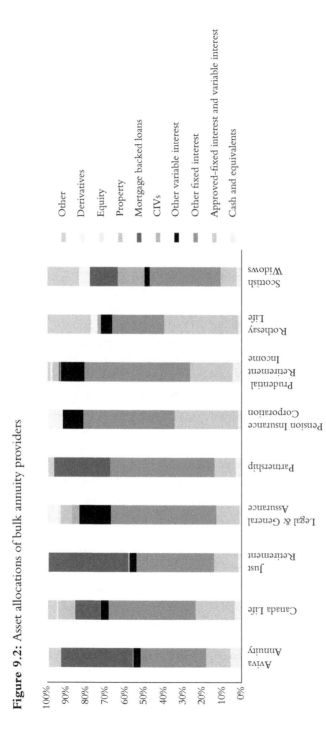

Source: Hymans Robertson (2016)

of pension liabilities to insurance companies essentially involves corporates buying their way out of an employer covenant, replacing it with risk capital.

Reordering the buyout field

In 2005, Cliff Speed quit his job as investment consultant to become the Chief Investment Officer of the start-up insurance company Paternoster. Paternoster was founded by Mark Wood, who had left his job as CEO of Prudential UK, reportedly when he was not appointed as the group CEO (Northedge, 2008). "Some people said it was a surprising thing to go and do", Speed recalls. "There's a polite way of saying, a lot of my colleagues said I was mad … you're going off to try and sell a product, which nobody wants." By the mid-2000s, only few insurers were active in the buyout market, and the transactions were rather expensive for pension funds. The market "was quite a niche", Andrew Stoker recalls. "You just had Legal & General and Pru [Prudential]. Pricing wasn't that competitive."

By the mid-2000s, the old order of the buyout market was uprooted by the introduction of new entrants that sought to redefine the rules of the game. Apart from Legal & General and Prudential, Aviva also joined the buyout market in 2006. Paternoster was the first in a series of insurance start-ups funded by investment firms specializing in the de-risking market. Other entrants included Lucida (set up by the former CEO of Prudential Jonathan Bloomer), the Pension Corporation (founded by the private equity investor Edmund Truell), and Synesis Life (founded by Isabel Hudson, a former distribution director at Prudential), which were all founded in 2006. These entrants were backed by private equity firms (the Pension Corporation and Lucida) and investment banks (Synesis Life). In 2007, Goldman Sachs set up its own insurance subsidiary, Rothesay Life. In 2006, Aviva also entered the market, perceiving the buyout market as an opportunity to scale their business in a declining annuity market. The motivations for financial firms, as reported by interviewees, were different. One interviewee, for instance, suggested that Goldman Sachs perceived their buyout subsidiary as a vehicle for dealing with the thorny question of pension liabilities troubling their merger and acquisition business. Another interviewee suggested that financial firms perceived the bulk annuity business primarily as an attractive source of funding for investment in asset-backed securities, the market for which peaked pre-financial crisis.

The perception that defined-benefit pension promises were more costly and risky than corporates had for a long time assumed had thus made entrance in the pension de-risking market seem attractive to a variety of business actors. Few of the newcomers, however, survived. In 2008, the Pension Corporation already acquired Synesis Life, which had failed to underwrite a single large transaction. In 2010, Rothesay Life acquired Paternoster;

Legal & General acquired Lucida. In 2012, Rothesay Life also acquired the de-risking business of MetLife, which had entered the British market in 2007. At the same time, established life insurance companies continued to enter the de-risking market. Canada Life and Scottish Widows entered the market in 2015, Phoenix Life entered in 2017. Another entrant was the Just Retirement Group, which originated from a merger between the Just Group – a relatively young insurance group focusing on retirement-related products – and Partnership Assurance – also a relatively young insurance group specialized in the annuity market – and entered the market in 2012.

Anecdotal evidence suggests competition in the market for pension liabilities was fierce, at least in the first years of the market's new activity. For instance, having struggled to secure large transactions, the Pension Corporation attempted to buy entire companies, including their pension funds, strip the company of its pension liabilities and then to sell the remaining assets at a premium. In late 2007, however, regulators put this strategy to a halt. The Pension Corporation had acquired the telecoms company Telent, and the trustees of Telent's pension scheme worried that the acquisition would lead to 'conflicts of interest', registering their concern with the Pension Regulator (Bandel, 2007). In 2006, its previous owner, the Marconi Group, sought to spin-off Telent in an attempt to make the group more attractive to a potential buyer. Telent held claims on a £490mln escrow account to meet future shortfalls in the scheme's funds; and the scheme's trustees worried that Pension Corporation sought to get their hands on this sum (Davies, 2009). Not trusting the takeover, the Pensions Regulator intervened and appointed three independent trustees to the scheme. Even if Pension Corporation did eventually come to an agreement with the regulator about the contributions it would make to the fund, the regulatory challenge had made company management wary of the acquisition strategy, which it ceased to pursue.

The buyout field emerged at the intersection of various adjacent fields. Apart from eroding the boundary between the pensions field and the field of life insurance, the buyout markets also established increased connections to the asset management field in general and the private equity field in particular. On the one hand, private equity firms had indirectly entered the insurance markets by putting capital into new insurance vehicles, which sometimes pursued rather aggressive private equity-like expansion strategies. The established insurance companies that had entered the buyout market, on the other hand, increasingly came to resemble asset management firms, whose business model consisted in optimizing the investment strategies backing the pension liabilities. The buyout market, however, also contributed to the strengthening of ties between British life insurers and foreign reinsurers. According to David Rule (2019), the Prudential Regulation Authority executive director of insurance supervision, the risk margin of Solvency

II (see Chapter 8) created excessive capital requirements for longevity risk in a low interest rate environment. To reduce these capital requirements, insurance companies active in the buyout market therefore sought to reinsure their longevity risk in offshore insurance centres, establishing a financial link between British pensioners and offshore insurance companies that started to worry regulators. 'UK insurers', Rule (2019) noted, 'are increasingly exposed to offshore reinsurers' (p 5). Thus, while previously, pension funds might have put pensioners' capital to work in foreign capital markets, now the risks embedded in these liabilities were also increasingly passed on to foreign insurance markets.

Insurance and asset management

A crucial aspect of any market is the pricing mechanism. The price of a buyout transaction is expressed as a spread over the interest rate on gilts (UK government bonds), for example gilts plus 50 basis points. As the consulting actuary Tiziana Perrella explained, the price of bulk annuity can be expressed this way because "you can look at a bulk annuity a bit like a gilt, but it's a better gilt, because it matches your longevity" (Perrella interview). One way to understand this is to say that in a buyout transaction, the insurance company borrows the assets of a pension scheme, and to the extent that the maturity of the assets match the longevity of the scheme's participants, the insurer runs little additional risk apart from investment risk. In a buyout transaction, in other words, the insurance company profits by re-investing the assets in fixed-income investments that yield higher returns than the net rate they pay for borrowing the assets ('gilts plus'). The difference between these returns and the price of the bulk annuity, expressed as a spread over gilt rates, is how insurers earn a profit in the de-risking market.

Placing the focus on the asset side of the balance sheet, the buyout field is situated downstream in the 'investment chain' (Arjaliès et al, 2017) relative to pension funds. This is one way of interpreting the claim that insurers have increasingly become like asset managers: the buyout market focuses insurers' attention on managing 'other people's money' rather than on making and marketing risk (compare: Kay, 2015). It extends the investment chain, linking savings to capital market investment. Most insurers, for instance, further outsource their investment to internal or external asset managers. In today's world of investment, asset management requires risk management and investment research departments, which can be rather expensive to set up. The diversity of assets in which insurers invest today is so large that it becomes difficult to manage all assets internally. The low interest rate environment, moreover, has pushed insurers to invest increasingly in 'alternative investments', which is an asset class that they have traditionally relatively little expertise in.

While particularly the smaller insurance companies may outsource investment to external asset managers, many of the largest insurers have internal asset management branches. Aviva and Legal & General, for instance, have large internal asset management units (Aviva Investors and Legal & General Investment Management) that manage £366 billion and £1,279 billion assets respectively, some of which are managed on behalf of external companies. Other large insurers have been taken over or usurped by their investment management branches. Prudential, for instance, merged with its internal asset manager, M&G, to form Prudential M&G in 2017. A few years later, the company demerged again, forming two separate companies: the insurance company Prudential plc, focusing on Asian, African and American insurance markets, and M&G, an investment management firm, which also incorporates the former Prudential UK brand. M&G has stopped writing annuity business and has sought to sell its £45 billion annuity back book to Rothesay Life, in a transfer that was blocked in court. In 2017, Standard Life merged with Aberdeen Asset Management to form Standard Life Aberdeen. It then sold its in-force life insurance business to the closed life insurance group Phoenix, focusing its activities more squarely on the asset management field.

The established insurance companies, in other words, became increasingly entangled with asset management firms, either by outsourcing asset management activities, by relying on internal asset managers, or by being usurped by existing asset management firms that sought to leverage insurers' large capital pools to scale their activities. Newly established insurance companies were set up by financial firms, such as investment banks or private equity firms. More generally, competition between insurance firms increasingly centred not just on insurers' capacity to make and insure risks but also on their capacity to source relatively high-yielding investments, creating a push towards expanding their expertise in asset management, whether internally or externally. The bulk annuity market was one factor contributing to this shift in emphasis. Another factor was the rising level of occupational pension savings put into defined contribution schemes, a large share of which is invested in capital markets mediated by insurance companies.

Without Solvency II, the increased emphasis on asset management in the insurance business would likely have been less pronounced. There are several reasons for this. First, the framework's emphasis on market-consistent valuation of both assets and liabilities pushed insurers to reorganize their investment strategies, putting more emphasis on asset-liability management – that is, the reduction of risk by investing in assets that 'match' the maturity profile of the liabilities. Second, the calibration of the risk margin, which in a low interest rate environment created relatively high capital requirements for risks like longevity risk, pushed many insurers to reinsure their longevity risk in offshore insurance centres, focusing insurers' activities on the management of assets instead. Third, the framework's matching adjustment allowed insurers to capitalize on risk premiums of the risky assets that matched their liability profile. This further focused their investment strategy on asset-liability management and gave insurers' an incentive to source long-term investments in alternative fixed-income investments that generate relatively high returns compared to the more traditional investments in high-grade corporate bonds and government bonds.

Conclusion

If anything, I hope this chapter has shown that the seemingly technical struggles over pension assets and liabilities are also deeply political struggles over the distribution of the costs and risks of pension promises. The gradual coming to an end of what the Pensions Commission called the fool's paradise of the 1980s and '90s has meant that pensioners have increasingly strengthened their claims over pension assets, pushing some of the costs and risks of the defined benefit pension schemes back to their corporate sponsors, who had previously benefitted from the pension schemes' relatively low levels of funding. In turn, however, employers have changed the terms on which corporate pensions are issued from defined benefit arrangements to defined contribution arrangements. This has created a twofold business opportunity for British life insurance companies: accumulating new assets by managing defined contribution funds and by buying out legacy defined benefit schemes. The buyout market allows corporate sponsors to de-risk their pension schemes. The question remains, however, at what cost? And to what extent do pension promises remain safe now their security relies on risk-based capital rather than on the sponsor covenant?

The changes in the second pillar of the retirement income system, which were induced by changes in the evaluation of the riskiness and costliness of pension promises, have thus created a business opportunity for British life insurers to manage the UK's pension assets. The shift in focus towards asset management has been further stimulated by the adoption of a market-consistent and risk-based capital regime. The introduction of this regime made the consideration of risk–reward trade-offs more important, pushing insurers to expand their expertise in alternative investment strategies in search of high-yielding assets that generate fixed cash flows. The changes in the UK's retirement income system and insurers' evaluation machinery, in other words, have together stimulated the demand for a particular kind of securities that transform capital investment into fixed-income streams. This is the other side of the asset management capitalism coin (Braun, 2016), the literature on which has predominantly focused on the creation of financial assets in areas of the economy such as infrastructure investment and social impact investing.

10

Financial Evaluation and the Future of Insurance Society

In the preceding chapters, I examined the processes of cultural change in the British life insurance business since the late 1960s and early 1970s, paying specific attention to the institutionalization of financial evaluation practices rooted in modern finance theory and the consequences thereof. At this point, I hope to have persuaded readers of the usefulness of my approach: to investigate financialization in the making by looking at the social forces that shape evaluation practices in insurance. Evaluation practices enable and constrain particular ways of viewing the world; they shape how we imagine the relations underlying the commoditization of an uncertain economic future and the concomitant long-term promises such as life insurance and pensions. Evaluation practices rooted in modern finance theory foster a particular way of imagining these relations, one that prioritizes a market-based enactment of 'economic value' and the logic of risk-based capital and perceives 'financial risk' as an intrinsic part of that commodity. With the introduction of modern finance theory in the life insurance business, in other words, the 'value model' (Christophers, 2015) of insurers has changed to incorporate financial risk into the insurance commodity, rejigging the social relations constitutive of private risk sharing arrangements.

Throughout the book, I argued that the uptake in British life insurance of evaluation practices of this kind shaped and was shaped by social forces of two broad kinds: the field dynamics in the life insurance market and in actuarial science and the competition among professional groups over their jurisdictional claims in the insurance business. Following this framework, the process of cultural change may be presented as a triptych.

On the first panel, we see newly established insurance companies challenge the dominance of the large and well-established insurers selling traditional with-profits insurance from the late 1960s onwards. The challenger firms deployed newly available information technologies and innovative marketing strategies to offer a model of insurance that undermined the capacity of the field's institutional structure to restrain competition. This new model of insurance promised to remove actuarial discretion from the insurance contract, tying policyholder's investments directly to the performance of underlying investments. By the early 2000s, the increased competition among insurers, the hybridization of unit-linked and with-profits insurance and the continuously declining interest rates had created difficulties for some insurers, precipitating the spectacular demise of the Equitable Life Assurance Society and raising doubts about the adequacy of actuarial expertise in the governance of life insurance in an age of high financial market volatility. One of the field effects produced by the introduction of the unit-linked insurance model was to weaken the jurisdictional claims of the actuarial profession in the life insurance business.

On the second panel, we can see a group of actuaries who by the 1990s had become familiar with modern finance theory due to their work in non-traditional actuarial fields. These actuaries viewed the appropriation of financial practices in the governance of the life insurance business as the preferred strategy to fend off allegations that the actuarial profession had become obsolete. This group of actuaries formed an alliance across professional ecologies, with supervisors from the newly established integrated Financial Services Authority (FSA) and with international accounting standard setters, to propagate the financial evaluation practices of market-consistent valuation and risk-based capital calculation as core features of the UK's insurance governance regime. When the FSA decided to move towards a market-consistent and risk-based capital regime in the early 2000s, the actuaries with extensive knowledge of economics and modern finance theory were the knowledge brokers who reformed actuarial expertise by building the models that allowed insurers to perform the calculations needed to comply with the new regulation and by educating other members of the profession on how the models should be used and how their results should be interpreted.

The third panel depicts the effects produced by the institutionalization of financial evaluation practices. The institutionalization of market-consistent valuation, risk-based capital regulation and financial risk management more generally strengthened the position of shareholders in the life insurance field, allowing for rationalized capital allocation decision making and for more short-term considerations of profitability in the insurance industry. The other side of this coin was that actuaries lost their powerful position within the insurance business as custodians of surplus, making discretionary decisions about when and how financial surpluses generated through investment and the non-profit business should be distributed across participating policyholders and shareholders. This is not to say that the actuarial profession has lost out altogether (actuaries may still earn handsome salaries in the insurance business); rather that actuaries have had to reimagine their claims to specialist expertise and that they acquired a more technical role rather than a managerial one. The institutionalization of financial risk management has also contributed to the emergence of a new market field in British life insurance, the pension de-risking market, which is dominated by some old companies and some new ones that have their roots in the financial sector more generally. The institutionalization of financial evaluation practices, in other words, changed the rules of the game, rejigged the relative position of actors in the market field and contributed to the emergence of new market fields.

Together, the three panels of the triptych paint an image of the changing boundaries between finance and insurance, whereby policyholder benefits are increasingly tied to the financial market performance of the underlying investments, whereby financial markets have displaced actuaries as the authoritative source for knowledge about the economic value and the financial risk embedded in insurance contracts, and whereby shareholders have gained a more powerful position within the insurance business. The flipside of this coin is that policyholders have ceased to participate in the profits generated by insurers' non-profit business, which are now almost entirely reserved for shareholders. Life insurance has lost its idiosyncratic organizational form and has become more like any other financial service than it has ever been before.

The performative power of modern finance theory

Why were the exemplary problem solutions of modern finance theory so influential in shaping insurers' evaluation practices? And what does their 'performative power' (Svetlova, 2012) consist of? The extant literature in the social studies of finance tends to address questions like these by looking at the organizational and institutional environment in which models are deployed (Beunza and Stark, 2004; MacKenzie and Spears, 2014; Svetlova, 2018; Wansleben, 2018). Seen from this perspective, the widespread usage of the Black–Scholes equation may be explained by its 'high academic standing', its practical utility in solving specific organizational problems, and its public availability (MacKenzie, 2007, p 71). The approach adopted in this book highlights several other factors that have likely contributed to the institutionalization of modern finance theory in the life insurance business.

A first feature that can be identified refers to a change in the professional ecologies in which actuaries were employed. The rapid growth of the actuarial profession and the increased employment of actuaries outside the traditional career paths at life offices and pension funds had created a group of insiders in the profession that one way or another had become familiar with the core models of modern theory. This group sought to propagate the benefits of modern finance theory from within, campaigning for its inclusion in the knowledge base of actuarial expertise, even if their efforts generated substantial animosity within the profession. Some of these actuaries were consultants working together with members of other professional groups to advise on mergers and acquisitions among insurance companies; others were employed directly at investment banks and were hired to help sell derivative products to insurance companies, thus having a direct interest in making modern finance theory part of the actuarial toolkit. Wherever they were employed, these actuaries formed an active part of the actuarial profession willing to form alliances with members of other professional groups to overhaul evaluation in insurance. The broadening employment of actuaries outside traditional lines of occupation had thus created a group of actuaries within the profession who perceived the appropriation of modern finance theory as a necessary strategy for the survival of the profession; once traditional actuarial expertise was increasingly discredited after the introduction of unit-linked insurance and ultimately the collapse of Equitable Life, this group managed to gain control over the professional project in a bid to maintain the profession's jurisdictional claims. While the actuarial profession first served as a bulwark of resistance against the transformation of life insurance, it later became an important catalyst of the institutionalization of modern finance theory.

Second, the more general move away from self-regulation to a British regulatory state had led to the establishment of a more assertive regulatory agent, the FSA, that perceived the alleged objectivity of modern finance as a major attraction. In contrast to the previous regulatory agent, the FSA was an integrated regulatory agent, which meant that many of the regulators and supervisors in charge of insurance regulation had past experience with banking supervision. This made the regulatory agent more susceptible to a reform of insurance governance based on market-consistent valuation and explicit risk-based capital regulation. These kinds of quantifications, moreover, were also regarded as more 'objective' and transparent, providing a more solid basis for increased supervisory oversight over the insurance business. Market-consistent valuation circumvents the need to forecast the future and turns the valuation problem into a synchronous problem (Langenohl, 2018). With the transition towards an integrated financial services supervisor, in other words, the propagation of modern finance theory formed a hinge strategy (Abbott, 2005; Seabrooke and Tsingou, 2009) that would generate rewards not only for the proponents of modern finance theory within the actuarial profession but also for an important group within the newly established supervisory agent.

Third, the discretionary elements associated with traditional with-profits insurance were increasingly met with suspicion. While some perceived actuaries as policyholder champions and custodians of surplus, others suggested that actuaries might well succumb to the pressure of shareholders at the expense of participating policyholders. It was, moreover, extremely difficult to assess how insurers and the actuaries they employed balanced the interests of shareholders and the different groups of policyholders. Within this context, unit-linked insurance seemed to offer a more transparent alternative that some perceived also as more equitable because there was no direct interference with the level of benefits policyholders would receive. Unit-linked insurance promised to alleviate the conflicts of interest embedded in with-profits insurance, but, in so doing, it also made the question of financial risk embedded in the guarantees written on unit-linked products seem more urgent. This was a concrete problem for which proponents of modern finance theory could promise what seemed an objective and transparent solution, even if it had many imperfections and was difficult to implement and understand in practice.

Fourth, the growth and increased international expansion of the insurance industry had made the management of at least the larger insurers look increasingly favourably at the institutionalization of modern finance theory. By the late 1990s, it had become clear that international accounting standards would embrace the concept of fair value accounting, making accounting standards conform to the valuation principles of modern finance theory. For the largest insurers, this meant that they would likely have to adopt some form of financial evaluation of insurance contracts anyway, making the resistance to the adoption of market-consistent valuation and risk-based capital regulation for the purpose of capital regulation seem futile. That the international accounting standard for insurance contracts was published only in 2017 hardly mattered in this regard. As the chapter on Solvency II made clear, moreover, the larger insurers viewed advocacy of market-consistent capital regulation also as an opportunity to pursue the goal of home country supervision, which would have made it a lot easier to access other European insurance markets. Just like the accounting standards, the fact that Solvency II was eventually adopted without a strong version of home country supervision hardly mattered.

Altogether, it becomes clear that the appropriation of modern finance theory in the life insurance business should not so much be seen as a financial colonization of the insurance business by financial interests; rather, the appropriation of financial evaluation practices seemed to offer significant rewards for a broad variety of relevant actors within the insurance business too, which throughout the 1990s made the overhaul of the evaluation machinery in insurance increasingly likely.

Rationalization and the authority of the market

The story of the appropriation of modern finance theory in insurance may be seen as a story of rationalization, an attempt to remake the evaluation machinery in insurance conform to the prescriptions of 'scientific' economic theory. The double meaning of the term rationalization here is convenient. In the most straightforward usage of the term, rationalization means making things – processes, businesses and so on – more efficient and more efficiency oriented, optimizing input relative to output. Rationalization, in this sense, refers to the ascendancy of instrumental reason and a process of socio-technical closure that is often associated with Weber's notion of the iron cage. Rationalization, however, may also refer to the act of justifying one's actions with logical reasons. This is where the efficiency-oriented rationality presupposed by the iron cage turns into its plural, rationalities. In this perspective, there are potentially many different ways to rationalize our actions. In contrast to the first meaning, this second meaning of rationalization is non-teleological. It also implies a different kind of question for social science research: rather than focusing on the question of whether society is becoming more rational, calculating and efficiency-oriented, it implies the question of what reasons and rationalities are deployed to justify action, what reasons and rationalities are considered more legitimate than others and why. This view of rationalization, in other words, leaves open the possibility of critical-political openness towards different kinds of instrumental reasoning (Feenberg, 1999; Overwijk, 2021).

In the context of life insurance, the appropriation of modern finance theory has often been linked to the notion of technical and scientific progress. In a 1993 debate at the Institute of Actuaries on the merits of modern finance theory, for instance, Wilkie likened the work of Redington (whose immunization theory was generally regarded as a major contribution to actuarial thought on investment) to the *Cutty Sark*, "one of the last great sailing ships in an age that was already being taken over by steamships" (Wilkie et al, 1993, p 398). Modern finance theory, in other words, relied on fundamentally different techniques and methods compared to traditional actuarial work and would potentially be much more efficient in reaching the same goal of maximizing returns and benefits to participating policyholders and shareholders while still maintaining a sufficient level of security to policyholders. As actuarial science entered the age of steamships, however, the relative weight given to the various goals also started to shift. In traditional with-profits arrangements, the aim was to produce stable returns to both shareholders and participating policyholders, smoothened across financial cycles. Uncertainty was dealt with by actuarial discretion and a degree of flexibility in the with-profits contract. Actuaries had to form judgements about what levels of reserves were appropriate and how many benefits different groups of policyholders and shareholders should receive, judgements that imply a view of how much insurers' liabilities are worth and how uncertain their returns are. In contemporary insurance, the delegated capacity of actuaries to make decisions about bonuses and dividends is reduced. Judgements about the adequacy of reserves, moreover, are delegated to evaluation practices that are partially tethered to financial markets (market-consistent valuation) and partially based in regulatory approved calculations of risk. Actuarial authority and discretion, in other words, is replaced by the authority of the market and the regulator, achieving a degree of socio-technical closure while foreclosing more mutualist conceptions of the insurance business.

The financial evaluation practices rationalize or frame the problem of uncertainty in insurance as a problem of risk, even if – as insurance practitioners seem well aware – uncertainty cannot be reduced just to calculable risk (Baker, 2021). This rationality of calculated risk, which does not just capture diversifiable risk but also non-diversifiable risk, privileges some organizational forms over others, making it harder for insurance arrangements alternative to the dominant form of large proprietary private insurance companies to flourish, for instance for insurance forms where financial uncertainty is dealt with at the level of the company rather than that of policyholders, or organizational forms where capital efficiency is only secondary to other values. Evidence from elsewhere, where similar practices have been institutionalized through the European directive Solvency II, indicates for instance that these practices make it harder to sustain organizational forms rooted in non-profit, cooperative and mutualist principles (Benoît, 2021). They also make it more difficult to sustain idiosyncratic profit sharing systems, such as that seen in Germany (Paetzmann, 2011). In the UK, the financial evaluation practices seem to have at least contributed to the demise of with-profits insurance by making the trade-offs embedded in the profit sharing arrangement amenable to regulatory scrutiny (Jennings et al, 2014). Rationalization of insurance arrangements seen through the models of modern finance theory imposes a limit on what insurance can be. It represents a form of closure that is underpinned by a particular form of instrumental reasoning that may (and perhaps should) be contested.

The future of insurance societies

It is of course well possible to say that the institutionalization of financial evaluation practices merely brought to light the weaknesses in traditional insurance arrangements that would have led to even more and larger insurance failures than Equitable had they not been stopped in their tracks. In this view, increased financial market volatility, secularly declining interest rates, increased competitive pressures among insurers and a failing system of corporate governance had turned prudence into imprudence, at least in some companies, and created an infeasible situation. In contrast to banking, where the introduction of risk-based capital regulation has often been associated with the excesses leading up to the global financial crisis, risk-based capital regulation actually made the insurance sector more efficient and more secure. In the age of financial capitalism, this view maintains, risk-based capital regulation is the most sensible framework for the governance of the insurance industry.

We might, however, equally well say that in the context of financial capitalism and increased privatization of the retirement income system there is an increased need for collective vehicles to organize financial uncertainty in such a way to protect individuals from excessive financial market volatility. This view highlights the fact that the institutionalization of financial evaluation practices has also individualized the responsibility for financial uncertainty, pushing the burden of financial market volatility to the level of the individual household and insulating shareholders from it. Proponents of this view, moreover, could point out that financial evaluation practices are often associated with procyclical investment behaviour, making insurance actually contribute to the financial market volatility that they sought to manage in the first place.

My aim here is not to take a stance on whichever of these views is the right one. Rather, I simply want to point out (at the risk perhaps of stating the obvious) that a system of governance rooted in market-consistent valuation and risk-based capital regulation obfuscates the fact that there are other mechanisms of dealing with financial uncertainty too, mechanisms that come with different advantages and drawbacks. Financial risk management provides a blueprint for how financial uncertainty can be managed through asset-liability management. Yet, as the financial crisis has made clear, this blueprint is by no means fail-safe, and the practical merits of financial risk management may be overstated. Financial risk management may even induce moral hazard by giving off a false sense of security, embedding actors in complex financial circuits that are prone to crashing. The traditional mechanisms of dealing with uncertainty, on the other hand, consist of contractual flexibilities and collective savings mechanisms that organize financial uncertainty around actuarial prudence and discretion and that allow policyholders to become participating members of the insurance firm. The question here is whether the actuary (or some other expert) can be trusted as the custodian of surplus to make equitable trade-offs between different groups of policyholders and shareholders. This certainly is no fail-safe method either, as the history of Equitable Life has shown, but it does make clear that there are other mechanisms for dealing with uncertainty that *may* under the right set of circumstances lead to a preferable arrangement for organizing uncertainty.

An important question here is how well these issues travel to other insurance markets. Life insurance is somewhat peculiar in its long-term orientation and its focus on saving and investment. Other forms of insurance may be much more focused on the spreading, absorbing or pre-empting of risk (Ericson and Doyle, 2004), which may give the impression that the developments described in this book are only relevant for the life insurance business. To some extent, this is true. The models of with-profits insurance and unit-linked insurance, for instance, have almost exclusively been deployed in the life insurance market. Nonetheless, non-life insurers have also had to adopt financial risk management practices in response to regulatory reforms (most notably Solvency II), and it seems likely that this has similarly strengthened the position of shareholders and shareholder-owned companies in the respective market fields. The introduction of financial evaluation practices in non-life insurance, moreover, may also highlight the fact that even relatively short-term insurance arrangements have a savings and investment component to them (Lehtonen and Liukko, 2015). The emergence of large insurance groups like AVIVA in the UK (and Allianz, Axa and Generali on the European continent), moreover, has increasingly tied the fate of general insurance companies to their life insurance counterparts. These observations make clear that much remains to be done in assessing how the institutionalization of modern finance theory through risk-based capital regulation and financial risk management enables and constrains particular ways of organizing economic and financial uncertainty in the various domains covered by insurance other than life insurance.

Looking ahead, the societal importance of private insurance is unlikely to subside, and these issues may become more important going into the future. On the one hand, changes in labour markets and ongoing welfare state retrenchment creates increased demand for private (non-profit) vehicles for organizing financial and economic uncertainty, raising important questions about access, risk sharing, the distribution of profits and risks, and the management of financial uncertainty more generally (van Leeuwen, 2016; Vriens et al, 2019). On the other hand, increased economic losses associated with climate change, cyber criminality and pandemics raise important distributional questions about who should carry the burden of these costs and what the role of private insurance should be therein (see Elliott, 2021). The question that remains here is whether the model of for-profit private insurance operating on the principles of financial risk management will provide the most equitable solution for organizing forms of uncertainty that are extremely difficult to calculate or whether we need alternative organizational forms to organize uncertainty, ones that do not seek to deal with financial uncertainty by dealing in uncertainty but by managing this uncertainty through solidaristic risk·sharing arrangements.

Notes

Chapter 1

[1] The figures on insurance spending are taken from the OECD. The figures on insurers' assets are taken from the Office for National Statistics.

[2] The figures are derived from the following sources: Wilkie (1996) and the Institute and Faculty of Actuaries (2017).

[3] Bretton Woods system. A system of monetary management agreed upon at an international conference held in Bretton Woods in 1944. This system revolved around the convertibility of dollars to gold at a rate of $35 to 1 ounce of gold. It came to an end in 1971, when the US terminated the convertibility of the dollar.

Chapter 2

[1] Though, as Baker (2021) rightly notes, insurers can never eliminate diversifiable forms of uncertainty entirely, and in some cases they can eliminate such forms of uncertainty hardly at all.

Chapter 4

[1] Actuaries used different valuation bases for different purposes. The basis used to determine premiums for non-profit business, for instance, was typically more 'prudent' than the one used for with-profits business.

[2] When using a 'best estimate' for the likelihood of certain cash flows arising, one expects that in half the cases the premium income would suffice to cover the outgoing claims. When using a 'prudent basis', however, the perceived likelihood of income exceeding outgo increases, leading in most cases to the emergence of additional surplus that could then be distributed across with-profits policyholders.

[3] Apart from some 'internalist' histories, little is known about the sociological conditions in which risk theory emerged. Considering its later influence on insurance practice, this is a topic that merits further investigation.

[4] In economic terms, maintaining such large reserves is considered to carry an 'opportunity cost'. The firm's owners could have used that capital differently, perhaps getting a better return on capital than when total capital investments for unit-linked business are considered. The amount of capital needed to finance particular lines of business is thus an important aspect of considering the commercial viability of such activities.

[5] This was possible because Wilkie had included data from the rather volatile 1971–5 period, which implied a significantly higher standard deviation.

[6] The working party was chaired by Hambro Life's Alan Ford, and further included Ford's colleague Phil Smith; David Hager, who was a colleague of Benjamin from Bacon & Woodrow; David Loades, who was a delegate from the Government's Actuary Department; and three others.

[7] British actuaries might have also encountered risk theory in an international context: the International Actuarial Assocation founded a group focused on general insurance (ASTIN) in the 1950s. In its journal, the *ASTIN Bulletin*, and its meetings risk theory was frequently discussed.

Chapter 5

[1] The stochastic models discussed in Chapter 4 did allow for such valuations but, as I noted in that chapter, the uptake of those models seems to have been limited to a relatively small number of insurers.

[2] This percentage is measured by the reported value of the underlying liabilities. In other words, £35bn of £304bn insurers' total liabilities contained guaranteed annuity options.

Chapter 6

[1] In fact, Black and Scholes had derived their famous Black–Scholes equation from the capital asset pricing model central in modern portfolio theory. It was Robert Merton's paper that provided the no-arbitrage arguments that would later become so influential. Hence, the model is often also referred to as the Black–Scholes–Merton model (see MacKenzie, 2006, pp 135–6).

[2] In contrast to an American option, which can be exercised at any point in time, a European option can only be exercised at maturity. This makes the analysis of a European option relatively simple compared to that of an American option.

[3] Martingale. A random process in which all expected future values of a variable are equal to the variable's present value, given all available present information and regardless of past values.

[4] The possibility of drawing an analogy between insurance guarantees and financial options was remarked on in other places too. When, for instance, Myron Scholes and Robert Merton were awarded the Nobel Prize in 1997 (Black had died by that point), the press release contained the following comment: 'A similar method [as the Black–Scholes–Merton model] may be used to value insurance contracts and guarantees. … A guarantee gives the right, but not the obligation, to exploit it under certain circumstances. Anyone who buys or is given a guarantee thus holds a kind of option. The same is true of an insurance contract. The method developed by this year's laureates can therefore be used to value guarantees and insurance contracts. One can thus view insurance companies and the option market as competitors' (The Royal Swedish Academy of Sciences, 1997).

[5] This is how Phelim Boyle, who was well respected in both the British actuarial profession and among financial economists, recounts this episode: 'After a short stint in Liverpool with a firm of consulting actuaries, I moved in 1973 to the University of British Columbia in Canada. The Dean, Philip White, was building a finance department and had recently hired Michael Brennan and Bob White from MIT, both of whom had learned about modern option pricing theory from Scholes and Merton. I recall giving an early seminar to the finance group and mentioning the problem of the maturity guarantees. Michael excitedly pointed out that this contract was a put option and that it could be priced and also hedged using the Black Scholes Merton technology. We wrote a few papers on how maturity guarantees could be handled in an option framework. This approach was treated with some healthy actuarial scepticism by the Maturity Guarantees Working Party' (Boyle, 2005, p 592).

[6] A survey held by KPMG in 2013 indicated that two thirds of the respondents used Barrie Hibbert's economic scenario generator.

[7]   Of course, as scholars in science studies have shown, scientific activity can seem as ad hoc (for example Latour and Woolgar, 1986). The point is, however, that most practitioners perceive the methods of modern finance theory as a coherent theory, more so than traditional actuarial science.

[8]   Redington's immunization theory, moreover, only applied to interest rate risk. It did therefore not seem to have shaped actuarial thought on the risks that come, for instance, with equity and real estate investment in any direct way.

[9]   Similarly, Prudential, the only UK firm that succeeded in building an in-house scenario generator, hired not only actuaries, but also people with a strong "programming and quantitative background", and "a number of CFAs [chartered financial analysts]" (Jakhria interview).

Chapter 7

[1]   As Cairns noted, however, "there were limits to how far you could go with that analogy" (Cairns interview). Nevertheless, the interest rate analogy provided the starting point for his own longevity modelling work.

Chapter 8

[1]   Although the directives were very similar, there was a six-year gap between their adoption. The main reason for this is that the thorny question of specialization (whether insurers should be able to sell both life and non-life insurance or whether they should specialize in one or the other) was left to be settled in the first life directive (Pool, 1990, p 33).

[2]   Initially, in 2004 there were separate groups for non-life and life insurers. Sharma first chaired the non-life group; the life group was chaired by Björn Palmgren from Sweden. In 2005, however, the two groups merged.

[3]   For a more detailed elaboration of this concept, see Van der Heide (2022).

[4]   Wilson in Treasury Committee, Oral evidence: EU Insurance Regulation, HC 852 (25 January 2017).

[5]   Woods in Treasury Committee, Oral evidence: EU Insurance Regulation, HC 852 (22 February 2017).

[6]   Woods in Treasury Committee, Oral evidence: EU Insurance Regulation, HC 852 (22 February 2017).

References

Aalbers, M.B. (2016) *The Financialization of Housing: A Political Economy Approach*. London: Routledge.

Abbott, A. (1995) 'Sequence Analysis: New Methods for Old Ideas', *Annual Review of Sociology*, 21(1): 93–113. doi: 10.1146/annurev.so.21.080195.000521

Abbott, A. (2005) 'Ecologies and Fields'. Available at: http://home.uchicago.edu/~aabbott/Papers/BOURD.pdf

Abbott, A.D. (1988) *The System of Professions: An Essay on the Division of Expert Labor*. Chicago: University of Chicago Press.

Abbott, A.D. (2005) 'Linked Ecologies: States and Universities as Environments for Professions', *Sociological Theory*, 23(3): 245–74.

Adams, T.L. (2015) 'Sociology of Professions: International Divergences and Research Directions', *Work, Employment and Society*, 29(1): 154–65. doi: 10.1177/0950017014523467

Alborn, T.L. (1994) 'A Calculating Profession: Victorian Actuaries among the Statisticians', *Science in Context*, 7(3): 433–68. doi: 10.1017/S0269889700001770

Alborn, T.L. (2002a) 'The First Fund Managers: Life Insurance Bonuses in Victorian Britain', *Victorian Studies*, 45(1): 65–92.

Alborn, T.L. (2002b) 'The Thrift Wars: Savings Banks and Life Assurance in Victorian Britain'. Unpublished manuscript, International Economic History Society conference, Buenos Aires.

Alborn, T.L. (2009) *Regulated Lives: Life Insurance and British Society, 1800–1914*. Toronto: University of Toronto Press.

Almezweq, M. (2015) 'How Does the Life Insurance Business Perform and Behave: The Case of the UK Industry'. PhD Thesis, Brunel University.

Anon (1974) 'The Men Who Decide What Your Life Assurance Is Worth Should Wise Up', *The Economist*, July, p 86.

Arjaliès, D., Grant, P., Hardie, I., MacKenzie, D. and Svetlova, E. (2017) *Chains of Finance: How Investment Management Is Shaped*. Oxford: Oxford University Press. doi: 10.1093/oso/9780198802945.001.0001

Arrighi, G. (1994) *The Long Twentieth Century: Money, Power, and the Origins of Our Times*. London: Verso.

Association of British Insurers (2018) 'UK Insurance and Long-Term Savings: The State of the Market'. London: Association of British Insurers. Available at: https://www.abi.org.uk/globalassets/files/publications/public/data/abi_bro4467_state_of_market_v10.pdf

Bachelor, L. (2001) 'Scottish Provident Members Vote for Demutualisation', *The Guardian*, 14 June.

Baker, T. (1996) 'On the Genealogy of Moral Hazard', *Texas Law Review*, 75(2): 237–92.

Baker, T. (2003) 'Containing the Promise of Insurance: Adverse Selection and Risk Classification', in R.V. Ericson and A. Doyle (eds) *Risk and Morality*. Toronto: University of Toronto Press, pp 258–83.

Baker, T. (2021) 'Uncertainty > Risk: Lessons for Legal Thought from the Insurance Runoff Market', Faculty Scholarship at Penn Law. Available at: https://scholarship.law.upenn.edu/faculty_scholarship/2141

Baker, T. and Simon, J. (eds) (2002) *Embracing Risk: The Changing Culture of Insurance and Responsibility*. Chicago: University of Chicago Press.

Bandel, C. (2007) 'Pensions Corporation Buys Out Telent Shell', Investment & Pensions Europe. Available at: https://www.ipe.com/news/pensions-corporation-buys-out-telent-shell/25451.article

Barnes, B. (1982) *T.S. Kuhn and Social Science*. London: MacMillan.

Barnes, B., Bloor, D. and Henry, J. (1995) *Scientific Knowledge: A Sociological Analysis*. Chicago: Chicago University Press.

Bartlett, D., Chaplin, M., Dowd, K., Kelliher, P., and O'Brien, C. (2005) *Risk Management by UK Life Assurers: A Survey*. London: Institute and Faculty of Actuaries..

Baud, C. and Chiapello, E. (2017) 'Understanding the Disciplinary Aspects of Neoliberal Regulations: The Case of Credit-Risk Regulation under the Basel Accords', *Critical Perspectives on Accounting*, 46: 3–23. doi: 10.1016/j.cpa.2016.09.005

Beckert, J. (2009) 'How Do Fields Change? The Interrelations of Institutions, Networks, and Cognition in the Dynamics of Markets', *Organization Studies*, 31(5): 605–27. doi: 10.1177/0170840610372184

Beckert, J. (2016) *Imagined Futures: Fictional Expectations and Capitalist Dynamics*. Cambridge, MA: Harvard University Press.

Benjamin, S. (1963) 'Computers and Actuarial Science', *Journal of the Institute of Actuaries Students Society*, 17(2): 93–153.

Benjamin, S. (1964, May 25) 'Toys for Magnates', *The Times*, viii.

Benjamin, S. (1966) 'Putting Computers on to Actuarial Work', *Journal of the Institute of Actuaries*, 92(2): 134–92.

Benjamin, S. (1971) 'A Study of Maturity Guarantees under Equity-Linked Policies'. Typescript, In Institute and Faculty of Actuaries Library.

Benjamin, S. (1976) 'Maturity Guarantees for Equity-Linked Policies', in *Transactions of the 20th International Congress of Actuaries in Tokyo*. Tokyo: DAI Nippon, pp 17–28.

Benjamin, S., Ford, A., Gillespie, R.G., Hager, D.P., Loades, D.H. and Rowe, B.N. et al (1980) 'Report of the Maturity Guarantees Working Party', *Transactions of the Faculty of Actuaries*, 37: 213–36.

Bennet, I.R., Barclay, K.J., Blakeley, A.G., Crayton, F.A., Darvell, J.N. and Gilmour, I. et al (1984) 'Life Assurance in Four European Countries', *Transactions of the Faculty of Actuaries*, 39: 170–250.

Benoît, C. (2021) 'Solvency II, the European Government of Insurance Industry and Private Health Insurance', in C. Benoît, M. Del Sol and P. Martin (eds) *Private Health Insurance and the European Union*. Cham: Springer International Publishing, pp 55–82. doi: 10.1007/978-3-030-54355-6_3

Benz, N. (1960) 'Some Notes on Bonus Distributions By Life Offices', *Journal of the Institute of Actuaries*, 86(1): 1–29.

Berland, N. and Chiapello, E. (2009) 'Criticisms of Capitalism, Budgeting and the Double Enrolment: Budgetary Control Rhetoric and Social Reform in France in the 1930s and 1950s', *Accounting, Organizations and Society*, 34(1): 28–57. doi: 10.1016/j.aos.2008.04.004

Besedovsky, N. (2018) 'Financialization as Calculative Practice: The Rise of Structured Finance and the Cultural and Calculative Transformation of Credit Rating Agencies', *Socio-Economic Review*, 16(1): 61–84.

Beunza, D. (2019) *Taking the Floor: Models, Morals, and Management in a Wall Street Trading Room*. Princeton: Princeton University Press.

Beunza, D. and Stark, D. (2004) 'Tools of the Trade: The Socio-Technology of Arbitrage in a Wall Street Trading Room', *Industrial and Corporate Change*, 13(2): 369–400. doi: 10.1093/icc/dth015

Beunza, D. and Stark, D. (2012) 'From Dissonance to Resonance: Cognitive Interdependence in Quantitative Finance', *Economy and Society*, 41(3): 383–417. doi: 10.1080/03085147.2011.638155

Birch, K. and Muniesa, F. (eds) (2020) *Assetization: Turning Things into Assets in Technoscientific Capitalism*. Cambridge, MA: MIT Press. doi: 10.7551/mitpress/12075.001.0001

Black, J. (2008) 'Forms and Paradoxes of Principles-Based Regulation', *Capital Markets Law Journal*, 3(4): 425–57. doi: 10.1093/cmlj/kmn026

Black, J. and Nobles, R. (1998) 'Personal Pensions Misselling: The Causes and Lessons of Regulatory Failure', *The Modern Law Review*, 61(6): 789–820. doi: 10.1111/1468-2230.00179

Black, J., Hopper, M. and Band, C. (2007) 'Making a Success of Principles-Based Regulation', *Law and Financial Markets Review*, 1(3): 191–206. doi: 10.1080/17521440.2007.11427879

Blake, D., Cairns, A., Coughlan, G., Dowd, K. and MacMinn, R. (2013) 'The New Life Market', *Journal of Risk and Insurance*, 80(3): 501–58. doi: 10.1111/j.1539-6975.2012.01514.x

Blake, D., Cairns, A.J.G. and Dowd, K. (2019) 'Still Living with Mortality: The Longevity Risk Transfer Market after One Decade', *British Actuarial Journal*, 24(1): 1–80.

Bloor, D. (1991) *Knowledge and Social Imagery*. Chicago: University of Chicago Press.

Boldyrev, I. and Svetlova, E. (2016) 'After the Turn: How the Performativity of Economics Matters', in I. Boldyrev and E. Svetlova (eds) *Enacting Dismal Science: Naturalism, Critique, and Performativity*. London: Palgrave Macmillan, pp 1–27.

Bolton, M.J., Carr, D.H., Collis, P.A., George, C.M., Knowles, V.P. and Whitehouse, A.J. (1997) 'Reserving for Annuity Guarantees: Report of the Annuity Guarantees Working Party', November. Available at: www. actuaries.org.uk/documents/reserving-annuity-guarantees

Booth, P.M. (2007) '"Freedom with Publicity": The Actuarial Profession and United Kingdom Insurance Regulation from 1844 to 1945', *Annals of Actuarial Science*, 2(1): 115–45. doi: 10.1017/S1748499500000282

Bouk, D. (2015) *How Our Days Became Numbered: Risk and the Rise of the Statistical Individual*. Chicago: Chicago University Press.

Bourdieu, P. (1997) 'Le champ économique', *Actes de la recherche en sciences sociales*, 119: 48–66.

Bourdieu, P. (2005) *The Social Structures of the Economy*. Cambridge: Polity Press.

Boy, N. (2014) 'The Backstory of the Risk-Free Asset: How Government Debt Became "Safe"', in C. Goodhart, D. Gabor, J. Vestergaard and I. Ertürk (eds) *Central Banking at a Crossroads*. London: Anthem Press, pp 177–87.

Boyle, P.P. (2005) 'Guest Editorial: Lost in Translation', *British Actuarial Journal*, 11(4): 591–4.

Boyle, P.P. and Schwartz, E.S. (1977) 'Equilibrium Prices of Guarantees under Equity-Linked Contracts', *The Journal of Risk and Insurance*, 44(4): 639–60.

Braun, B. (2016) 'From Performativity to Political Economy: Index Investing, ETFs and Asset Manager Capitalism', *New Political Economy*, 21(3): 257–73. doi: 10.1080/13563467.2016.1094045

Brennan, M.J. and Schwartz, E.S. (1976) 'The Pricing of Equity-Linked Life Insurance Policies with an Asset Value Guarantee', *Journal of Financial Economics*, 3(3): 195–213. doi: 10.1016/0304-405X(76)90003-9

Bridgen, P. and Meyer, T. (2009) 'The Politics of Occupational Pension Reform in Britain and the Netherlands: The Power of Market Discipline in Liberal and Corporatist Regimes', *West European Politics*, 32(3): 586–610. doi: 10.1080/01402380902779105

Brine, K.R. and Poovey, M. (2017) *Finance in America*. Chicago: University of Chicago Press.

Brown, M. (2004) 'EIB, PartnerRe, and BNP Paribas Create First Longevity Hedge', *Euromoney*, December, p 32.

Bruce, D.H. (2006) 'ICAS: The Challenge Ahead', *The Actuary*, April, pp 28–9.

Bryer, R.A. (2000) 'The History of Accounting and the Transition to Capitalism in England: Part One; Theory', *Accounting, Organizations and Society*, 25(2): 131–62. doi: 10.1016/S0361-3682(99)00032-X

Burt, R.S. (1992) *Structural Holes: The Social Structure of Competition*. Cambridge, MA: Harvard University Press.

Burt, R.S. (2007) *Brokerage and Closure: An Introduction to Social Capital*. Oxford: Oxford University Press.

Cairns, A., Blake, D. and Dowd, K. (2004) 'Pricing Frameworks for Securitization of Mortality Risk', in *14th Annual International Colloquium, Boston, November 8–9, 2004*. Boston: np, pp 509–40.

Çalışkan, K. and Callon, M. (2009) 'Economization, Part 1: Shifting Attention from the Economy towards Processes of Economization', *Economy and Society*, 38(3): 369–98. doi: 10.1080/03085140903020580

Çalışkan, K. and Callon, M. (2010) 'Economization, Part 2: A Research Programme for the Study of Markets', *Economy and Society*, 39(1): 1–32. doi: 10.1080/03085140903424519

Callon, M. (1998a) 'An Essay on Framing and Overflowing: Economic Externalities Revisited by Sociology', *The Sociological Review*, 46(1_ suppl): 244–69. doi: 10.1111/j.1467-954X.1998.tb03477.x

Callon, M. (1998b) 'Introduction: The Embeddedness of Economic Markets in Economics', in M. Callon (ed) *The Laws of the Markets*. Oxford: Blackwell, pp 1–57.

Callon, M. (2007) 'What Does It Mean to Say that Economics is Performative?', in D.A. MacKenzie, F. Muniesa and L. Siu (eds) *Do Economists Make Markets? On the Performativity of Economics*. Princeton: Princeton University Press, pp 311–57.

Carroll, P.M. (1975) 'The Net Premium Method of Valuation', *Journal of the Institute of Actuaries Students Society*, 21(2): 121–38.

Carruthers, B.G. (2015) 'Financialization and the Institutional Foundations of the New Capitalism', *Socio-Economic Review*, 13(2): 379–98. doi: 10.1093/ser/mwv008

Carruthers, B.G. and Espeland, W.N. (1991) 'Accounting for Rationality: Double-Entry Bookkeeping and the Rhetoric of Economic Rationality', *American Journal of Sociology*, 97(1): 31–69.

Carter, R.L. and Falush, P. (2009) *The British Insurance Industry since 1900*. Basingstoke: Palgrave Macmillan.

Cevolini, A. and Esposito, E. (2020) 'From Pool to Profile: Social Consequences of Algorithmic Prediction in Insurance', *Big Data & Society*, 7(2): 2053951720939228. doi: 10.1177/2053951720939228

Chiapello, E. (2015) 'Financialisation of Valuation', *Human Studies*, 38(1): 13–35. doi: 10.1007/s10746-014-9337-x

Chiapello, E. (2016) 'How IFRS Contribute to the Financialization of Capitalism', in D. Bensadon and N. Praquin (eds) *IFRS in a Global World*. Cham: Springer, pp 71–84.

Chiapello, E. and Walter, C. (2016) 'The Three Ages of Financial Quantification: A Conventionalist Approach to the Financiers' Metrology', *Historical Social Research*, 41(2): 155–77. doi: 10.12759/hsr.41.2016.2.155-177

Christophers, B. (2015) 'Value Models: Finance, Risk, and Political Economy', *Finance & Society*, 1(2): 1–22.

Clark, G.W. (1999) *Betting on Lives: The Culture of Life Insurance in England, 1695–1775.* Manchester: Manchester University Press.

Clarkson, R.S. (1996) 'Financial Economics: An Investment Actuary's Viewpoint', *British Actuarial Journal*, 2(4): 809–973.

Clarkson, R.S. (1997) 'An Actuarial Theory of Option Pricing', *British Actuarial Journal*, 3(2): 321–409.

CMI (2002) 'An Interim Basis for Adjusting the "92" Series Mortality Projections for Cohort Effects'. CMI Working Paper 1. Available at: www.actuaries.org.uk/learn-and-develop/continuous-mortality-investigation/cmi-working-papers/mortality-projections/cmi-wp-1

Coates, J. and Lynam, E. (2005) 'Change in the Balance of Power for UK Pensions', *Pensions: An International Journal*, 10(4): 308–16. doi: 10.1057/palgrave.pm.5940310

Cohen, N. (2008) 'Pension Funds Face a Shortfall of Billions', *Financial Times*, 14 February.

Collier, S.J. (2008) 'Enacting Catastrophe: Preparedness, Insurance, Budgetary Rationalization', *Economy and Society*, 37(2): 224–50. doi: 10.1080/03085140801933280

Collins, D., Dewing, I. and Russell, P. (2009) 'The Actuary as Fallen Hero: On the Reform of a Profession', *Work, Employment & Society*, 23(2): 249–66. doi: 10.1177/0950017009102857

Collins, T.P. (1982) 'An Exploration of the Immunization Approach to Provision for Unit-Linked Policies with Guarantees', *Journal of the Institute of Actuaries*, 109(2): 241–84.

Conference of Insurance Supervisory Services of the Member States of the European Union (2002) 'Prudential Supervision of Insurance Undertakings'. Available at: https://web.archive.org/web/20220816052016/https://www.knf.gov.pl/knf/pl/komponenty/img/Prudential_supervision_of_insurance_undertakings_18431.pdf

Coombs, N. and Van der Heide, A. (2020) 'The Calculative and Regulatory Consequences of Risk Management', in P. Mader, D. Mertens and N. van der Zwan (eds) *Routledge International Handbook of Financialization*. Abingdon: Routledge, pp 358–68.

Corby, F.B. (1977) 'Reserves for Maturity Guarantees under Unit-Linked Policies', *Journal of the Institute of Actuaries*, 104(3): 259–96.

Corley, R. (2001) 'Report of the Corley Committee of Inquiry Regarding the Equitable Life Assurance Society'. London/Edinburgh. Available at: http://www.cookham.com/community/equitable/pdfs/CorleyRepor tonEquitableLife_200109.pdf

Coughlan, G., Epstein, D., Sinha, A., and Honig, P. (2007) 'q-Forwards: Derivatives for Transferring Longevity and Mortality Risks'. JP Morgan white paper.

Daston, L. (1988) *Classical Probability in the Enlightenment*. Princeton, NJ: Princeton University Press.

Davies, H. (2002) 'Life Insurance: A More Realistic Approach'. Speech, McKinsey's annual insurance ceo's roundtablerome.

Davies, P.J. (2009) 'Truell Deal Over Telent Scheme', *Financial Times*, November 25, 2009. Available at: https://www.ft.com/content/5ebc0 1da-d931-11de-b2d5-00144feabdc0

Davies, P.J. (2011) 'Insurers wary of new capital regime', *Financial Times*, March 14.

Davis, A. and Etheridge, M. (2006) *Louis Bachelier's Theory of Speculation: The Origins of Modern Finance (M. Davis & A. Etheridge, Trans.)*. Princeton: Princeton University Press.

Day, J.G. (1966) 'Some Reflections on the Actuarial Contribution to Investment Thought', *Journal of the Institute of Actuaries*, 92(3): 253–95.

Daykin, C.D. (1992) 'The Developing Role of the Government Actuary's Department in the Supervision of Insurance', *Journal of the Institute of Actuaries*, 119(2): 313–43.

Daykin, C.D. (1999) 'The Regulatory Role of the Actuary', *British Actuarial Journal*, 5(3): 529–74.

de Goede, M. (2005a) 'Resocialising and Repoliticising Financial Markets: Contours of Social Studies of Finance', *Economic Sociology: European Electronic Newsletter*, 6(3): 19–28.

de Goede, M. (2005b) *Virtue, Fortune, and Faith: A Genealogy of Finance*. Minneapolis, MN: University of Minnesota Press.

Deeg, R. and Hardie, I. (2016) 'What Is Patient Capital and Who Supplies It?', *Socio-Economic Review*, 14(4): 627–45. doi: 10.1093/ser/mww025

Deighton, S.P., Dix, R.C., Graham, J.R. and Skinner, J.M.E. (2009) 'Governance and Risk Management in United Kingdom Insurance Companies', *British Actuarial Journal*, 15(3): 503–72.

Dennett, L. (2004) *Mind over Data: An Actuarial History*. Cambridge: Granta Editions.

Deringer, W. (2017) 'Pricing the Future in the Seventeenth Century: Calculating Technologies in Competition', *Technology and Culture*, 58(2): 506–28.

Derrick, V.P.A. (1927) 'Observations on (1) Errors of Age in the Population Statistics of England and Wales, and (2) the Changes in Mortality Indicated by the National Records', *Journal of the Institute of Actuaries*, 58(2): 117–59.

DiMaggio, P.J. and Powell, W.W. (1983) 'The Iron Cage Revisited: Institutional Isomorphism and Collective Rationality in Organizational Fields', *American Sociological Review*, 48(2): 147–60.

Dionne, G. (2013) 'Risk Management: History, Definition, and Critique', *Risk Management and Insurance Review*, 16(2): 147–66. doi: 10.1111/rmir.12016

Dodds, J.C. (1979) *The Investment Behaviour of British Life Insurance Companies*. London: Croom Helm.

Dowd, K. and Blake, D. (2006) 'After VaR: The Theory, Estimation, and Insurance Applications of Quantile-Based Risk Measures', *The Journal of Risk and Insurance*, 73(2): 193–229.

Dowd, K., Bartlett, D.L., Chaplin, M., Kelliher, P. and O'Brien, C. (2008) 'Risk Management in the UK Insurance Industry: The Changing State of Practice'. CRIS Discussion Paper Series. doi: 10.1504/IJFSM.2008.016696

Drehmann, M., Borio, C. and Tsatsaronis, K. (2012) 'Characterising the Financial Cycle: Don't Lose Sight of the Medium Term!' Available at: https://www.bis.org/publ/work380.htm.

Dumbreck, N. and Sanders, A. (1993) 'Demutualisation: A Growing Trend?', *The Actuary*, October, pp 30–1.

Dyson, A.C.L. and Exley, C.J. (1995) 'Pension Fund Asset Valuation and Investment', *British Actuarial Journal*, 1(3): 471–557.

Eastwood, A.M., Ledlie, M.C., Macdonald, A.S. and Pike, D.M. (1994) 'With Profits Maturity Payouts, Asset Shares and Smoothing', *Transactions of the Faculty of Actuaries*, 44: 497–575.

The Economist (1957) 'The Unicorn in Town', *The Economist*: 437.

The Economist (1958) 'Pensions and Inflation', *The Economist*: 789.

The Economist (1969) 'Life Offices Must Define Their Objectives', *The Economist*, pp 11–14.

EIOPA (2016) 'Consultation Paper on the Methodology to Derive the UFR and Its Implementation'. EIOPA-CP-16/03. Available at: https://www.eiopa.europa.eu/document-library/consultation/methodology-derive-ufr-and-its-implementation_en

Elliott, R. (2021) *Underwater: Loss, Flood Insurance, and the Moral Economy of Climate Change in the United States*. New York: Columbia University Press.

Ellis, D., Ward, A., Stone, B. and Rajagopalan, S. (2020) *The Impact of Pension Risk Transfer on the Share Prices of UK Sponsoring Employers*. Mercer.

Ericson, R.V., Doyle, A. and Barry, D. (2003) *Insurance as Governance*. Toronto: University of Toronto Press.

Ericson, R.V. and Doyle, A. (2004) *Uncertain Business: Risk, Insurance, and the Limits of Knowledge*. Toronto: University of Toronto Press.

Erturk, I. (2020) 'Shareholder Primacy and Corporate Financialization', in P. Mader, D. Mertens and N. van der Zwan (eds) *The Routledge International Handbook of Financialization*. Abingdon: Routledge, pp 43–55.

Espeli, H. (2020) 'Insurance Cartels and State Policies in Norway, 1870s– 1990s', *Scandinavian Economic History Review*, 68(3): 222–38. doi: 10.1080/ 03585522.2019.1703802

Ewald, F. (1991) 'Insurance and Risk', in G. Burchill, C. Gordon and P. Miller (eds) *The Foucault Effect: Studies in Governmentality*. London: Harvester Wheatsheaf, pp 197–210.

Exley, C.J., Mehta, S.J.B. and Smith, A.D. (1997) 'The Financial Theory of Defined Benefit Pension Schemes', *British Actuarial Journal*, 3(4): 835–966.

Exley, C.J., (2002) 'The Trouble with FRS17', *The Actuary*, April, pp 30–1.

Exley, C.J., Mehta, S.J.B. and Smith, D.A. (2000) 'The Trend towards Using Market Values', *The Actuary*, pp 34–5.

Eyal, G. (2013) 'For a Sociology of Expertise: The Social Origins of the Autism Epidemic', *American Journal of Sociology*, 118(4): 863–907. doi: 10.1086/668448

Fagan, J. (1977) 'Maturity Guarantees under Investment-Linked Contracts'. Typescript. In Institute and Faculty of Actuaries Library.

Fama, E.F. (1965) 'The Behavior of Stock-Market Prices', *The Journal of Business*, 38(1): 34–105.

Fama, E.F. (1970) 'Efficient Capital Markets: A Review of Theory and Empirical Work', *The Journal of Finance*, 25(2): 28–30. doi: 10.2307/ 2325486

Feenberg, A. (1999) *Questioning Technology*. London: Routledge.

Field, M.H. (1987) 'Address', *Journal of the Institute of Actuaries*, 114(1): 1–14.

Field, M.H., Needleman, P.D., Smith, W.W.C and Shedden, A.D. (1991) 'Demutualisation: A Discussion', *Transactions of the Faculty of Actuaries*, 42: 277–90.

Fine, A.E.M., Headdon, C.P., Hewitson, T.W., Johnson, C.M., Lumsden, I.C. and Maple, M.H. et al (1988) 'Proposals for the Statutory Basis of Valuation of the Liabilities of Linked Long-Term Insurance Business', *Transactions of the Faculty of Actuaries*, 41: 369–443.

Finsinger, J. and Pauly, M.V. (eds) (1986) *The Economics of Insurance Regulation: A Cross-National Study*. Basingstoke: Palgrave Macmillan. doi: 10.1007/978-1-349-18397-5

Fligstein, N. (1990) *The Transformation of Corporate Control*. Cambridge, MA: Harvard University Press.

Fligstein, N. (1996) 'Markets as Politics: A Political-Cultural Approach to Market Institutions', *American Sociological Review*, 61(4): 656–73. doi: 10.2307/2096398

Fligstein, N. (2001) *The Architecture of Markets: An Economic Sociology of Twenty-First Century Capitalist Societies*. Princeton: Princeton University Press.

Fligstein, N. and McAdam, D. (2012) *A Theory of Fields*. New York: Oxford University Press.

Fligstein, N. and Shin, T. (2007) 'Shareholder Value and the Transformation of the U.S. Economy, 1984–2001', *Sociological Forum*, 22(4): 399–424. doi: https://doi.org/10.1111/j.1573-7861.2007.00044.x

Ford, A., Benjamin, S., Gillespie, R.G., Hager, D.P., Loades, D.H., Rowe, B.N., et al (1980) 'Report of the Maturity Guarantees Working Party', *Journal of the Institute of Actuaries*, 107(2): 103–231.

Ford, J. (2020) 'Pension Buyouts Carry Needless Credit Risks', *Financial Times*, 25 October. Available at: https://www.ft.com/content/89c312d0-5fa8-4453-8152-3291335f3508.

Fourcade, M. (2007). Theories of markets and theories of society. American behavioral scientist, 50(8), 1015-1034.

François, P. (2015) 'La fabrique sociale d'une tabula rasa: Le lancement de Solvency II'. Working Paper. Paris: Chaire PARI. Available at: https://www.chaire-pari.fr/wp-content/uploads/2015/11/Fran%C3%A7ois-_S2-Tabula-rasa.pdf

François, P. (2019) 'Le jour sans find d'Omnibus II'. Working Paper 16. Paris: Chaire PARI. Available at: https://hal-sciencespo.archives-ouvertes.fr/hal-02965555

François, P. (2021) *Financiariser l'assurance: Enquête sur Solvabilité II*. Paris: Presses de Sciences Po.

Franklin, P.J. and Woodhead, C. (1980) *The UK Life Assurance Industry*. London: Croom Helm.

FSA (2003) 'Enhanced Capital Requirements and Individual Capital Assessments for Life Insurers'. CP195. Available at: https://www.abi.org.uk/globalassets/sitecore/files/documents/consultation-papers/2003/11/cp190.pdf

FSA (2005) 'ICAS: One Year On'. Insurance Sector Briefing.

FSA (2009) 'The Turner Review: A Regulatory Response to the Global Banking Crisis'. Available at: http://www.actuaries.org/CTTEES_TFRISKCRISIS/Documents/turner_review.pdf

Funk, R.J. and Hirschman, D. (2014) 'Derivatives and Deregulation Financial Innovation and the Demise of Glass–Steagall', *Administrative Science Quarterly*, 59(4): 669–704. doi: 10.1177/0001839214554830

Fytros, C. (2021) 'The Aporetic Financialisation of Insurance Liabilities: Reserving under Solvency II', *Finance & Society*. Available at: http://financeandsociety.ed.ac.uk/ojs-images/financeandsociety/FS_Fytros_EarlyView.pdf

Garfield, A. (2000) 'Equitable Life Management "Blew 238 Years of History"', *The Independent*, 18 December, p 16.

Geoghegan, T.J., Clarkson, R.S., Feldman, K.S., Green, S.J., Kitts, A. and Lavecky, J.P. et al (1992) 'Report on the Wilkie Stochastic Investment Model', *Journal of the Institute of Actuaries*, 119(2): 173–228.

Glen, J. (2022) 'Speech by John Glen MP, Economic Secretary to the Treasury, to the Association of British Insurers Annual Dinner'. Available at: https://www.gov.uk/government/speeches/speech-by-john-glen-mp-economic-secretary-to-the-treasury-to-the-association-of-british-insurers-annual-dinner

Goodhart, C. (2011) *The Basel Committee on Banking Supervision: A History of the Early Years 1974–1997*. Cambridge: Cambridge University Press.

Granovetter, M. (1985) 'Economic Action and Social Structure: The Problem of Embeddedness', *American Journal of Sociology*, 91(3): 481–510.

Grant, A.T. and Kingsnorth, G.A. (1966) 'Unit Trusts and Equity Linked Endowment Assurances', *Transactions of the Faculty of Actuaries*, 30(225): 17–80.

Greenspan, A. (2003) 'Corporate Governance', speech given at the 2003 Conference on Bank Structure and Competition, May 8.

Gulledge, E., Roscoe, P. and Townley, B. (2015) 'Economizing Habitus', *Journal of Cultural Economy*, 8(6): 637–54. doi: 10.1080/17530350.2015.1047785

Gupta, A.K. and Westall, G. (1993) 'Distribution of Financial Services', *Journal of the Institute of Actuaries*, 120(1): 25–65.

Hacking, I. (1990) *The Taming of Chance*. Cambridge: Cambridge University Press.

Haldane, A., Goldin, I., Gupta, A., Bowie, R., Breeden, S. and Davies, P., et al (2014) 'Procyclicality and Structural Trends in Investment Allocation by Insurance Companies and Pension Funds'. Bank of England Discussion Paper. Available at: https://www.bankofengland.co.uk/-/media/boe/files/paper/2014/procyclicality-and-structural-trends-in-investment

Hall, W. (1982) 'Hambro Life and the Revolution', *Financial Times*, 25 September, p 7.

Hannah, L. (1986) *Inventing Retirement*. Cambridge: Cambridge University Press. doi: 10.1017/CBO9780511720611

Hardwick, P. (1997) 'Measuring Cost Inefficiency in the UK Life Insurance Industry', *Applied Financial Economics*, 7(1): 37–44. doi: 10.1080/096031097333835

Hare, D.J.P. (1989) *Immunization: A Match for Investment Managers.* Glasgow: Glasgow Actuarial Students' Society.

Hare, D. J. P., Dickson, J. A., McDade, P. A. P., Morrison, D., Priestley, R. P., & Wilson, G. J. (2000) 'A Market-Based Approach to Pricing With-Profits Guarantees', *British Actuarial Journal*, 6(1): 143–213.

Harrison, J.M. and Kreps, D.M. (1979) 'Martingales and Arbitrage in Multiperiod Securities Markets', *Journal of Economic Theory*, 20(3): 381–408. doi: 10.1016/0022-0531(79)90043-7

Harrison, J.M. and Pliska, S.R. (1981) 'Martingales and Stochastic Integrals in the Theory of Continuous Trading', *Stochastic Process and Their Applications*, 11: 215–60.

Hautcoeur, P.-C. (2004) 'Efficiency, Competition, and the Development of Life Insurance in France (1870–1939): Or: Should We Trust Pension Funds?', *Explorations in Economic History*, 41(3): 205–32. doi: 10.1016/j.eeh.2004.01.004

Head, S.J., Adkins, D.R., Cairns, A.J.G., Corvesor, A.J., Cule, D.O. and Exley, C.J. et al (2000) 'Pension Fund Valuations and Market Values', *British Actuarial Journal*, 6(1): 55–141.

Hibbert, B.A.J. and Turnbull, C.J. (2003) 'Measuring and Managing the Economic Risks and Costs of With-Profits Business', *British Actuarial Journal*, 9(4): 725–86.

HM Treasury (2016) 'Equitable Life Payment Scheme: Final Report'. London. Available at: https://www.gov.uk/government/publications/equitable-life-payment-scheme-final-report

Holton, G.A. (2002) 'History of Value-at-Risk: 1922–1998'. Available at: http://stat.wharton.upenn.edu/~steele/Courses/434/434Context/RiskManagement/VaRHistlory.pdf

Horan, C. (2021) *Insurance Era: Risk, Governance, and the Privatization of Security in Postwar America.* Chicago: University of Chicago Press.

House of Lords (2000) 'Judgments: Equitable Life Assurance Society v. Hyman'. 20 July.

Huault, I. and Rainelli-Le Montagner, H. (2009) 'Market Shaping as an Answer to Ambiguities: The Case of Credit Derivatives', *Organization Studies*, 30(5): 549–75. doi: 10.1177/0170840609106113

Huber, P.P. (1997) 'A Review of Wilkie's Stochastic Asset Model', *British Actuarial Journal*, 3(1): 181–210.

Hymans Robertson (2016) 'Risk Transfer Report'. Available at: https://www.hymans.co.uk/media/uploads/Risk_Transfer_Report_2016.pdf

Institute and Faculty of Actuaries (2017) 'Our Members: At a Glance 2016'. Institute and Faculty of Actuaries. Available at: https://www.actuaries.org.uk/system/files/field/document/Our%20Members%202016.pdf

Jakhria, P., Frankland, R., Sharp, S., Smith, A., Rowe, A. and Wilkins, T. (2019) 'Evolution of Economic Scenario Generators: A Report by the Extreme Events Working Party Members', *British Actuarial Journal*, 24(e4): 1–25.

Jarvis, S., Southall, F. and Varnell, E. (2001) 'Modern Valuation Techniques', *Staple Inn Actuarial Society*, 6. Available at: http://www.planchet.net/EXT/ISFA/1226.nsf/0/aa9471c5c0f22a12c1256cfc00272276/$FILE/mvt.pdf

Jarzabkowski, P., Bednarek, R. and Spee, P. (2015) *Making a Market for Acts of God: The Practice of Risk Trading in the Global Reinsurance Industry*. Oxford: Oxford University Press.

Jauho, M. (2015) 'The Mutual Shaping of Life Insurance and Medicine in Finland', *Social Studies of Science*, 45(4): 501–24. doi: 10.1177/0306312715599850

Jennings, K., Rowley, N., Diggins, D. and Roberts, P. (2014) 'Working Party Report: The Management of With-Profits Funds in Run-off'. Institute and Faculty of Actuaries.

Johnston, J. and Murphy, G. (1957) 'The Growth of Life Assurance in UK since 1880', *The Manchester School*, 25: 107–82.

Jones, G.L. (2003) 'A Longer Life', *The Actuary*, November, pp 34–5.

Jones, R. (1999) 'Widows Out of Mourning', *The Guardian*, November, p 14.

Kavanagh, B. (2003) 'A Retrospective Look at Market Risk', in P. Field (ed) *Modern Risk Management: A History*. London: Risk Books, pp 251–60.

Kay, J. (2015) *Other People's Money: Masters of the Universe or Servants of the People?* London: Profile Books.

Kemp, M.H.D. (1997) 'Actuaries and Derivatives', *British Actuarial Journal*, 3(1): 51–180.

Kemp, M.H.D. (2009) *Market Consistency: Model Calibration in Imperfect Markets*. Chichester, UK: Wiley.

Kindleberger, C.P. (2015) *Manias, Panics and Crashes: A History of Financial Crises*. London: Palgrave Macmillan.

Kingston, C. (2014) 'Governance and Institutional Change in Marine Insurance, 1350–1850', *European Review of Economic History*, 18(1): 1–18. doi: 10.1093/ereh/het019

Knights, D. and Vurdubakis, T. (1993) 'Calculations of Risk: Towards an Understanding of Insurance as a Moral and Political Technology', *Accounting, Organizations and Society*, 18(7–8): 729–64. doi: 10.1016/0361-3682(93)90050-G

KPMG (2002) 'Study into the Methodologies to Assess the Overall Financial Position of an Insurance Undertaking from the Perspective of Prudential Supervision'. Brussels: European Commission. Available at: https://www.knf.gov.pl/knf/pl/komponenty/img/Assessment_of_the_overall_financial_position_of_an_insuranc_18428.pdf

Krippner, G.R. (2005) 'The Financialization of the American Economy', *Socio-Economic Review*, 3(2): 173–208. doi: 10.1093/SER/mwi008

Langenohl, A. (2018) 'Sources of Financial Synchronism: Arbitrage Theory and the Promise of Risk-Free Profit', *Finance and Society*, 4(1): 26–40.

Langley, P. (2006) 'The Making of Investor Subjects in Anglo-American Pensions', *Environment and Planning D: Society and Space*, 24(6): 919–34. doi: 10.1068/d405t

Langley, P. (2008) *The Everyday Life of Global Finance Saving and Borrowing in Anglo-America.* Oxford: Oxford University Press.

Langley, P. and Leaver, A. (2012) 'Remaking Retirement Investors', *Journal of Cultural Economy*, 5(4): 473–88. doi: 10.1080/17530350.2012.691893

Larson, M.S. (1977) *The Rise of Professionalism: A Sociological Analysis.* Oakland, CA: University of California Press.

Larsson, M. and Lönnborg, M. (2015) 'Regulating Competition of the Swedish Insurance Business: The Role of the Insurance Cartel Registry', in S. Fellman and M. Shanahan (eds) *Regulating Competition: Cartel Registers in the Twentieth-Century World.* New York: Routledge, pp 248–67.

Latour, B. and Woolgar, S. (1986) *Laboratory Life: The Construction of Scientific Facts.* Princeton: Princeton University Press. doi: 10.1017/CBO9781107415324.004

Laux, C. and Leuz, C. (2009) 'The Crisis of Fair-Value Accounting: Making Sense of the Recent Debate', *Accounting, Organizations and Society*, 34(6–7): 826–34. doi: 10.1016/j.aos.2009.04.003

Lee, R.D. and Carter, L.R. (1992) 'Modeling and Forecasting U.S. Mortality', *Journal of American Statistical Association*, 87(419): 659–71. doi: 10.2307/2290201

Legal & General (2016) 'Rolls-Royce Buyout: Legal & General Completes Largest Pension Buyout of 2016 with £1.1 Billion Vickers Group Pension Scheme'. Available at: /media-centre/press-releases/

Lehtonen, T. and Van Hoyweghen, I. (2014) 'Insurance and the Economization of Uncertainty', *Journal of Cultural Economy*, 7(4): 532–40. doi: 10.1080/17530350.2013.875929

Lehtonen, T.-K. and Liukko, J. (2010) 'Justifications for Commodified Security: The Promotion of Private Life Insurance in Finland 1945–90', *Acta Sociologica*, 53(4): 371–86. doi: 10.1177/0001699310382674

Lehtonen, T.-K. and Liukko, J. (2015) 'Producing Solidarity, Inequality and Exclusion through Insurance', *Res Publica*, 21(2): 155–69. doi: 10.1007/s11158-015-9270-5

Leins, S. (2018) *Stories of Capitalism: Inside the Role of Financial Analysts.* Chicago: University of Chicago Press.

Leland, H. and Rubinstein, M. (1988) 'The Evolution of Portfolio Insurance', in D. Luskin (ed) *Dynamic Hedging: A Guide to Portfolio Insurance.* New York: John Wiley & Sons. Available at: https://www.researchgate.net/profile/Hayne-Leland-2/publication/265430746_The_Evolution_of_Portfolio_Insurance/links/568c160208ae197e42689833/The-Evolution-of-Portfolio-Insurance.pdf

Lengwiler, M. (2015) 'Competing Globalizations: Controversies between Private and Social Insurance at International Organizations, 1900–60', in R. Pearson (ed) *The Development of International Insurance*. London: Routledge, pp 167–86.

Lengwiler, M. (2016) 'Risky Calculations: Financial Mathematics and Securitization since the 1970s', *Historical Social Research/Historische Sozialforschung*, 41(2): 258–79.

Lever, C.D. (1992) 'Memoir: Sidney Benjamin', *Journal of the Institute of Actuaries*, 119(2): 383–4.

Levy, J. (2012) *Freaks of Fortune: The Emerging World of Capitalism and Risk in America*. Cambridge, MA: Harvard University Press.

Lewin, C.G., Evans, J.V., Goodare, K.J. and Packer, L.R. (1989) 'Calculating Devices and Actuarial Work', *Journal of the Institute of Actuaries*, 116(2): 215–87.

Lintner, J. (1965) 'Security Prices, Risk, and Maximal gains from Diversification', *The Journal of Finance*, 20(4): 587–615. doi: 10.1111/j.1540-6261.1965.tb02930.x

LiPuma, E. (2017) 'The Social Dimensions of Black Scholes'. Presented at: Chains of Value: How Intermediaries Evaluate Financial Instruments, 2017, May 4-5, University of Edinburgh.

List, T. (2011) 'Allianz-Vorstand wettert gegen Solvency II', *Börsen-Zeitung*, 17 November.

Liu, S. and Emirbayer, M. (2016) 'Field and Ecology', *Sociological Theory*, 34(1): 62–79. doi: 10.1177/0735275116632556

Lockwood, E. (2015) 'Predicting the Unpredictable: Value-at-Risk, Performativity, and the Politics of Financial Uncertainty', *Review of International Political Economy*, 22(4): 719–56.

Lockwood, E. (2020) 'From Bombs to Boons: Changing Views of Risk and Regulation in the Pre-Crisis OTC Derivatives Market', *Theory and Society*, 49(2): 215–44. doi: 10.1007/s11186-020-09386-1

Lowrey, W. and Sherrill, L. (2020) 'Fields and Ecologies: Meso-Level Spatial Approaches and the Study of Journalistic Change', *Communication Theory*, 30(3): 247–67. doi: 10.1093/ct/qtz003

Macdonald, K.M. (1995) *The Sociology of the Professions*. London: Sage.

MacKenzie, D.A. (1981) *Statistics in Britain, 1865–1930: The Social Construction of Scientific Knowledge*. Edinburgh: Edinburgh University Press.

MacKenzie, D.A. (2001) 'Physics and Finance: S-Terms and Modern Finance as a Topic for Science Studies', *Science, Technology, & Human Values*, 26(2): 115–44.

MacKenzie, D.A. (2003) 'Long-Term Capital Management and the Sociology of Arbitrage', *Economy and Society*, 32(3): 349–80. doi: 10.1080/03085140303130

MacKenzie, D.A. (2006) *An Engine, Not a Camera: How Financial Models Shape Markets*. Cambridge, MA: MIT Press.

MacKenzie, D.A. (2007) 'Is Economics Performative? Option Theory and the Construction of Derivatives Markets', in D.A. MacKenzie, F. Muniesa and L. Siu (eds) *Do Economists Make Markets? On the Performativity of Economics*. Princeton: Princeton University Press, pp 54–86.

MacKenzie, D.A. (2009) *Material Markets: How Economic Agents Are Constructed*. Oxford: Oxford University Press.

MacKenzie, D.A. (2011) 'The Credit Crisis as a Problem in the Sociology of Knowledge', *American Journal of Sociology*, 116(6): 1778–841. doi: 10.1086/659639

MacKenzie, D.A. (2019) 'Market Devices and Structural Dependency: The Origins and Development of "Dark Pools"', *Finance and Society*, 5(1): 1–19. doi: 10.2218/finsoc.v5i1.3015

MacKenzie, D.A. and Millo, Y. (2003) 'Constructing a Market, Performing Theory: The Historical Sociology of a Financial Derivatives Exchange', *American Journal of Sociology*, 109(1): 107–45.

MacKenzie, D.A. and Spears, T. (2014a) '"A Device for Being Able to Book P&L": The Organizational Embedding of the Gaussian Copula', *Social Studies of Science*, 44(3): 418–40. doi: 10.1177/0306312713517158

MacKenzie, D.A. and Spears, T. (2014b) '"The Formula That Killed Wall Street": The Gaussian Copula and Modelling Practices in Investment Banking', *Social Studies of Science*, 44(3): 393–417. doi: 10.1177/0306312713517157

Mader, P., Mertens, D. and van der Zwan, N. (eds) (2020) *The Routledge International Handbook of Financialization*. Abingdon: Routledge. doi: 10.4324/9781315142876

Markowitz, H. (1952) 'Portfolio Selection', *The Journal of Finance*, 7(1): 77–91. doi: 10.1111/j.1540-6261.1952.tb01525.x

Martin, R. (2002) *Financialization of Daily Life*. Philadelphia: Temple University Press.

Martin-Löf, A. (2014) 'Harald Cramér and Insurance Mathematics', in D. Silvestrov and A. Martin-Löf (eds) *Modern Problems in Insurance Mathematics*. Basel: Springer International Publishing, pp 7–15. doi: 10.1007/978-3-319-06653-0

McFall, L. (2009) 'The Agencement of Industrial Branch Life Assurance', *Journal of Cultural Economy*, 2(1–2): 49–65. doi: 10.1080/17530350903063933

McFall, L. (2011) 'A "Good, Average Man": Calculation and the Limits of Statistics in Enrolling Insurance Customers', *The Sociological Review*, 59(4): 661–84. doi: 10.1111/j.1467-954X.2011.02033.x

McFall, L. (2015) *Devising Consumption: Cultural Economies of Insurance, Credit and Spending*. Abingdon: Routledge.

McFall, L. (2019) 'Personalizing Solidarity? The Role of Self-Tracking in Health Insurance Pricing', *Economy and Society*, 48(1): 52–76. doi: 10.1080/03085147.2019.1570707

Mehta, S.J.B. (1992) 'Allowing for Asset, Liability and Business Risk in the Valuation of a Life Office', *Journal of the Institute of Actuaries*, 119: 385–455.

Melville, G.L. (1970) 'The Unit-Linked Approach to Life Insurance', *Journal of the Institute of Actuaries*, 96(3): 311–67.

Meyers, G. and Van Hoyweghen, I. (2018) 'Enacting Actuarial Fairness in Insurance: From Fair Discrimination to Behaviour-Based Fairness', *Science as Culture*, 27(4): 413–38. doi: 10.1080/09505431.2017.1398223

Mikes, A. (2011) 'From Counting Risk to Making Risk Count: Boundary-Work in Risk Management', *Accounting, Organizations and Society*, 36(4–5): 226–45. doi: 10.1016/j.aos.2011.03.002

Millo, Y. and MacKenzie, D.A. (2009) 'The Usefulness of Inaccurate Models: Towards an Understanding of the Emergence of Financial Risk Management', *Accounting, Organizations and Society*, 34(5): 638–53. doi: 10.1016/j.aos.2008.10.002

Modigliani, F. and Miller, M.H. (1958) 'The Cost of Capital, Corporation Finance and the Theory of Investment: Reply', *The American Economic Review*, 48(3): 261–97. Available at: http://www.jstor.org/stable/1809766

Morecroft, N.E. (2017) *The Origins of Asset Management From 1700 to 1960*. Cham: Palgrave Macmillan. doi: 10.1007/978-3-319-51850-3

Morris, S.D. (2005) 'Morris Review of the Actuarial Profession: Final Report'. London: HM Treasury.

Müller, J. (2014) 'An Accounting Revolution? The Financialisation of Standard Setting', *Critical Perspectives on Accounting*, 25(7): 539–57. doi: 10.1016/j.cpa.2013.08.006

Muniesa, F. (2014) *The Provoked Economy: Economic Reality and the Performative Turn*. London: Taylor & Francis.

Muniesa, F. and Callon, M. (2007) 'Economic Experiments and the Construction of Markets', in D. MacKenzie, F. Muniesa and L. Siu (eds) *Do Economists Make Markets? On the Performativity of Economics*. Princeton,: Princeton University Press, pp 163–89.

Needleman, P.D. and Westall, G. (1991) 'Demutualisation of a United Kingdom Mutual Life Insurance Company', *Transactions of the Faculty of Actuaries*, 43: 278–375.

Newman, A. and Posner, E. (2016) 'Transnational Feedback, Soft Law, and Preferences in Global Financial Regulation', *Review of International Political Economy*, 23(1): 123–52. doi: 10.1080/09692290.2015.1104375

Northedge, R. (2008) 'Paternoster Chief "Chopper" Carves Out His Success', *The Telegraph*, 16 February.

O'Brien, C.D. (2006) 'The Downfall of Equitable Life in the United Kingdom: The Mismatch of Strategy and Risk Management', *Risk Management and Insurance Review*, 9(2): 189–204. doi: 10.1111/j.1540-6296.2006.00093.x

O'Brien, C.D., Gallagher, G.A., Green, R.J., Hughes, D.W., Liang, F., Robinson, S.A. et al (2015) 'The Roles of Actuaries in UK Life Offices: Changes and Challenges'. Institute and Faculty of Actuaries, March. Available at: https://www.actuaries.org.uk/system/files/docume nts/pdf/role-actuaries-uk-life-offices-changes-and-challengesfinal.pdf

O'Malley, P. (2000) 'Uncertain Subjects: Risks, Liberalism and Contract', *Economy and Society*, 29(4): 460–84. doi: 10.1080/03085140050174741

O'Neill, J.E. and Froggatt, H.W. (1993) 'Unitised with Profits: Gamaliel's Advice', *Journal of the Institute of Actuaries*, 120(3): 415–69.

Ossandón, J. (2014) 'Reassembling and Cutting the Social with Health Insurance', *Journal of Cultural Economy*, 7(3): 291–307. doi: 10.1080/17530350.2013.869243

Overwijk, J. (2021) 'Paradoxes of Rationalisation: Openness and Control in Critical Theory and Luhmann's Systems Theory', *Theory, Culture & Society*, 38(1): 127–48. doi: 10.1177/0263276420925548

Paetzmann, K. (2011) 'Discontinued German Life Insurance Portfolios: Rules-in-Use, Interest Rate Risk, and Solvency II', *Journal of Financial Regulation and Compliance*, 19(2): 117–38. doi: 10.1108/13581981111123843

Penrose, G. (2004) 'Report of the Equitable Life Inquiry'. London. Available at: https://www.gov.uk/government/publications/report-of-the-equita ble-life-inquiry

Pensions Commission (2004) 'Pensions: Challenges and Choices'. London.

Pensions Commission (2005) 'A New Pension Settlement for the Twenty-First Century: The Second Report of the Pensions Commission'. London.

Pepper, G.T. and Thomas, R.L. (1973) 'Cyclical Changes in the Level of the Equity and Gilt-Edged Markets', *Journal of the Institute of Actuaries*, 99(3): 195–247.

Plackett, R.L. (1970) 'Risk Theory', *Transactions of the Faculty of Actuaries*, 32(237): 337–62.

Pool, B. (1990) 'The Creation of the Internal Market on Insurance'. Luxembourg: Office for Official Publications of the European Communities.

Porter, T.M. (1986) *The Rise of Statistical Thinking, 1820–1900*. Princeton: Princeton University Press.

Porter, T.M. (1995) *Trust in Numbers: The Pursuit of Objectivity in Science and Public Life*. Princeton: Princeton University Press.

Porter, T.M. (2000) 'Life Insurance, Medical Testing, and the Management of Mortality', in L. Daston (ed) *Biographies of Scientific Objects*. Chicago: University of Chicago Press, pp 226–46.

Power, M. (2005) 'Organizational Responses to Risk: The Rise of the Chief Risk Officer', in B. Hutter and M. Power (eds) *Organizational Encounters with Risk*. Cambridge: Cambridge University Press, pp 132–48.

Power, M. (2007) *Organized Uncertainty: Designing a World of Risk Management*. Oxford: Oxford University Press.

Power, M. (2012) 'Accounting and Finance', in K. Knorr Cetina and A. Preda (eds) *The Oxford Handbook of the Sociology of Finance*. Oxford: Oxford University Press, pp 293–314. doi: 10.1093/oxfordhb/9780199590162.013.0016

Preda, A. (2007) 'Where Do Analysts Come From? The Case of Financial Chartism', *The Sociological Review*, 55(2): 40–64. doi: 10.1111/j.1467-954X.2007.00729.x

Preda, A. (2009) *Framing Finance: The Boundaries of Markets and Modern Capitalism*. Chicago: University of Chicago Press.

Quaglia, L. (2011) 'The Politics of Insurance Regulation and Supervision Reform in the European Union', *Comparative European Politics*, 9(1): 100–22. doi: 10.1057/cep.2009.12

Ralph, O. (2018) 'Identity Crisis: The Insurers Moving Away from Insurance', *Financial Times*, 6 August. Available at: https://www.ft.com/content/2916c128-918d-11e8-b639-7680cedcc421

Ralph, O. and Pfeifer, S. (2019) 'Rolls-Royce Agrees Record £4.6bn Deal for Pensions', *Financial Times*, 6 June. Available at: https://www.ft.com/content/aaf7f942-87ae-11e9-a028-86cea8523dc2

Ranson, R.H. and Headdon, C.P. (1989) 'With Profits, without Mystery', *Journal of the Institute of Actuaries*, 116(3): 301–45.

Ranson, R.H. and Headdon, C.P. (1990) 'With Profits, without Mystery', *Transactions of the Faculty of Actuaries*, 42: 139–86.

Redington, F.M. (1952) 'Review of the Principles of Life-Office Valuations', *Journal of the Institute of Actuaries*, 78(3): 286–340.

Redington, F.M. (1981) 'The Flock and the Sheep and Other Essays', *Journal of the Institute of Actuaries*, 108: 361–404.

Richards, K. and Colenutt, D. (1975) 'Concentration in the UK Ordinary Life Assurance Market', *The Journal of Industrial Economics*, 24(2): 147–59.

Ritchie, D.A. (2003) *Doing Oral History: A Practical Guide*. Oxford: Oxford University Press.

Ronen, J. (2008) 'To Fair Value or Not to Fair Value: A Broader Perspective', *Abacus*, 44(2): 181–208.

Rosen, D. (2003) 'The Development of Risk Management Software', in P. Field (ed) *Modern Risk Management: A History*. London: Risk Books, pp 135–50.

The Royal Swedish Academy of Sciences (1997) 'The Bank of Sweden Prize in Economic Sciences in Memory of Alfred Nobel, 1997'. Available at: https://www.nobelprize.org/prizes/economic-sciences/1997/press-release/

Rule, D. (2019) 'An Annuity Is a Very Serious Business: Part Two'. Speech. Available at: https://www.bankofengland.co.uk/-/media/boe/files/speech/2019/an-annuity-is-a-very-serious-business-part-two.pdf?la=en&hash=6BF86C21B2C85232A0A22D7D4D36344DF34B4610

Scholes, M.S. (2000) 'Crisis and Risk Management', *American Economic Review*, 90(2): 17–21.

Scott, H., Abbott, R.W., Clayton, G., Corbett, J.T., Dow, J.B., and Fletcher, G.H. et al (1973) 'Linked Life Assurance: Report of the Committee on Property Bonds and Equity-Linked Life Assurance'. London: Her Majesty's Stationery Office. In Institute and Faculty of Actuaries Library.

Scott, P. (2002) 'Towards the "Cult of the Equity"? Insurance Companies and the Interwar Capital Market', *Economic History Review*, 55(1): 78–104. doi: 10.1111/1468-0289.00215

Scott, W.F. (1977) 'A Reserve Basis for Maturity Guarantees in Unit-Linked Life Assurance', *Transactions of the Faculty of Actuaries*, 35: 365–415.

Seabrooke, L. (2014) 'Epistemic Arbitrage: Transnational Professional Knowledge in Action', *Journal of Professions and Organization*, 1(1): 49–64. doi: 10.1093/jpo/jot005

Seabrooke, L. and Tsingou, E. (2009) 'Revolving Doors and Linked Ecologies in the World Economy: Policy Locations and the Practice of International Financial Reform', CSGR Working Paper 260/09, pp 37–41.

Sharma, P. and Cadoni, P. (2010) 'Solvency II: A New Regulatory Frontier', in C. Kempler, M. Flamée, C. Yang and P. Windels (eds) *Global Perspectives on Insurance Today: A Look at National Interest versus Globalization*. New York: Palgrave Macmillan, pp 53–67.

Sharpe, W.F. (1964) 'Capital Asset Prices: A Theory of Market Equilibrium under Conditions of Risk', *The Journal of Finance*, 19(3): 425–42.

Shedden, A.D. (1977) 'A Practical Approach to Applying Immunisation Theory', *Transactions of the Faculty of Actuaries*, 35(251): 313–64.

Singer, D.A. (2007) *Regulating Capital: Setting Standards for the International Financial System*. Ithaca, NY: Cornell University Press.

Smith, A.D. (1996) 'How Actuaries Can Use Financial Economics', *British Actuarial Journal*, 2(5): 1057–193. doi: 10.1017/S1357321700004876

Spears, T. (2014) 'Engineering Value, Engineering Risk: What Derivatives Quants Know and What Their Models Do'. PhD Thesis, University of Edinburgh.

Speed, C., Clarke, M., Bowie, D. and Hawkins, J.W. (2008) 'The Annuity Bulk Buy-Out Market: A Discussion Meeting', *British Actuarial Journal*, 14(2): 237–56.

Squires, R. (1974) 'Unit-Linked Assurance: Observations and Propositions', *Journal of the Institute of Actuaries*, 101(1): 1–51.

Squires, R.J. and O'Neill, J.E. (1990) 'A Unitised Fund Approach to With-Profit Business', *Journal of the Institute of Actuaries*, 117: 279–317.

Story, J. and Walter, I. (1997) *Political Economy of Financial Integration in Europe.* Manchester: Manchester University Press.

Strange, S. (1997) *Casino Capitalism.* Manchester: Manchester University Press.

Suddaby, R. and Viale, T. (2011) 'Professionals and Field-Level Change: Institutional Work and the Professional Project', *Current Sociology,* 59(4): 423–42. doi: 10.1177/0011392111402586

Svetlova, E. (2009) 'Theoretical Models as Creative Resources in Financial Markets', in S.A. Jansen, E. Schröter and N. Stehr (eds) *Rationalität der Kreativität?* Wiesbaden: VS Verlag für Sozialwissenschaften, pp 121–35.

Svetlova, E. (2012) 'On the Performative Power of Financial Models', *Economy and Society,* 41(3): 418–34. doi: 10.1080/03085147.2011. 616145

Svetlova, E. (2018) *Financial Models and Society.* Cheltenham: Edward Elgar.

Tait, N. and Felsted, A. (2008, June 10) 'Insurers fear political delay to EU reform', *Financial Times,* 4.

Thiemann, M. (2018) *The Growth of Shadow Banking: A Comparative Institutional Analysis.* Cambridge: Cambridge University Press.

Thiemann, M. and Lepoutre, J. (2017) 'Stitched on the Edge: Rule Evasion, Regulatory Networks and the Evolution of Markets', *American Journal of Sociology,* 122(6): 1775–821.

Thompson, P. (1988) *The Voice of the Past: Oral History.* Oxford: Oxford University Press.

Thomson, A. (2010) 'Memory and Remembering in Oral History', in D.A. Ritchie (ed) *The Oxford Handbook of Oral History.* Oxford: Oxford University Press, pp 77–95. doi: 10.1093/oxfordhb/9780195339550.013.0006

Thornton, M.D. (1979) 'Actuaries and Long-Term Insurance Business', *Transactions of the Faculty of Actuaries,* 37: 24–62.

Treynor, J.L. (1961) 'Toward a Theory of Market Value of Risky Assets'. doi: 10.2139/ssrn.628187

Turnbull, C. (2017) *A History of British Actuarial Thought.* Basinstoke: Palgrave Macmillan.

Underhill, G.R.D. and Zhang, X. (2008) 'Setting the Rules: Private Power, Political Underpinnings, and Legitimacy in Global Monetary and Financial Governance', *International Affairs,* 3: 535–54.

Van der Graaf, A.E.A. (2018) 'Managing Financial Risks: Protecting the Organisation'. PhD Thesis, Sciences Po.

Van der Heide, A. (2020) 'Model Migration and Rough Edges: British Actuaries and the Ontologies of Modelling', *Social Studies of Science,* 50(1): 121–44. doi: 10.1177/0306312719893465

Van der Heide, A. (2022) 'Talk the Talk and Walk the Walk? European Insurance Capital Regulation and the Financial Vocabulary of Motive', *Socio-Economic Review,* Available at: https://academic.oup.com/ser/adva nce-article/doi/10.1093/ser/mwac032/6643555

Van Hoyweghen, I. (2007) *Risks in the Making: Travels in Life Insurance and Genetics*. Amsterdam: Amsterdam University Press.

Van Hulle, K. (2019) *Solvency Requirements for EU Insurers: Solvency II Is Good for You*. Cambridge: Intersentia.

Van Leeuwen, M.H.D. (2016) 'The Age of the Friendly Societies: Mutual Insurance in the Nineteenth Century', in M.H.D. Van Leeuwen (ed) *Mutual Insurance 1550–2015: From Guild Welfare and Friendly Societies to Contemporary Micro-Insurers*. London: Palgrave Macmillan UK (Palgrave Studies in the History of Finance), pp 83–165. doi: 10.1057/978-1-137-53110-0_3

Van der Zwan, N. (2014) 'Making Sense of Financialization', *Socio-Economic Review*, 12(1): 99–129. doi: 10.1093/ser/mwt020

Velthuis, O. and Coslor, E. (2012) *The Financialization of Art*. Oxford: Oxford University Press. Available at: http://minerva-access.unimelb.edu.au/han dle/11343/90894

Von Fürstenwerth, J. (2008) 'Einzelinteressen dürfen Solvency II nicht verwässern'. Börsen-Zeitung, April 26.

Vriens, E., Buskens, V. and de Moor, T. (2019) 'Networks and New Mutualism: How Embeddedness Influences Commitment and Trust in Small Mutuals', *Socio-Economic Review*, 19(3): 1149–1170, doi: 10.1093/ser/mwz050

Waine, B. (1992) 'Workers as Owners: The Ideology and Practice of Personal Pensions', *Economy and Society*, 21(1): 27–44.

Wansleben, L. (2018) 'How Expectations Became Governable: Institutional Change and the Performative Power of Central Banks', *Theory and Society*, 47(6): 773–803. doi: 10.1007/s11186-018-09334-0

Ward, D. (2002) 'The Costs of Distribution in the UK Life Insurance Market', *Applied Economics*, 34(15): 1959–68. doi: 10.1080/00036840 210129428

Weinberg, M. (1973) 'A Non-Actuary's View of the Role of the Actuary'. Jubilee Lecture, 9 February. In Institute and Faculty of Actuaries Library.

Weisberg, M. (2013) *Simulation and Similarity: Using Models to Understand the World*. Oxford: Oxford University Press.

Westall, O.M. (2006) 'Domestic Distortions and the Early Emergence of the International Trade in Fire Insurance from the UK', *The World Economy*, 29(11): 1629–41. doi: 10.1111/j.1467-9701.2006.00859.x

Whelan, S.F. (2002) 'Actuaries' Contributions to Financial Economics', *The Actuary*, pp 34–5.

Whelan, S.F., Bowie, D.C. and Hibbert, A.J. (2002) 'A Primer in Financial Economics', *British Actuarial Journal*, 8(1): 27–74.

White, H.C. (1981) 'Where Do Markets Come From?', *American Journal of Sociology*, 87(3): 517–47.

Whitley, R. (1984) *The Intellectual and Social Organization of the Sciences*. Oxford: Clarendon Press.

Whitley, R. (1986) 'The Transformation of Business Finance into Financial Economics: The Roles of Academic Expansion and Changes in U.S. Capital Markets', *Accounting, Organizations and Society*, 11(2): 171–92. doi: 10.1016/0361-3682(86)90029-2

Wigan, D. (2009) 'Financialisation and Derivatives: Constructing an Artifice of Indifference', *Competition and Change*, 13(2): 157–73. doi: 10.1179/102452909X417033

Wilkie, A.D. (1964) 'Valuation of Ordinary Life Assurance Business Using a Medium-Sized Electronic Computer and Magnetic Tape Files', *Transactions of the Faculty of Actuaries*, 29(220): 89–207.

Wilkie, A.D. (1977) 'Maturity (and Other) Guarantees Under Unit Linked Policies', *Transactions of the Faculty of Actuaries*, 36: 27–41.

Wilkie, A.D. (1984) 'A Stochastic Investment Model for Actuarial Use', *Transactions of the Faculty of Actuaries*, 39: 341–403.

Wilkie, A.D. (1987) 'An Option Pricing Approach to Bonus Policy: In Memoriam Anthony P. Limb', *Journal of the Institute of Actuaries*, 114(1): 21–90. doi: 10.1017/S0020268100019004

Wilkie, A.D. (1995) 'More on a Stochastic Asset Model for Actuarial Use', *British Actuarial Journal*, 1(5): 777–964.

Wilkie, A.D. (1996) 'The Future of the Profession: A Study Looking Out to 2005 to Identify Challenges for the Profession', *British Actuarial Journal*, 2(2): 325–427.

Wilkie, A.D. and Horsmeier, H.J. (1990) 'On the Calculation of Technical Reserves for Life Insurance in the Countries of the European Communities'. Report by the Groupe Consultatif des Associations d'Actuaires des Pays des Communutés Européennes for the Commission of the European Communities. In Institute and Faculty of Actuaries Library.

Wilkie, A.D., Tilley, J.A., Arthur, T.G. and Clarkson, R. (1993) 'This House Believes That the Contribution of Actuaries to Investment Could Be Enhanced by the Work of Financial Economists', *The Journal of the Institute of Actuaries*, 120(3): 393–414.

Willets, R. (1999) 'Mortality in the Next Millennium'. Paper presented to the Faculty of Actuaries Students' Society. In Institute and Faculty of Actuaries Library.

Willis Towers Watson (2021) 'Keep Calm and Carry On De-Risking'. De-risking report 2021. Willis Towers Watson. Available at: https://www.wtwco.com/-/media/WTW/Insights/2021/01/de-risking-report-2021-keep-calm-and-carry-on.pdf?modified=20201224110107

Yakoubov, Y.H., Teeger, M.H. and Duval, D.B. (1999) 'The TY Model: A Stochastic Investment Model for Asset Liability Management'. Available at: https://www.semanticscholar.org/paper/The-TY-Model-A-Stochastic-Investment-Model-for-and-Yakoubov-Teeger/c6a4de068c454000a9b994a583c44058db8185d3

Yates, J. (1999) 'The Structuring of Early Computer Use in Life Insurance', *Journal of Design History*, 12(1): 5–24.

Yates, J. (2004) *Structuring the Information Age: Life Insurance and Technology in the Twentieth Century*. Baltimore, MD: Johns Hopkins University Press.

Zhang, Y. and Andrew, J. (2014) 'Financialisation and the Conceptual Framework', *Critical Perspectives on Accounting*, 25(1): 17–26. doi: 10.1016/j.cpa.2012.11.012

Zorn, D.M. (2004) 'Here a Chief, There a Chief: The Rise of the CFO in the American Firm', *American Sociological Review*, 69(3): 345–64. Available at: https://doi.org/10.1177/000312240406900302

Index